# OVE FUNDIN
## SPEEDWAY SUPERSTAR

# OVE FUNDIN
## SPEEDWAY SUPERSTAR

JOHN CHAPLIN

TEMPUS

For all the speedway fans that there have ever been... or ever will be. And for my parents: Doris, who loved speedway, and Jack, who preferred football.

Front cover image © Trevor Meeks

First published 2006

Tempus Publishing Limited
The Mill, Brimscombe Port,
Stroud, Gloucestershire, GL5 2QG
www.tempus-publishing.com

© John Chaplin, 2006

The right of John Chaplin to be identified as the Author
of this work has been asserted in accordance with the
Copyrights, Designs and Patents Act 1988.

British Library Cataloguing in Publication Data.
A catalogue record for this book is available from the British Library.

ISBN 0 7524 2944 2

Typesetting and origination by Tempus Publishing Limited
Printed in Great Britain

# CONTENTS

Acknowledgements                                    7
Author Profile                                      8
Sources of Reference                                9
Foreword by Reg Fearman                            11
Preface: A Walk With Kings                         15
Introduction: Simply the Best                      17

One       Country Boy                              25
Two       The Real Beginning                       29
Three     Figure It Out For Yourself               35
Four      Is That the Greatest Rider in the World? 55
Five      Can You Cope?                             75
Six       Norwich Track Spare No. 2                89
Seven     Passion and Privilege                    97
Eight     Mona... in her Own Write                119
Nine      Marriage                                131
Ten       The Cancer                              139
Eleven    Murderous Moments                       147
Twelve    The Governor                            171
Thirteen  The Man They Loved to Hate              211
Fourteen  Ove and the EsO                         227

          Epilogue                                257
          Innerviews                              263
          Ove's Career Record                     286

'*Ove Fundin was the world's worst sport – in that he had an absolute hatred of not winning. It must have been something deep in his past. But in reality he is a very caring man.*' – Eric Linden

# ACKNOWLEDGMENTS

For their patient and generous assistance in the preparation of this book I would like to record my grateful thanks to: Guy Allott, Bob Andrews, Eileen Arnison, Sheila Blakeman-Shead, Jim Blanchard, Nigel and Cynthia Boocock, Gillian Bowen, Roy Bowers, Barry Briggs, Eddie Bull, Brian Burford, Alan Clark, Phil Clarke, Brian Darby, Carina Davidsson of the Tranas Tourist Office, Reg Duval, Keith Farman, Reg Fearman, Mona Forsberg-Fundin, Annika Fundin, Ioanna Fundin, Monica Fundin, Niclas Fundin, Harold Gardner, Anne Gillespie, Jimmy Gooch, Bert Harkins, Ernie Hancock, Karen Hart-Fundin, Trevor Hedge, Ron How, James Howarth of Tempus Publishing, Norman Jacobs, Igor Kalashnik, Mike Kemp, Bjorn Knutson*, Dave Lanning, Don Lawson, Rosemarie Lawson-Quinn, Eric Linden, Ronnie Moore, Shani Moore, Gote Nordin, Les Mullins, Olle Nygren, Peter Oakes, Tony Olsson, Philip Rising, Martin Rogers, Mark Sawbridge, Bill Smith, Ian Thomas, Roy Waller, Hugo Wilson of *Classic Bike* magazine, Vic White, Eric Williams, Fred Williams, Peter Williams, Archie Windmill, Jim Yacoby and, of course, Ove Fundin.

*Bjorn told me that his family from the 1920s spelled Knutson with one 's' – and that he 'happened to have a second "s" when I started riding in England, but I changed it back and one "s" is correct today'.

# AUTHOR PROFILE

John Chaplin watched his first speedway meeting as a teenager in the 1940s at Perry Barr, Birmingham in the Tiger Hart/Graham Warren/Arthur Payne/Alan Hunt era. He had already decided that he wanted a career in journalism, and submitted reports of the meetings to whomever and wherever he could.

He was eventually offered a job on a local newspaper and then spent almost forty years in Fleet Street with the *Daily Mirror* and *Daily Mail*, finally becoming deputy editor of *UK Mail International*, the global edition of the *Daily Mail*. He founded *Vintage Speedway Magazine*, which he edited for ten years, has built up a substantial knowledge of speedway racing and is an authority on its history. He has broadcast about the sport on radio and television, written several books about it and has contributed articles on speedway racing to magazines in Britain and throughout the world. He is married with three sons and lives in Spain.

# SOURCES OF REFERENCE

*Stenner's Speedway Annuals 1946-1954*
*Speedway Championship World Final*, Maurice Jones
*Ove Fundin (This Was Part of Your Speedway Life)*, Bob Spence
*Speedway in East Anglia*, Norman Jacobs
*Norwich Speedway*, Mike Kemp & Norman Jacobs
*Peter Craven: The Wizard of Balance*, Brian Burford
*British Speedway Leagues 1946-1964,* Peter Morrish
*A History of the World Speedway Championship*, Robert Bamford &
    Glynn Shailes
*Triple Crown Plus*, Ivan Mauger with Peter Oakes
*The Ronnie Moore Story* as Told to Rod Dew
*Briggo: Barry Briggs Speedway Champion: His Own Story*
*Classic Bike* magazine
*Vintage Speedway Magazine*
*The Complete History of the British League*, Peter Oakes (ed.)
*Five-One* magazine
*Ride It: The Complete Book of Speedway*, Cyril May
*Speedway World*
*Speedway Post*
*Barry Briggs's Speedway World*
*Speedway Star & News*
*Speedway Star*
Various World Final programmes.

# FOREWORD

By Reg Fearman, former England Speedway Test rider, Great Britain and England team manager, British Speedway Promoters' Association chairman and Veteran Speedway Riders' Association president 1992.

*'Victory goes to the player who makes the next to last mistake.'*

This book is the coming together of two determined personalities who both became masters of their own profession. One is a Swede who, as a very young man, had his sights set upon becoming a professional speedway rider. The other is an Englishman who took up the pen. But it is primarily about Ove Fundin of Sweden.

Several of Ove's passions are golf, flying, keeping fit, reading, travel and speedway, not necessarily in that order. And, of course, Norwich, for whom he raced from 1955 until the speedway was closed in 1964. He is revered in Norwich even now, more than forty years later.

He began his speedway career in 1951 with the Filbyterna club in the town of Linkoping, which, at one time, was the capital of Sweden. The King's name was Folke Filbyter. It was with Filbyterna that Ove made his first speedway visit to Britain in 1953. The side was a Swedish 'B' team that raced on the Southern League (Third Division) tracks at Rayleigh, Exeter, Oxford, Plymouth and Swindon. At the same time, a Swedish 'A' team was touring the First Division tracks. On their night off the 'B' team went to Wimbledon to watch the 'A' team in action, and that was where Ove first saw his idol, Ronnie Moore, and world-class speedway.

In 1954 he qualified for the World Championship rounds in England. It was not an easy ride. He was twenty-one years old and knew little English. He had to make his way from Sweden and then to Norwich by train, pushing his machine between stations. Aub Lawson, then captain of Norwich, arranged for him to be met at the station and Aub became Ove's mentor and friend, as he had been mine in 1948. We both had great affection and respect for Aub as well as a great friendship with him until his untimely death on his farm at Northam, fifty miles from Perth, Western Australia, in 1976 at the age of only sixty-two.

Ove scored 13 points at Norwich. Then, after being taken by Aub to the Fearman family home in London for a cup of tea, for which my mother was famous (the kettle was always on!), he scored another 13 points at West Ham and qualified for his first World Final. It was the start of a long and enduring friendship between Ove and my family, so much so that he asked my father, Arthur, to be his mechanic on the big night at Wembley that September. My dad was christened 'Cyclone' by Aub Lawson because he was no whirlwind, but patient, methodical and thorough in everything he did – absolutely ideal as Ove's mechanic on a big occasion.

The first of Ove's five World titles came in 1956 at Wembley, a phenomenal performance considering that he'd had a mere four years of real racing experience. That he went on to win another four World Championships made him one of the all-time greats in the sporting world.

It was on board the SS *Oronsay* on the way to Australia, a voyage of four weeks, late in 1954 that Ove and I – both twenty-one-year-olds – really got to know each other. It is a friendship that has endured for more than fifty years, and we have shared some of the highs as well as the lows of life. Ove was travelling with fellow Swedes Ulf Ericsson and Goran Norlen. They had been invited by the great English international Jack Parker, who took touring teams to Australia regularly during the European close season. I was on honeymoon with my late wife Joan on our way to Auckland, New Zealand, where I had a contract to race at Western Springs.

When my racing career ended, I turned to speedway promoting in 1960, and it was in 1966 when promoting at Long Eaton that I needed to strengthen the team. Since the closure of Norwich in 1964 Ove had been unattached, so I telephoned him in Sweden and asked him to ride for me. He replied: 'Sure, Reg, I would like to.' And he did, with no strings. His stay at Long Eaton was short-lived. The Swedish motor federation, SVMO, wanted him to ride in Sweden, which he refused to do, so they promptly withdrew his racing licence – in effect banning him from that year's World Championship. Had he been allowed to compete, he might well have been a six-times World Champion ahead of Ivan Mauger of New Zealand, who topped Ove's record in 1979, and his fellow Swede Tony Rickardsson who won a sixth world title in 2005.

Ove's passion for golf is such that when he and his wife Ioanna moved to a new home in the south of France in 1990, he would not commit himself to the property until he was sure that he could become a member of the local golf club. He and I have enjoyed many games of golf together, here in the south of France and in Britain. One of our great delights was when I organised a small party to play The Old Course at St Andrews. Ove took the wheel from me on the drive to Scotland, and pushed our speed up to 90mph on the motorway. When he was pulled over by the police a request for his driving licence was answered in fluent Swedish – and, with a warning, a disgruntled policeman waved us on our way. Ove's usual time to tee-off is at daybreak – eighteen holes and then home for breakfast. It is not unusual for him to decide on another eighteen holes in the late afternoon.

It is amazing how many speedway riders have taken up flying. Ove started flying aeroplanes in the late 1950s but it wasn't until the early 1970s that he did a three-week crash course (excuse the pun!) in Florida, passing all his exams. We have shared many flying exploits over the French countryside. You will read more in this book about Ove's airborne experiences. And you will learn what a remarkable individual he is, what made him a five-times World Champion, about his dedication to fitness (I am sure he could still get into his racing leathers of fifty years ago), his amazing cycle ride from the south of France to Tranas to celebrate his sixty-fifth birthday and of his even more amazing long walk from France to Tranas for his seventieth birthday party. This reminds me of a time that I joined Ove some years ago on a twelve-mile mountain walk. Our wives were to drive up and meet us at a restaurant at noon. At 12.15 p.m. they hadn't arrived and Ove announced that if they didn't turn up within five minutes we would start walking back. He told me Swedes were never, never late! He has always been impatient. I said, 'Ove, you walk back! I shall have to wait for the girls to arrive so that they know we have not had an accident.' In no way was I going to walk back. Fortunately, within minutes, they arrived.

Ove has always enjoyed travel and on one occasion we took a Nile cruise. We were enthralled by the tombs of the Pharaohs and the Valley of the Kings, but several of us fell foul of Egyptian (gippy) belly, except Ove and his wife Ioanna who, I later learned, were in the habit of taking a slug of vodka, neat, before dinner. This evidently kills the bugs. You learn something every day!

I married Eileen, who was a great friend of Joan's for many years, in 2004 and we are very pleased to be living close to Ove and Ioanna. Of course, we now see much more of each other, usually at dinner. Ove is extremely well read and he and I frequently have heated discussions on various topics, not least on speedway racing of which we are both passionately fond.

I have enjoyed Ove's friendship over the past fifty years. And I know that, with John Chaplin's eloquent writing skills and his dedication to his subject, you will find this book compulsive reading. You will certainly discover there is much, much more to Ove Fundin than just a speedway rider.

The ultimate measure of a man is not where he stands in moments of comfort and convenience, but where he stands in times of challenge and controversy.

Reg Fearman
Valcros, La Londe, France,
*February 2005*

# A WALK WITH KINGS

*'You have to be ruthless. And, as with any other individual sport, you have to be selfish. I am the first to admit that I am very selfish. Every good rider I have seen has always been selfish. Except maybe Ronnie Moore. Ronnie could have gone much further had he been much more selfish.'* – Ove Fundin

*'The stars were idols who possessed secrets of perfection I knew nothing about. That they were actually human beings was a swift shock to my system, almost beyond my comprehension.'* – Shirley MacLaine

For nigh on half a century it has been my immense honour and privilege to walk with the kings of the most exciting, exhilarating, skilful, thrilling, spectacular, demanding and dangerous modern sport on the face of this planet – speedway racing. The kings of the cinder tracks were the idols of my youth, my role models. I aspired to be like them, to have their courage, their bravery, their skill and their glamour. I never had the money or the determination to become like them. Instead I became a journalist and wrote about them. Even so, I never allowed myself to get close to them, because I considered that a close relationship with anyone I would have to write about could compromise my job as a reporter.

There were three exceptions. The first was Phil 'Tiger' Hart, who was the unfortunately accident-prone captain of Birmingham when I first saw speedway racing in 1946. We became friends in his later years and we delighted in sending each other saucy postcards – him from his holiday home in Majorca. The second was my unashamed boyhood hero, the hugely charismatic England captain and Golden Helmet maestro Jack Parker, whom I got to know after he had given up racing. The third was Ove Fundin of Sweden, who fascinated me not merely because of his outstanding achievements on the track, but because of his complex and volatile personality. Also I felt that, unlike those other icons of the sport, New Zealand's terrible triplets Ronnie Moore, Barry Briggs and Ivan Mauger, whose careers have all been recorded for posterity in books – as, posthumously, have the exploits of their brilliant and tragic contemporary Peter Craven – true and proper justice has not been done to Ove's contribution to speedway racing, not only at Norwich, the club to which he dedicated most of his extraordinary career, but to British and world speedway as a whole.

Here I should point out that this chronicle of his life in and out of public scrutiny does not claim to be a definitive statistical record of his speedway career. I am quite likely to be caught out on some of them, because the statistics that are available are far too imprecise, and one reason for this is that the gentlemen – and I use the term advisedly – who ran the Speedway Control Board at the time failed to keep any proper archives. But with the able assistance of several statistical wizards, I have done the best I can. So the blame for any inaccuracies lies solely with the author.

I was never privileged to be around the great Ove while he was at his magnificent height, so the stories of his fiery temperament reached me second hand. But I don't doubt them, and he has never denied them to me – in fact he has readily confirmed them. The thing about Fundin is that he not only set the standard of achievement – five World titles and six other rostrum places in twelve years – he was the epitome of what every ambitious speedway rider should aspire to be. One reason for writing this book is because I wanted to show that quality. Another is to at least attempt to reveal the complex personality behind the idol of the thousands who knew him only as a speedway rider.

Ove was supreme as a sportsman, yet is described elsewhere as 'the world's worst sport'. The reason is that he positively loathed losing. He is not ashamed of that part of his character. It is what drove him to achieve such outstanding success. Since I have come to know him well, I have discovered that he is also, in the true sense of the word, a gentleman.

John Chaplin

# SIMPLY THE BEST

*'With Fundin there is nothing to watch beyond the perfection of style that makes racing look simple. It's pretty useless hoping he might make a mistake. The guy just doesn't.'* – Angus Kix

Ove Fundin won the individual speedway World Championship five times, setting new standards, and they thought it could never be bettered. It was. Ivan Mauger won one more and so did Tony Rickardsson. Yet still, Fundin's astonishing record of standing on the World Final rostrum ten consecutive times has not been equalled in the entire sixty-year history of the competition. At over seventy he still races in Golden Greats meetings.

When I set out to write this book about his life, I thought it would be an easy task. There has been a book about the life of the other great equivalent superstar of his era, Barry Briggs. There has been a book about the life of the man who came after and had the temerity – or determination – to win six World Championships, Ivan Mauger. There has been a book about the life of the man who went before, Ove's acknowledged own hero, the superbly gifted Ronnie Moore. Ove Fundin: five World Championships, European Champion four times, Swedish Champion nine times, the first foreign rider to hold the Golden Helmet British Match Race Championship, and numerous other Continental titles as well. It appeared to me that the sporting chronicles had obviously done the man less than justice.

You think: Sit down with one of these icons and they will deliver chapter and verse, in great detail, all the thrills and spills, triumphs and tragedies of their life and career. That wasn't Ove's scene. Unlike some speedway riders not remotely of his eminence, he does not have total recall of his racing exploits. One of his most frequent – and journalistically frustrating – expressions is 'I can't remember now'. And one of the reasons is that, amazingly, he is an incredibly modest man. I once asked him publicly if, given all those achievements, it made him feel good. He considered for a moment and then said, 'No.' He could, he said, have tried even harder.

Sure, he has the qualities I have discerned in nearly all the World Champions it has been my privilege to interview: the certainty and total conviction that he was – and is – simply the best. If World Speedway Champions had not believed that of themselves, they would never have been World Speedway Champions. But at one stage Ove said to me, 'I hope it's not going to be one of those books that says "He scored so many points in this meeting and so many points in that meeting". That would be bloody boring, wouldn't it?'

During his distinguished career – there has been none more distinguished in the near-eighty-year history of speedway racing – Fundin has been accused of being boring. There was a spat with journalist Angus Kix in *Speedway Star & News* in 1958. Ove had been turning in his immaculate performances for a few seasons. He had won the 1956 World Championship and was to come perilously close to winning it again for the next three years. (Kix was really the writer Eric Linden wearing another hat and Ove was in on the professional deception, which is why he always called Eric 'Angus'. But throughout this book quotes from Linden and Kix will be attributed to each of them separately for the purpose of simplicity.) Above a piece written by Kix, billed as 'The Columnist With Punch', there appeared the headline 'Fundin Can Be Boring'. And he went on to ask, 'Want to know who my number one bore is? Ove Fundin. It's simple enough. Fundin wins his races too easily, too often, too much. With Fundin there is nothing to watch beyond the perfection of style that makes racing look simple. It's pretty useless hoping he might make a mistake. The guy just doesn't.' And the sting in the Kix tale was, 'Ove – your individualism is showing!'

The following week a tit-for-tat headline appeared: 'Kix Bores Ove Fundin'. The magazine's Norwich reporter Bill Cooper leapt to Ove's defence. Fundin did not team ride because, wrote Cooper, 'his partners cannot keep up with him'. Fundin came up in a hard school, Cooper went on. The only nursing he got was when others succeeded in knocking him off. Could he be blamed for having an individual tendency? Judging by the expression on Ove's face when he read the offending article, concluded Cooper, 'Kix bores Fundin!' All good knockabout stuff.

Too many books on the sport have dwelt ad infinitum and ad nauseam on the minutiae of who did what and where and when, indeed to the threshold of boredom and beyond. And so I promised Ove I would try not to make this chronicle of his life and times 'bloody boring', though inevitably there are sections when you will learn that 'he scored so many points in this meeting and so many points in that meeting'. It is, after all, about his speedway career. However, I am unable to recall a single moment in his company that was 'bloody boring'. The experience of being privy to his innermost thoughts and trust has been not only pleasurable but infinitely stimulating, and anything but boring.

About his house, a hillside villa among the pines and vineyards of southern France, there are few mementoes of his glory days on the track. There are one or two prized and tasteful silver trophies – by no means the Aladdin's cave of silverware favoured by some, though I did notice, with some satisfaction, that the Farndon Trophy, given to him by me as editor and founder of *Vintage Speedway Magazine* when he was president of the Veteran Speedway Riders' Association in 1993, was one of them. There are also one or two very fine cartoons and a plaque with his head in relief, plus a first-day cover of the stamp issued in Sweden in honour of his achievements in the world of motor sport, as well as those of his fellow countryman Olle Nygren. There is a fine piece of artwork of him in action on the wall by the bend in his staircase, and on the ledge below it sits his crash helmet. His speedway life is completed by a sparse picture gallery, prominent among which is an action study of one of the track rivals he held in high regard during his halcyon racing days, the late, great Peter Craven.

Ove keeps a fairly spacious 'Pandora's Box' of memorabilia upstairs in a wicker basket. It contains photographs, old diaries, school exercise books, passports, newspaper cuttings and letters from fans – including one of mine I had sent to him thirty or more years ago. And after being allowed to view evidence of his hectic and demanding racing commitments at the time, I now know why I never got a reply. Had I been female it might have been different. Ove's personal life and relationships with the opposite sex have been as varied, colourful and controversial as his exploits on the international speedway circuit. Speedway, he once told me, is a great way to meet girls. Mona, Ove's first wife with whom he has seven children, says of him, 'He was a Mick Jagger-type. He just couldn't resist the temptations of girls hanging around.' Only a few years ago he discovered he has an eighth child from another relationship, a daughter who was adopted by an English couple. She tracked him down through newspaper cuttings. The delightful Ioanna, from Romania and a former actress, is his third wife.

When you glance through his diaries you realise why he had no time to answer the many letters he received that were similar to mine and the numerous others he had from fans. These days he communicates with his admirers – and they are legion, even now – if they are interesting enough, through the internet. He has his own website (www.ove-fundin.com), presided over by our mutual friend, the very talented motorsport artist Jim Blanchard, which he updates regularly, and there is a visitors' book to sign.

'Only the other day, someone wanted to know something about a meeting that took place in the 1960s,' Ove said. 'It was a four-team meeting. He had the results from only three of the teams and wanted to know if I could supply the rest. And a couple of months ago there was someone who wanted to start a speedway history club.' Like myself, Ove is not a man who is a slave to statistics. I wouldn't be at all surprised if the answer he sent back was 'I can't remember now.' After all, he says, it was all so long ago. There is also a small collection of telegrams – 'that was in the days when they sent telegrams' – congratulatory and wishing him well – delivered to him at various World Finals.

Mona says of their early relationship, 'I had noticed of course that Ove was an intelligent guy. Although I had studied more than he had, I found out that he had a good general knowledge of a lot of things, and he liked to read a lot. He was also a health-minded young man – he neither drank liquor nor did he smoke.' In the Fundin library are books by such diverse authors as Oscar Wilde, Nelson Mandela, Boris Pasternak, Vladimir Nabokov, Kirk Douglas, Britt Ekland, Sebastian Faulks, Michael Crichton, Graham Greene, Maeve Binchy, Joanna Trollope and volumes on travel and flying. It is such intellectual ammunition that prompted Barry Briggs to remark, 'Ove was really too intelligent to be a speedway rider. He was different – that's why he was so good.'

Ove likes Kipling's poem *If*, a good pub sing-song, Toblerone chocolate, traditional jazz and Italian singers. He has strong right-wing views and was a keen Scout; he loves walking and golf. He is particularly keen on golf and is a five-times winner of the 'Rider Cup', traditionally competed for by like-minded speedway riders on the eve of the Veteran Speedway Riders' Association annual dinners. He is passionate about flying, is a qualified pilot and recently passed his annual medical, which cleared him to fly for another year. He has just bought a microlight aircraft, has made more than 1,000 parachute jumps and is an accomplished parachute instructor.

During my stay with him to interview him for this book, we walked at least three miles a day. He would be up and out fairly early to play a round of golf. Then he would come back, and while having breakfast – traditionally an item of his own invention: Swedish crispbread, Emmenthal cheese topped with apricot jam, christened The Breakfast Ove by his great friend and neighbour Reg Fearman – he liked to take in the world news on television. If he felt like talking we would. If not, it was a walk in the hills surrounding his home. And I recorded our conversation as we went. He took particular delight in introducing me to the local café/bars and his favourite out-of-the-way restaurants in which we would sample the rather splendid French cuisine.

You haven't really had a proper automotive experience until you have been driven at 140kph along the Autoroute Cote D'Azur by Ove Fundin. With him in the pilot's seat, it's hold-on-to-your-hat time as he vents his frustrations on erring drivers, curses women behind the wheel, blasts bewildered pedestrians and puts his state-of-the-art VW (he also has two Saabs, plus a virtual wreck he uses to transport his golf clubs, a BMW R1300 RT shaft-driven motorcycle and a pedal cycle) through the chicanes and hairpins of that unforgiving, rugged road. It might just occur to you that though the best part of four decades has passed since he won the last of his five World Speedway Championships, little has changed of the acerbic and aggressively competitive personality that made him such a formidable opponent during a unique racing career in which, throughout the world that knew his special talent and beyond, he was at once feared and respected, hated and adored. 'You may have noticed,' he says, 'that I do not have very much patience. It's still there, isn't it? Very much so. I'm retired. I've got nothing to fight for now, I don't have to be first in anything, but I still have no patience.' It is an inherent characteristic of the star sign under which he was born: Gemini.

On our drive he contains himself long enough to negotiate sedately the strip of expensive Continental European walkway that is the sparkling Mediterranean seafront known as the Boulevarde de la Croisette, at Cannes, pointing out the wedding-cake edifice of the Carlton Hotel and also the Picasso Museum as we pass. It is but a few hundred yards, yet the place fair reeks of wealth and privilege. Its paved-with-gold sidewalk is the place the world's glitterati like to tread to see and be seen, especially during the famous annual film festival.

But he insists on taking the longer coast road leading back to his villa, which is perched high and insulates him from the crowds and the pretensions of the super-rich. He is at pains that you fully appreciate the wild and rugged beauty of the Les Maures Massif that is one of France's National Parcs. It's a roller-coaster ride – sheer cliffs on one side, the sea on the other – as he weaves his way through the garish beach resorts before threading back home through the vineyards and pinewoods. It is through these ribbons of roads in the mountains of La Maures that he cycles, when the fancy takes him. Not long ago he decided to pedal the 1,500 miles from his home in the south of France to Tranas, his home town in Sweden, sleeping in the open when it was fine and taking a hotel room when it wasn't.

At other times he wheels out his motorcycle, once again puts on a crash helmet and leathers – plain black, 'just like the old speedway riders', none of those fancy coloured suits for him – and takes to the road. One of his latest trips was to Lourdes – 'to see what all the fuss is about' – and to the Campostilla monastery in north-west Spain, because he wanted to see it. He recently rode 600 miles in a day to join me and some thirty speedway-minded people in the south of Spain for a lunch with the newly formed Speedway Amigos Europe, and then there was the recent trip into the Pyrenees mountains with half a dozen former airline captains who shared with him the sheer exhilaration of motorcycling. During his racing career, he wanted to see Russia, so he took up ice speedway. For very similar reasons (he was told he stood a chance of getting into the Swedish Olympic team) he tried his hand at bobsleighing. He recently drove the length of the legendary American Route 66, from Chicago to Los Angeles, and so passionate is he still about motorcycling that, though now in his eighth decade, in July 2006, along with fellow Swedes Olle Nygren and former Ice Speedway World Champion Per-Olof Serenius, Ove planned to take part in a Trans-Asia Expedition by riding the 7,500 miles between Korea and Stockholm via Siberia, Mongolia, Kazakhstan, Slovakia and Poland, which means spending 55 days in the saddle.

By way of a secret celebration to mark his seventieth birthday, he decided to walk the 650 miles from Lille in northern France to Sweden, timing his arrival once more in Tranas to coincide with the party he had previously arranged and invited all the family and numerous special guests. He calculated it would take him twenty-one days. He said, 'I plan to arrive on 23 May, my seventieth birthday. I have already arranged a big family party for seventy people.' He did it with a few days to spare, averaging almost thirty-one miles a day. And it was a secret because, though he told me his plans weeks before, he did not tell his wife, Ioanna, until he was almost ready to set off.

He is, indeed, a remarkable man. He is a man of outstanding determination. He has strong and firmly held opinions – on everything from politics, music and art to human integrity and honesty. He has a highly developed, though he admits virtually untrained, intelligence. I wouldn't mind betting he has a fairly high IQ.

It is easy to be overawed by him, because of his stature and achievements, yet if you can become close to him and penetrate the at times formidable exterior, he reveals himself – when he has come to trust you – as a most vulnerable human being. One of the things he revealed to me was that he did not expect to live until he was seventy, let alone walk from France to Sweden, or even pull on modern brightly coloured Kevlars and race a speedway machine again in one of those Golden Greats meetings organised by his great rival and friend Barry Briggs. Or take on 2000 World Speedway Champion Mark Loram in a race commemorating British speedway's seventy-fifth anniversary – a Match Race he was winning until the final bend when the engine of the bike he was riding died under him.

He did not expect to reach the age of seventy because a few years ago Ove Fundin, the five-times World Speedway Champion, the hard man of the toughest and cruellest motor sport in the world, the man with a reputation for unmatched determination and iron will, the battler, the bruiser, the volatile personality swiftly roused to anger – usually with himself – if he lost even an insignificant race on the track, suddenly found himself about to fight the biggest battle of his career. He had to take on an opponent more formidable and frightening than facing a 100,000 World Final crowd at Wembley, more exacting than the split-second instinctive reactions needed to avoid disaster when hurtling round an enclosed speedway circuit at high speed on a powerful motorcycle with no brakes.

Because Ove Fundin was told he had cancer.

# ONE

# COUNTRY BOY

*'When I first saw speedway I thought it was fun.'* – Ove Fundin

Ove Fundin was a country boy, born of a country family. Ove's grandfather and father both came from the countryside. Yet he could so easily have been an American. All the record books say that his home town is Tranas, but the family came from an area around forty miles away. It was moorland and forest and only the timber was worth anything. There were a few old farms there. It was a very poor area of central Sweden. Because it was so poor people had to think of starting small businesses. Many of them were run by just a family.

'My grandfather, Franz Svensson, was a professional soldier, and when he gave it up he moved to Tranas. There he became the owner of the town's first motor car. He made that into a taxi and he built the first of the larger houses. They used to build them of wood, but he built his of stone and brick, and then he started all kinds of businesses – he was an entrepreneur. He married a Swedish-American girl, Hulda, who became my grandmother.

'At the end of the eighteenth century [1800 to 1899 was the eighteenth century in Sweden, the nineteenth, it seems, everywhere else] so many people from the poorer classes emigrated to America that Sweden was almost empty. To this day there are more Swedish people in Chicago than there are in Gothenburg, which is the second largest city in Sweden.'

Hulda's family was one of those who joined the exodus across the Atlantic and migrated to America. But, like so many others, when she was able, she could not resist going back to the 'old country' to see where her parents came from. And when she did she met Ove's grandfather. They had five sons and one daughter, but the daughter died when she was a baby. They became Fundins even though Franz was born a Svensson. In Sweden the sons take the names of the fathers: Svensson, Johansson – everyone in Sweden used to be named one or the other. But young men who became soldiers were normally given the name of the place they came from, and Franz came from a place called Fundsboda, which became Fundin.

Ove's proper first names are Knut Owe, pronounced Ow!

'But when I came to England, well I would just have been Ow, wouldn't I? It would have been hopeless. And I wanted to be known as Ove.

'Of my grandparents' five sons, there was David who became the manager of a bank in Tranas. The next one, Helmer, worked for a company that made bicycles, lawnmowers and guns. He was a private chauffeur for the boss. The next was my father, Arvid. He became a furrier and had a fur factory in Tranas that was a centre for the fur business. Axel was after him, who was a car dealer, and the youngest one was Gustav. He was an economic adviser, but he died when he was thirty-four.'

Ove's father did not live long enough to see his son's fabulous later success on the speedway tracks of the world. Though several people have laid claim to being the first to 'discover' the great Ove Fundin, Arvid could possibly legitimately say he was really the first because he lent Ove the money to buy his first speedway bike. Arvid Fundin died at the age of forty-nine from kidney problems, a complaint, says Ove, that is curable today. He died in 1953, the year Ove started to make the speedway world sit up and begin to take note that a new and special talent had emerged during a tour by the Swedish side Filbyterna on British Third Division tracks. The fledgling multi-World Champion had begun to barnstorm his way to the top in the sport in 1951.

'My mother, Ruth, and her family came originally from Linkoping, which is about sixty miles north of Tranas. Her parents, Johanis and Emma, moved to Tranas when they married. You know where they take animal hides and make them into leather. Her father had a tanning factory – it's not there any more, it went years and years ago – and also a shoe shop. My mother had four brothers.'

And she played the piano to accompany the silent flickering black-and-white images at the once-a-week local cinema.

'My father also wanted to migrate to America. They had bought the tickets and everything and then they found out that my mother was pregnant with my sister Elsie. She was born in 1931 – I was born in 1933 and my brother Torsten was born in 1934. So I suppose I could have been American. Torsten went into the services like my father and now he is retired. Elsie was a dental nurse. The family business was sold when my father died – just as well because the fur business was going right down, though it is coming back now. It is not so long ago that if a woman was wearing a fur coat she would be spat on.

'My childhood was happy I suppose. I wouldn't say I enjoyed school, but I was fairly good. A couple of times I received honours, normally in geography and history. I didn't show any mechanical aptitude, but I was very good at running. I always used to win the competition for running and also for cross-country skiing.

'You mustn't forget that I was at school during the Second World War. One day the teacher brought a banana to school, just when the war finished. They got some bananas in Sweden and he was one of the lucky ones to get one and he brought it to school to show us how to peel a banana – because none of us had ever seen a banana or an orange. Strange that one of the things you learned at school was how to peel a banana. I was six when the war started. Compulsory school then began at seven and you went to school for seven years. I went for only seven years – I never went any further because I had no interest whatsoever. My sister went on to college.

'Sweden was never occupied in the war. We had lots of refugees – most came as children – evacuees, Danes and Finns. Sweden, Spain and Switzerland were neutral countries. I never saw anything of the war. We saw American bomber crews who couldn't make it back to England. They diverted to Sweden and as Sweden was neutral they were kept until the end of the war. To send them back would have been an act of war. Quite a lot of Swedish people – including one of my uncles – fought against the Germans in the Finland army.

'The only concept of the war I had was I remember some people had gas masks and we had bomb shelters and they practised an invasion, so we had to black out the lights. We had an alarm system with sirens. Really the war went past me, but later on I was looking forward to doing my national service – I wouldn't have minded being an officer. I did my national service in 1953, but I had just started speedway and I was allowed a lot of time off to do my racing.'

It was in 1951, at the age of eighteen, that the young Fundin first became aware of speedway racing. He started motocross when he bought an old Matchless 350cc. All his young tearaway friends were interested in motorcycles and together they built a motocross track on land given by the community of Tranas. The local motor club pitched in to help the youngsters. 'I didn't ride my bike on the road. We started racing straight away – which was much more fun.'

Really, speedway discovered him rather than him discovering speedway. Someone from the local club came to the motocross track and saw him and invited him to go for a trial. He had never seen speedway before. They said to him: 'Here is a bike, this is what you do, go out and try it.' And he did.

'When I first saw speedway I thought it was fun.'

It was to consume him, become the core of his very existence and, for a while at least, be more important to him than any other single thing in his life.

# TWO

# THE REAL BEGINNING

*'When they first asked me to go and try it I knew I could do it without them telling me. I noticed I was quite good at it when I started beating everybody.'* – Ove Fundin

The history of Tranas can be traced back 4,000 years. Today it has retained its small-town atmosphere but has succeeded in combining the ancient with a modern outlook. The town is set in picturesque and peaceful countryside on the northern borders of the Smaland and Oland region of central Sweden, around sixty miles south of Linkoping and two hours by train from the capital, Stockholm. Lake Sommen is nearby and it is surrounded by beautiful forests. There is a population of 18,000 and a centuries-old market. Its traditional crafts include early farming implements and a furniture industry and until fifteen years ago it was the centre of Sweden's fur trade. It has the oldest wooden castle in Sweden and the only college course in the country for firefighters.

On Saturdays there is a brass band procession, and regular water pageants are held on Sundays. Tranas has the oldest wood-burning steamboat in Sweden and an ice hockey team. It was one of the first places in the world to have a fibre-optic network for modern information technology and there is a lively arts movement including music and drama. They have been talking about it for some time and have not quite got around to it yet, but there is every likelihood that in the not-too-distant future the good people of Tranas will erect a statue to their most famous son, Ove Fundin. When he lived in Tranas his hime was in Stjarngatan, which means in English – perhaps appropriately – Star Street. There is even talk about renaming a street after him. But that probably won't be until after he is dead because they never do that while people are still alive. At least, not in Tranas they don't.

'I grew up in the small town of Tranas, and you had to follow what the other kids did. Motorcycling became very popular. After the Second World War and all that, you could ride a bike again and buy a bike. I would be about seventeen or eighteen, and the boys I used to hang around with started getting into motorbikes. So I followed them. All of us bought English ex-army bikes that somebody imported. They came camouflaged and all. Mine was a 350 Matchless, I remember that. There was no rear suspension in those days, but mine did have telescopic forks – it was a very modern, nice one. Straight away we wanted to do something else, so we built ourselves a motocross track and I rode motocross for two seasons. Then somebody came around to the motocross meetings and he said to me, "I can see from your style that you should try speedway. Come over to Linkoping. We'll give you a bike. We practise at night." So I went there – my father took me. And they gave me a bike to try, and I seemed to be going very good.

'They must have been short of riders because they said, "Next Sunday we have a meeting and we'd like you to come and be in it as a reserve." So I went there as a reserve, and someone fell off, so I was in the very first meeting. And I scored a few points. That's how I started. I thought speedway was very much easier than motocross. It suited me more. I was never strong enough for motocross. In those days you used to do so many laps, and you used to go on and on. I just wasn't strong enough to keep that up.

'And then I remember the bike that they gave me to race. My father lent me the money to buy that bike. I don't even know if I repaid him because he died before the next season. It was the red bike I rode in that first World Final at Wembley, and that is the one that had been used by a leg-trailer. It is the one I had in England when I rode for the Swedish touring team Filbyterna in 1953, and I took it to Australia.'

But out in the wider speedway world the young Fundin discovered
there were infinitely higher rewards and much greater opportunities
on offer than there ever were to be had on the small town and country
tracks in the Swedish backwoods.

'In Sweden the speedways were all clubs. They did pay you – but
not very much. They paid you points money and start money, which,
as far as I remember, was about the equivalent of £1 a start and £1
a point, and therefore there weren't any professional speedway riders
in Sweden then. I was still working in my father's fur company at the
time. I was a furrier by trade.

'I become aware of the wider aspects of the sport the very next
year, 1953. I went to England with the Filbyterna club. It was really
a Swedish 'B' team and we raced on Southern League tracks – really
Third Division standard. Another senior team labelled Sweden, that
included Olle Nygren, Sune Karlsson, Stig Pramberg, Rune Sormander
and Dan Forsberg, raced on the First Division tracks at the same time
– but we did a bit better than them. We raced at Rayleigh, Exeter,
Oxford, Plymouth and Swindon and I was the top scorer everywhere,
strangely enough. We went across – two teams – on the boat from
Gothenburg to Tilbury in those days – and that was the first time I
met Olle Nygren.'

But also on that trip, Ove discovered how prim and was proper the
British attitude to the association of the sexes compared with the more
relaxed attitude in Sweden. He travelled with Dan Forsberg and both
had their girlfriends with them. Ove took along Mona, who was later
to become his first wife.

'That's when we found out that we couldn't share a room with
our girlfriends. So the girls had one room and we had another. Olle
at the time was not only a celebrated motorcyclist but let's say he
was at least as big then as David Beckham is now. He was always in
the papers. I would say that if Tony Rickardsson can win ten World
Championships he will never be as big as Olle Nygren – because
those days are gone. You don't have those super speedway stars any
more. They were like rock stars – Olle was. So you can imagine how
big he was.'

Throughout his racing career, Ove says, he was never conscious of any influence on his speedway style, which was unique. On the track he looked awkward and it is difficult to see how he could have modelled himself on anyone else. As a young, up-and-coming novice it would have been natural for him to have been eager to learn and to seek advice from other more experienced riders. But, he says, he never did.

'From the first day, no one influenced me. I was considered very much a loner, even as a small boy. I always went my own way. Nobody taught me about style or how to ride a bike. When they first asked me to go and try it, I knew I could do it without them telling me. I noticed I was quite good at it when I started beating everybody. And that encourages you. Oh, I'm good at this. I'll see how good I can be.'

It is often said that, in speedway, to be good you have to have a good engine, a fast engine. Ove disagrees.

'That's not true. Not true at all. Because my engines were very normal. I never had anything but a very plain, very normal engine. Les Mullins, who looked after my engines at Norwich, wasn't one of those who experimented. He just had a good engine. I wanted to experiment a couple of times with camshafts, but when I brought one over once he tried it but he didn't like it so he didn't use it. He wanted just a good, reliable engine.'

Ove was very firm about that, and he also remembered one incident that helped his style to evolve when he was starting out in Sweden. A friend of his who was, he said, 'a leg-trailer' – which was the method employed by the early dirt-track stars who trailed their left legs to power slide their machines round the bends rather than the modern method that has riders placing their left foot forward of the machine – fitted his bike with straight handlebars.

'When I got to England I saw that Jack Young, Fred Williams, Barry Briggs and Ronnie Moore all had what they call cow-horn handlebars, great big things, and they were sitting down, whereas I stood up with my tiny handlebars – and now today they are back to the tiny handlebars again.'

Wherever he went, throughout his riding career, those tiny, straight handlebars went with him. But what it all really came down to was that he was an absolute natural.

'I also fought hard for it. I do not think there is any such thing as a natural in anything. You have to be a natural in certain things. You do not become a good basketball player unless you are tall. You do not become a good boxer unless you are... well, you can figure that out. And you cannot become a good speedway rider if you become too tall or too heavy. With my 174 centimetres I was considered rather small in Sweden, but when I came to England I was considered tall.

'I never drank. I didn't even drink beer. But I loved going to pubs. And what I miss is that you can never come into a pub today where there is a singsong. There used to be a singsong in every second pub on a Friday or Saturday night.

'I believe that if somebody is good at their sport, they would be good at any sport if they just put their mind to it, because I think sporting success has a lot to do with determination and the will to win. Also, coming from a little place like Tranas, they kind of looked down on you, you know. All our cars in Sweden finish with "A" and that's the postal code – A, B, C and so-on. Where I came from it was "S", and we were really considered country bumpkins. The big shots – Olle and all of them – they looked down on us. Something the cat had dragged in from the fields. They more or less ignored us. But that made me feel more determined.

'And of course I had red hair, and they say that people with that are sort of angry and so on. Surely you have noticed that I have no patience. I have no patience for anything. I just can't sit there. There is something within me that clicks and I go wild.'

Olle Nygren remembers Fundin's beginning differently:

'Well, we are different people. I come from Stockholm – like London – and he came from Tranas in the country – like down in Devon. I came from the big city and was happy-go-lucky. I didn't give a damn, because I was brought up like that, during the war. I had an adventurous life before I started racing. I was expelled from school, all sorts. Fundin probably read about this 'botherall' – me. In those days you couldn't start on racing bikes. I think he started on little motorbikes and gradually got in, then motocross. Then he got a speedway bike and went to the Linkoping circuit. Always he was very aggressive and determined to win. He started out like that – rode like an idiot always to win, even though he couldn't handle it. That's how I remember him when he started. That's the way he came up. Then he got quite good because we had quite big tracks. Right from the start, he had a win or bust attitude.

'I suppose once you get up with the top boys, you don't think of them as the top boys. It's like if you see them in the pub every evening. You get used to them, and then you probably get to learn a little bit more about them so you know how to beat them. You are not overawed by them any more.

'I tried to suss him out and try and beat the bugger, but I couldn't. And once he got on that inside white line... I mean, they rode the white line in those days. He'd got what it takes to win at speedway. Win the gate. Being tough. He wasn't very polite.'

# THREE

# FIGURE IT OUT
# FOR YOURSELF

*'That first final, I was scared like hell. I didn't even know what gear to pull. No wonder I was hopeless.'* – Ove Fundin

The Empire Stadium, Wembley. Thursday 16 September 1954. World Final night, and great thundering waves of sound roll round the packed terraces from the voices of nearly 100,000 fiercely partisan speedway fans chanting the names of their favourites, their ranks soaring away into the night sky. It is an electrifying noise, focused with laser-like intensity on the floodlit central arena. The broad racing surface of red shale contrasts starkly with the brightness of the narrow ribbon marking the inner white line. And beyond is the green of the famous Wembley turf, fading away to blackness. To speedway enthusiasts the soccer pitch at Wembley, which spread at the corners almost to the safety fence, was always an intrusion. Wembley just did not look right unless the asymmetrical oval of the racing track – one bend was rounded, the other pointed – was in place. The Empire Stadium is the Mecca of sporting achievement, and the supercharged atmosphere is at once intoxicating, invigorating, terrifying and intimidating. It is the forum in which some are inspired to greatness and are granted the ecstasy of triumph, and where others know the despair of seeing their dreams dashed to pieces around them.

The colour, and the sound of the watching multitude, which all but drowns out the rumble of men warming up the engines of high-powered motorcycles to the temperature at which they will be at their most potent, combine to turn this into a night like no other. The sport of speedway racing's night of the year, when its biggest names, its star attractions, its most accomplished and skilful performers – yes, and ruthless practitioners, too – compete for the highest honour it can bestow: the World Championship.

At one end of the great stadium, a pall of blue smoke hangs in the air above the racing pits as mechanics in white overalls keep the rear wheels of the machines spinning above their metal stands. Riders, all in black leather and wearing colourful racing waistcoats bearing their national flags, watch and wait, and nervously assemble their equipment – crash helmets, goggles, gloves and scarves. White-coated officials with clipboards hover around, observing and checking.

Among all the chaos one young man, barely twenty-one years old, tries to make sense of it all. He is tall and slim, with strikingly red hair. He looks – and is – bewildered and alone. He is Ove Fundin, one of two Swedes among the eight Englishmen, four New Zealanders, three Australians and one Welshman all determined that the night will conclude with their name on the championship trophy. Fundin is awed by the entire spectacle. He is literally shaking with apprehension and nerves – a condition that will never go away, that in the years ahead he will never conquer, and that will affect profoundly those he loves most, though he will go on to achieve fabulous and undreamed of success throughout the world.

'That first final, I was scared like hell. When I saw that stadium. I'd never been in a big stadium like that – and I don't mean having anything to do with speedway – not even as a spectator. I don't think the big crowd bothered me. It was the stadium. When you came down and saw those twin towers and the whole building, it reminded me more of a castle. It was very imposing, very impressive. I was used to small country tracks in Sweden. There were no buildings around or anything. If you were lucky there might have been a small grandstand – but no big buildings – more just natural terraces.'

He is not the only one affected. And even the experienced Jack Young, whose fifth final this is and who has already had his name engraved on the magnificent *Sunday Dispatch* Trophy twice, is showing the signs of extreme stress.

'I know some of the other riders were all nervous. I remember I was shaking. And I remember Jack Young, who was the biggest at the time – he was completely gone. I thought he was going to throw up, the way he looked in the pits. So he must have been nervous. He was one of those who you thought nothing bothered.'

Fundin was ill-equipped to deal with the situation. He had never been told that there was a practice facility a few days before the final so that riders could set up their racing machines for the particular condition of the track, the track of which he had no prior knowledge and had never seen before. No one had told him it was compulsory to have a mechanic in attendance. No one had told him that mechanic had to wear white overalls on the night.

To attempt to ease the anxiety that plagued him, he had gone to the cinema that afternoon. It was something he would do before all except one of the twelve Wembley finals in which he was to appear. 'I used to like going to the movies. I went to the movies before every World Final but the 1967 one, when I won my fifth title. And I took the chocolate bars to Wembley hoping that it would be a good enough movie to forget about what I was about to do – otherwise I would have had the shakes. It's not good being nervous hours before if you can help it. I didn't go to the movies before the last one I won in 1967 because I was at Belle Vue and drove down from Manchester and there was not enough time. I was with Wilf Lucy, Belle Vue's chief mechanic, and not looking after myself. At Norwich I always went to a movie on a Saturday afternoon before a meeting.'

Going to the cinema also helped to improve his English as well as calm his nerves before a meeting. But he would never rid himself completely of the pre-meeting nerves that, at times, threatened to overwhelm him. At that first really 'big' meeting at Wembley in 1954, all around him his rivals busied themselves with their machines. The overhead track lights and the harsh intrusion of the Press photographers' flashbulbs bounced startling reflections off their shiny black leather racing suits. His own machinery was a bike with its frame painted bright red and, legend has it, saved from falling apart only by bits of old wire and string. It was a second-hand JAP for which his father had lent him the money to buy back home in Sweden. But it is extremely unlikely that it was held together with bits of string and wire – the machine examiners on World Final night would never have allowed him to race on a bike in such a condition.

'The red bike – that "shitty bike" – I rode in that first World Final is the one my father helped me to buy. It had been used by a leg-trailer. I'd ridden it in England the previous year when I toured with the Swedish Filbyterna team, and it was the one I had ridden in my World Championship qualifying rounds. After the championship rounds I left it in England. They talked me into leaving it because I didn't pay my own fare and they said I should leave the bike and come back for it for the World Final.

'So I left it there with a fellow called Bill Smith who used to be a mechanic at West Ham. The only trouble was he saw that the rear fork was broken and he welded it up and repaired it. But that was one of my features – I wanted to have it broken. I thought it was a great thing. The tube on the driving side was already broken. It was probably cheaper to buy a new one, but the fellow who helped me in Sweden put a smaller tube inside it and then it was still broken but it was flexible. And he said to me that it was a good thing. And I believed in it, so when I came back to race at Wembley in the World Final, Bill Smith had welded it up. And I thought, "Oh, he has destroyed my bike!"

'I think that put me off a bit. Really I also got a little bit upset because nobody had told me you could come two days ahead for practice. It was so badly organised. The Swedish Motor Federation organised it and they sent me there with someone to look after me, and this man spoke even worse English than me. So we came on the plane together and I had to show him round London Airport because I could read a little English. Fortunately Don Lawson was there to meet me. Aub had sent him.'

Aub Lawson, one of the sport's all-time great speedway artists, was to become something of a mentor – if not altogether an out-and-out Svengali – to Ove. He had taken a shine to the young Swedish upstart after observing his performances closely in the qualifying rounds leading up to the final. Chance had thrown them together as opponents when they had both been drawn to ride at Norwich and West Ham, two similar tracks. West Ham was a full quarter-mile. Norwich was almost as big at 425 yards. Aub and Norwich were to play more significant parts in Ove Fundin's life and career than he could possibly know at the time.

Known throughout the speedway world as 'Gentleman Aub' – though the attribute was questioned by some – Lawson had been a bit of an overnight sensation himself in his younger days. He had first arrived in Britain from Australia in 1939 to ride for Wembley but was loaned for a while to Second Division Middlesbrough. In that debut season he had qualified for the World Championship Final, the final that was never held because war was declared four days before it was due to take place. He became a world star at West Ham in the seasons immediately following the conflict and then, in 1953 after a two-year retirement from British racing, Norwich manager Fred Evans tempted him back to shore up a side that badly needed strengthening after the departure of top-rated Bill Gilbert and Bob Leverenz.

Fundin had shaken the British speedway aficionados with his performances in the World Championship qualifiers. His only previous experience of racing in what was at the time the toughest and best speedway league in the world had been the previous year while touring with the Swedish side Filbyterna on what amounted to British Third Division tracks.

On his red bike that he insisted was virtually 'home made', he had finished second to Aub at Norwich on 24 August, dropping only two points – one to Aub, unbeaten on 15 points, and one to Norwich's Fred Rogers. It was Fred's only win of the night. Among Ove's victims in his last ride were England's Split Waterman of Harringay, who had twice been World number two, and Wimbledon's Barry Briggs of New Zealand, who was just emerging into the top rank and was on the threshold of a glittering career that was to win him four World titles and see him become one of Ove's greatest track rivals. In the second qualifier ten days later, delayed because of rain, Ove, against all that was reasonable, was again right up among the big names and – where he had no right to be – among the top scorers. Former double World Champion Jack Young of West Ham was the round winner on 14 points. Ove dropped a point to Young in his opening ride and another to Dick Dradley of Second Division Bristol to again finish on 13, joint second with wonder-boy Ronnie Moore and two points ahead of Aub Lawson. It was a remarkable performance from a virtually unknown foreigner.

He had qualified for his first World Final without the benefit of sustained British racing experience, something that was to be considered essential for decades, in joint-third place on 26 points. He was equal with Wimbledon's other two New Zealanders, Ronnie Moore and Geoff Mardon, Wembley's Brian Crutcher of England and Aub Lawson, the only man who in the future Ove would acknowledge as a teacher. Ahead of Ove in the qualifiers was Young on 29 points, with Peter Craven of Belle Vue and England and Eddie Rigg of Bradford and England next on 28 points each. Way behind him on 24 points was Olle Nygren, the fellow Swede of whom he was in awe. Nygren at that time was huge in Sweden, a motorcycle star in virtually all disciplines – speedway, TT, grass, long track and road racing – and he enjoyed pop-star status. Nygren also happened to be at that second qualifier at West Ham. He remembers: 'Jack Young was there. And lots of other good riders. And Fundin was there. He had this bloody awful bike and, I mean, nobody expected him to get a point on it. Anyway, he knocked somebody off, and had somebody else over the fence, and they came up to me complaining about this bloody guy who could come and ride the way he did. They couldn't talk to him anyway because he couldn't speak English. I said it's nothing to do with me. He's an up-and-coming rider and he's just trying to win. I suppose he can't turn. It is difficult. You have to learn to turn. It takes a bit of time.'

Ove says: 'I was overdoing it. Trying to ride better than I could, or going into corners faster than I could or was good enough to do. But

I still think that everyone who wants to become good has to start that way – a little bit too wild and then be lucky enough to stay out of trouble. If you run into trouble you can hurt yourself. But if you're lucky you will sooner or later learn that it is impossible to come into a corner that fast or go through where there is no gap. But when you are young and inexperienced you just go for it.'

Ronnie Moore remembers: 'When Ove first came to England, his bike was an old welded-up wreck and his riding was ragged. He was a real tearaway. He would think nothing of cutting a corner and meeting you halfway round the other side.' Which was always all right, according to Ove, 'as long as both wheels didn't go over the white line'.

In spite of what was to prove to be a rapidly emerging disruptive reputation, when Ove arrived back in Britain to prepare for the big night – as well as he could – Aub Lawson took Ove, the innocent abroad, into virtual protective custody. He had arranged for his half-brother Don to meet Ove off his plane and take him to the home of the Fearman family in Plaistow, just round the corner from the West Ham track. The Fearmans, whose son Reg was to go on to ride not only for West Ham and England but also become one of the sport's top administrators, had provided board and lodging for many a young speedway hopeful arriving virtually penniless and homeless in Britain and helped them to get established. In the early post-war days, Aub Lawson had been one of them.

'Don took me to stay with Reg Fearman's mum and dad. I had no mechanic with me, so Reg's father was my mechanic. It was so poorly organised. I don't even know if they knew I could have been there for practice.'

But now all the razzmatazz was over. Looking at the strange, unfamiliar track, the bewildered young man wondered what gear he should use.

'I remember my good friend Olle Nygren was there – at least I thought he was my good friend because we were the only Swedes there. It was just him and me. So naturally I asked him what gear I should pull for this track. He just shrugged and said, "You have to figure that out for yourself." He wasn't very friendly, but probably that was because he was so nervous himself. I have been onto him ever since. We laugh about it. I didn't even know what gear to pull. No wonder I was hopeless.'

Nygren says: 'He went out in one race without a steel shoe. He was so nervous he forgot to put it on.'

...And now the vast crowd is hushed in expectation as the terrace lights are dimmed. Four riders emerge onto the dazzling illuminated track and approach the tapes for heat one. The spectators cannot know it but tonight three young men are making their first appearance in this Blue Riband event, and they will go on to dominate the sport and the competition for more than a decade to come: Ove Fundin, Barry Briggs and Peter Craven. Lining up for the opening race are Lawson, Fred Brand of England and Norwich, an outsider; former World Champion Tommy Price of England on his home track; and Arthur Forrest of England and Bradford, known as The Black Prince because of him always riding in immaculate, shiny black leathers. He is one of the favourites. The crowd's roar blends with the roar of the bikes into a crescendo of sound as the first sensation of the night unfolds before them. Lawson and Forrest get in each other's way on the first bend and it is the unfancied Brand who streaks into an uncatchable lead.

From the pits the young Fundin watches Lawson and Price disputing the minor placings. Under pressure from Lawson, Price's front wheel lifts and the Australian shoots through on the inside. Forrest is nowhere. Fundin sees the other whizzkid, Briggs, at least open his score in the next race with a third, and then it is his turn to take to the track. It couldn't be a tougher World Final baptism. His opponents are Jack Young, Craven and – ironic that they should meet in their first ride – his 'unfriendly' friend, Nygren.

'When I first walked in there, and on the parade when the stadium filled up with all those thousands of people, it was overwhelming to me. But as soon as I put on my helmet for my first ride I didn't hear the noise.'

Young makes a lightning start from the tapes. So much for his 'nerves'. Craven falls at the first bend, leaving Fundin and Nygren in a flat-out duel. In his desperation, Fundin narrowly avoids colliding with the fence on the pits turn. Nygren gets the better of him, but with Craven out of it – and sportingly pulling his bike to the fence to prevent the race being stopped – Fundin has one lucky point to his name.

In his second ride, heat eight, he reaches turn one level with Mardon and Harringay's Australian star Jack Biggs. But they leave him behind, and Brand also gets by him. On the fourth bend of the third lap Fundin blasts back under him, overslides and Brand surges through again. On the next bend Fundin goes for Brand once more but fails to move him. Two rides, one point.

His third ride nets him one more – at the expense of the vastly more experienced Lawson. Aub is taken wide by Waterman on the first turn of heat ten, and on the next bend Fundin charges underneath him to snatch the point. In heat thirteen Fundin loses a fight for third with Forrest, and Ronnie Moore takes his wins to three on the trot. He begins to look like the new World Champion.

Fundin is starting to congratulate himself on his two points because he has noticed that Craven has scored no points at all after four rides. Ove thinks that at least he won't come last in his first World Final. But in heat eighteen Craven romps to an all-the-way win over a wildly challenging Briggs. It wipes away Fundin's complacency. He knows that he needs two points in the very next race, heat nineteen and his final ride, if he is not to end the night ignominiously in sixteenth place.

*Speedway Star* editor Eric Linden, in his heat-by-heat report, saw that race like this: 'Fundin finally over-rides himself and comes down on the top bend starting second lap. Brings Redmond down with him. Swede is excluded from re-run. Crutcher comfortably ahead when race is stopped. Long delay while Redmond's machine is sorted out. Then three Wembley riders (Crutcher, Price, Redmond) line up at tapes with Crutcher needing a win to stay in the running... there's no doubt about his win. It's all of twenty yards.'

The night ends for Fundin with him sitting in the middle of the Wembley first turn looking into the disgruntled eyes of New Zealander Trevor Redmond. It is an incident that will remain with them for the rest of their lives.

'Of course Trevor Redmond always said that I knocked him off. It was one of Trevor's funny stories. The only World Final he ever rode in, you know, in 1954. I knocked him off and I fell off myself, and there I was sitting on the ground and I turned to him and excused myself. I heard him say it so many times.'

After the embarrassing heat nineteen tangle with Trevor Redmond, Ove returned to the pits downcast and disconsolate, straight into 'a real rollicking' from Redmond's Wembley teammate and former World Champion Fred Williams. In the pits watching the drama was Linden, the sometime editor of *Speedway Echo* and *Speedway Star & News*, prolific columnist under various pseudonyms, commentator and author of several books on the sport. It was the first time that he and Fundin came into contact, and he recalled: 'Ove was sitting in the pits with his head in his hands, as near to crying as he could be, and I remember telling Fred that he'd said enough. Ove brightened up a bit after that. But he was the world's worst sport – in that he had an absolute hatred of not winning. It must have been something deep in his past. But in reality he is a very caring man. He discovered I was "Angus Kix" and he always called me Angus, never Eric.'

The night and the glory belonged to another twenty-one-year-old, Ronnie Moore, who had been threatening to take the title ever since he had burst upon the international scene four years before. His maximum score was even more of an achievement because little more than two months previously he had been lying in a Danish hospital bed with a broken left leg. He had ridden with the injured limb encased in a metal brace. Nygren had been steadily piling up the points all night to remain in with a real chance. Had he beaten Moore in a climactic heat twenty both men would have had to race in a decider for the title. As it was, Olle lost the run-off for second place with Crutcher and was never to come so close again. And neither would Crutcher. But for Fundin, it was only the beginning.

The 1950s were the worst years to begin a speedway career. The fabulous post-war boom was over. Speedway was on one of its periodic slides towards apparent oblivion. The entertainment-starved, austerity-bound, still-rationed public had taken the thrilling spectacle of speedway racing to their hearts and an all-time high in the years immediately following the outbreak of peace. It wasn't as if the British needed the thrills. After all, they had experienced almost six years of a total and brutal war, and all that went with it. That meant constantly disturbed nights dodging bombs and doodlebugs – Adolf Hitler's pilot-less flying bombs – seeing their homes reduced to rubble and their towns go up in flames, having their children evacuated to goodness knows where in the country without knowing whether they would ever see them again. And those who were not engaged on the Home Front were in uniform and fighting for their very existence in the tanks, planes, ships and on foot throughout Europe and the Far East.

The first season of racing after the Second World War, 1946, was speedway enthusiasm with the lid off. Never before in the history of the sport had there been anything like the nationwide interest and adulation shown to the stars of the dirt tracks as there was at the beginning of those first post-war years. It almost certainly surpassed the 'gold rush' of the early pioneer days of the late 1920s and early 1930s. From 1928 the new sport, imported from Australia, captured the imagination of a world changing into a motorised and speed-conscious society hell-bent on a hedonistic existence in the carefree – for some – years between the conflicts. Tracks had sprung up almost overnight all over the land, only for many to disappear as suddenly.

Speedway's amazing ability to reinvent itself first became apparent with the introduction of properly organised league racing. The soccer-style arrangement stabilised an enterprise that previously had come to be thought of as little more than a circus attraction into a truly international sporting spectacle. It survived even the years of the Great Depression, which gripped the world by the economic throat in late 1929 and lasted for about a decade until the start of the Second World War.

Speedway was kept tenuously alive between 1940 and 1945 at the only track that never closed, Belle Vue in Manchester, where three million people watched racing programmes made up of any rider who could get time off from his war duties. When league racing resumed full time after the war, a total of 1,211,355 paid to see the sport at

Wembley alone during the 1946 season. That is four times as many (250,573) as attended meetings at the Empire Stadium in 1939. It was a similar story on the other side of London. West Ham drew 919,925 spectators that first post-war year compared with a third of that number in 1939.

London was the Mecca of the game with six tracks: Wimbledon (Mondays), West Ham (Tuesdays), New Cross (Wednesdays), Wembley (Thursdays) and Harringay and Walthamstow (Fridays). With such a wealth of opportunity, the national dailies of Fleet Street gave the sport due recognition. Major newspapers such as the *Daily Mail*, the *News Chronicle*, the *Star*, the *Evening News*, *News of the World*, the *People*, *Sunday Dispatch* and *Sunday Pictorial* all gave their names to speedway competitions. In the provinces the local newspapers were equally supportive, and Norwich and Birmingham, though in a lower division than the London sides, shared in the fabulous success, attracting almost half a million fans through each of their turnstiles in the 1946 season.

Such was the clamour for the glamour of the leather-clad heroes then that when Wembley were the opposition at West Ham's opening meeting on Good Friday, 19 April 1946 – a friendly – there was a crowd of 57,000. On the same day at Wimbledon there was a record attendance of 28,681, and 10,000 more were locked outside. At the final meeting of the 1946 season at the Empire Stadium a demonstration on a rocket-assisted bike by Wembley captain Bill Kitchen drew a crowd far in excess of a football cup final. 'It was memorable,' wrote Basil Storey, editor of one of the sport's major publications, *Speedway Gazette*, 'not from a racing point of view, but because half of Fleet Street's representatives failed to gain admission until shortly before the interval. Inside the vast stadium was a crowd of 85,000, while locked outside more than 20,000 fans followed the meeting by loudspeaker commentary. Extra police were rushed in to marshal the multitude outside.

Speedway was so popular that in a 1947 *Daily Mail* national sports poll it rated fourth place ahead of horse racing, rugby union, athletics, tennis, rugby league and golf. Soccer topped the poll, followed by cricket and boxing. And in the *Sporting Record*'s Sportsman of the

Year competition in 1948, Belle Vue and England captain Jack Parker was fourth ahead of Stanley (later Sir Stanley) Matthews (soccer), Gordon (later Sir Gordon) Richards (horse racing), Bill Edrich (cricket) and Bruce Woodcock (boxing). Denis Compton (cricket) was top with Reg Harris (cycling) second and Tommy Lawton (soccer) third. While they lasted, the late 1940s and very early 1950s were heady days and speedway, though still young compared with other national sports, came of age.

Wembley had the greatest following of any speedway team in 1946 with its 52,601 paid-up members of the supporters' club, a figure that was to rise to 61,000 within two years. Bristol Speedway's supporters' club could claim film stars Laurel and Hardy and Bing Crosby among its members. In 1948, the year speedway attained its majority – twenty-one it was in those days – a total of 10,694,000 customers paid to see racing in Britain. The Duke of Edinburgh – the Queen's consort, although she was then Princess Elizabeth – went to Wembley to present Australia's Vic Duggan with the winner's trophy at the Speedway Riders Championship Final, the event that had temporarily replaced the World Final. It really was boom time.

But we all know what usually follows a phenomenal boom: an equally phenomenal bust!

Riding the crest of that phenomenal boom at the time were veterans who had pioneered the sport twenty years earlier, many of them then in or near their forties. They were still the master craftsmen of the game and naturally reluctant to surrender the easy rider pickings they enjoyed to any bright, brash, up-and-coming youngster knocking on the door of speedway stardom, no matter how talented they were. And there were plenty. Eager ex-servicemen, unwilling to settle for a mundane existence after their wartime experiences, were queuing up to spend their demobilisation gratuities on speedway bikes and ride off in search of fame and, hopefully, fortune. One of those daringly ambitious and wide-eyed youngsters challenging the old order at the beginning of the 1950s was a young New Zealander named Barry Briggs. He was so challenging at the time that he was considered unsafe and there was even a move to have him banned from the tracks. But he was to go on to win four World titles and become one of the best-known and dominant figures in the sport. He followed his boyhood friend Ronnie Moore from New Zealand. Moore, recognised as probably the most naturally gifted speedway rider the sport has known, arrived in Britain as a raw seventeen-year-old in 1950 on the recommendation of Norman Parker, the highly experienced veteran Wimbledon captain, and was an immediate success with Parker's club. In his first season in Britain he qualified for the first of the fourteen World Championship Finals he appeared in during his career, and by the time he was twenty-one he was the sport's youngest World title holder.

Briggs recalled: 'Some of those old boys were really lethal. Ronnie had it hard from them I think, because he came in when they were a group like the Mafia. They had all that speedway money – their great big fat pay packets – riders like the Parker brothers, Jack at Belle Vue and Norman at Wimbledon – they had it all. And it was easy. They'd just cruise in and shut off. Then suddenly Ronnie came in, flat out... They wanted to kill Ronnie. There was one night at New Cross, Ronnie was sitting between the two Parkers and Jack leaned across to Norman and said, "Tell your boy I'll break his f——ing legs if he comes near me!"

'Then I came along. But Ronnie was really wild as well. And then they let him into their club. And he kind of cleaned up a bit. But they didn't start closing the gap on him or shutting off on him, because on the speedway, if someone shuts off on you, you have nowhere to go. You are supposed to be racing, but these old boys thought "bugger that!"

'Pricey [Tommy Price of Wembley and in 1949 the first Englishman to become World Champion] was another. Because Pricey couldn't take it back. I went to Wembley one night and in one race I'd keep passing him, and when we came into the straight he'd keep passing me. I got pissed off with it. All I did when we came out of the corner was just ride down the middle of the straight. He had to go out to the fence and I passed him. Tommy went nuts.'

Briggs had 'a certain reputation' on the track at the time. He was described as 'Tearaway Barry Briggs'. He said: 'There was one World

Championship qualifier at Wimbledon when I knocked two blokes off. I knocked Peter Clark off. Well, it was my first World Championship so I was nervous. And normally I was slap-happy. But Peter was my mate. He was a Kiwi. I got under him, and the way I learned speedway you had to keep the wheels spinning. Otherwise you just go straight. So I'm under him spinning, and I ease it off so I don't hit him. In those days the throttle cable went under the handlebars and mine got caught over the lifting handle on his rear mudguard. So as I eased off a bit, he pulled away, which put my bike flat out and I hit him hard. If you look at the pictures from those days, I'm the first rider to have the throttle cable to go up over the top of the handlebars. Suddenly the throttle cables go over the bars. And that was because of me, because I hit Peter Clark.

'And Pat Clarke – I knocked him off too. He probably deserved it. Everybody patted me on the back over Pat Clarke. He did nothing. I was just racing him. He probably didn't give me enough room. I probably needed a bit more room than he gave me. I remember they had to take his front wheel out to get his leg out of the bike, but I had no real regrets over that one. If you give it out you've got to take it. I have found myself underneath a fence now and again and thought, "I might have deserved that."'

On the face of it, though the sport may have been beginning to falter in Britain in the early 1950s, the speedway gospel had begun to spread to other parts of the world. As well as Australia and New Zealand, it was taking a hold in South Africa and in Continental Europe, with Austria, Belgium, Denmark, Finland, Germany, Holland, Norway, Sweden and Switzerland all beginning to throw up names that would become familiar before very long. Listing the rankings for Scandinavia, the *Stenner's Speedway Annual* for 1952 commented that there were only three Norwegians in the top fifteen. The rest were Swedish, indicating 'that Sweden is striding away from her near neighbours'. Olle Nygren at number one, Sune Karlsson at number four. Rune Sormander at number eight, Dan Forsberg at number ten and Stig Pramberg at number 13 were all destined for stardom, as were Norwegians Basse Hveem and Henry Andersen.

Denmark's Morian Hansen had led the way well before the Second World War, qualifying for the 1936 World Final with 10 bonus points, the same as Australia's Bluey Wilkinson – the man who scored an unbeaten 15-point, five-ride maximum on the night and did not win the championship because others took more bonus points to the final than he did. This was an infamous system that was dropped after the war. Hansen qualified again in 1937. It was not until 1952 that Dan Forsberg became the first Swedish rider to make the breakthrough and ride in a post-war World Final. Forsberg had joined First Division Birmingham, helping them to second place in the league behind Wembley. It was his first season in Britain and he was only eighteen. It was a remarkable achievement yet completely overshadowed by the Ronnie Moore phenomenon. Nygren had had a brief stay with Harringay the previous year but – ever the maverick – had been suspended for four months by the draconian Swedish authorities when he failed to return to Sweden for a fixture and rode instead for Harringay in the London Cup Final.

The harsh disciplinarians at SVEMO, the Swedish Motor Federation that governed the sport, were to impose their strict rulings on Ove Fundin in the years ahead, actions that almost certainly were to ensure that he did not become a six-times World Champion ahead of Mauger and Rickardsson.

The Swedes had introduced league racing in 1948, so with the usual speedway apprenticeship reckoned to be about five years, Dan Forsberg's elevation to world class and an appearance in the 1952 World Final put him a year ahead of his time. After scoring 9 points with one ride to go, Forsberg was in with a chance of a rostrum place – which was even better than Ronnie Moore's first World Final performance two years earlier. A win in heat twenty would have put him into a run-off with England's Bob Oakley of Wembley for third place. But a tangle with the highly experienced Jeff Lloyd, of England and Harringay, sent him crashing through the pit gates – an incident that he has always claimed, though never been able to prove, was a deliberate attempt to make sure he didn't finish among the points in his last race.

From a thirteen-club set-up in two divisions in 1946, the sport had expanded rapidly in Britain, and within five years there was a total of thirty-six clubs in three divisions. But there then began a slow haemorrhaging that had turned into a torrent by the end of the decade until there were a mere nine teams in the National League (First Division), which also ran sides in a Reserve League, plus a Southern Area League of five teams. In his excellently researched book on British speedway leagues between 1946 and 1964, the very knowledgeable Peter Morrish described the situation in 1959 British speedway as 'chaotic'. There appeared to be utter confusion about the number of heats in a league match, the number of riders in a team and in which part of the programme the reserve match should take place.

Belle Vue at first declined to take part in the Reserve League, but the speedway authorities waved their big stick at the Aces and gave them twenty-eight days to comply, which they did. Morrish reported that the result of all this was that the National Reserve League never stood a chance, the Southern Area League caught the general malaise and the National League suffered because Wimbledon were too powerful and won the title with plenty to spare. 'The sport,' wrote Morrish, 'got into a terrible mess.'

But then, just as it appeared to be on the point of expiring, speedway was resuscitated. The kiss of life was given to it by an entrepreneur and, reportedly, Manchester slum owner named Mike Parker who gathered together some like-minded risk-takers to form a Provincial League from previously moribund tracks. The Provincial League was to gain enough strength to break away from mainstream speedway and run 'black' for a year. What amounted to open warfare between the speedway establishment and Parker's provincials was finally resolved by the Shawcross Inquiry, which resulted in the amalgamation of the rival factions into the British League in 1965 and led to the great revival in the sport in the following two decades.

The warning bells had begun to ring in 1953 when Sir Arthur Elvin, the boss at Wembley – that well-known barometer of the sport's fortunes – revealed that no profit was made at the twenty-two meetings held at the Empire Stadium that year, even though another

Wembley rider, Fred Williams, had won his second World title. Yet almost £12,000 (an astonishing £207,840 in today's money) was paid out in entertainment tax, a government levy that at one time increased to more than fifty per cent and was slowly crippling the sport. Elvin continued to campaign for a reduction in the tax, but the reality was that speedway was losing its appeal. It was Coronation year and people were finding other interests. New Cross promoter Fred Mockford, who had pioneered speedway at Crystal Palace, was refused permission to sign Nygren. The Speedway Riders' Association – the very influential riders' union – was against foreigners riding regularly for British clubs, something it tried many times to enforce over the years, always eventually failing.

The SRA relented enough in April to allow Nygren to fill in for the injured Merv Harding at New Cross, but then Mockford warned that he would close the club if Olle's work permit was not renewed. It was not and, in June, he pulled the plug. His action jolted the complacent London promoters – it was the sort of thing that might happen in the provinces, but not London. The catharsis was such that they began to advertise each other's meetings in their programmes and even made concessions to supporters' clubs of rival tracks. Mockford blamed the increasing interest in television, and a new directive forbade promoters to allow television to film at their tracks without first getting permission from the Speedway Control Board. He also cited the entertainment tax burden, a rise in transport charges, lack of travel facilities and a shortage of spending money because people were choosing to spend their spare cash on the Coronation celebrations. But the killer blow was being banned from using Nygren, who was later given permission to ride for Bristol. Mockford never promoted speedway again.

It was perhaps ironic that a Swedish rider should precipitate such a hiatus, and maybe Nygren's growing success prompted Sweden, supported by Germany, to start throwing their World Championship weight about by proposing that, in the following year's title race, Continental riders should be given a 1-point-a-meeting start. Predictably, Britain rejected the idea. But Sweden, the sleeping giant, was about to awaken. In 1952 a tour of Southern League (Third

Division) tracks by a Swedish side that included Olle Nygren, Sune Karlsson, Stig Pramberg, Rune Sormander and Dan Forsberg, earned itself a small accolade in Stenner's annual review of the year under the headline 'Swedes brilliant *v.* Southern League'.

It was reported: 'Touring Swedes, in a visit that pulled top-of-the-season gates, turned in a brilliant performance *v.* Southern League, winning four matches, losing two, drawing one in eight days. Tour showed that the Swedes are ready for a higher class of opposition. Commented John Wick in *Speedway World*: "There is no doubt that Sweden is ready for a full international series against the best England can find."' The following season they came again, ready for the higher class of competition. This time there were two Swedish teams touring Britain. The senior side were on First Division tracks, and with the likes of Nygren, Karlsson, Pramberg, Sormander and Forsberg again included, naturally most of the publicity was directed at them. The other was by the Filbyterna club side on the Southern League tracks.

Many people may have overlooked the match reports in *Speedway Star* charting the progress of the 'junior' side, but the clues that a rising star was on the horizon were there. One, headed 'Exeter 47 Filbyterna 37', revealed: 'The rider who impressed most in this match was twenty-year-old Ove Fundin. Scoring two wins and a second, he was second in heat five when engine trouble forced him to pull out.' It must have been that old red painted 'shitty' bike again! 'Heat eleven produced the thrill of the match, when Fundin fought out a thrilling duel with [Johnny] Sargeant. For the whole race it was wheel to wheel, Sargeant just pulling away in the run-in for a win by half a wheel.' The senior side lost their series 3-2. Filbyterna lost their first match at Rayleigh by 20 points, their second by 10 at Exeter, but by the time they got to Oxford, Plymouth and Swindon they had the hang of it, winning all three. Their top scorer, with totals of 7, 8, 12, 15 and 12, was Ove Fundin.

Their best win was at Plymouth, running up a 66-42 score, where 'Ove Fundin's flat-out riding while seemingly glued to the white line was positively brilliant.' And at Swindon, where Filbyterna won 44-40,

'Ove Fundin, "babe" of Filbyterna, rode the track like a master and his maximum was one of the finest ever recorded at Swindon.' The English commentators considered Fundin 'easily up to First Division heat leader standard'. The Filbyterna travelling press representative told British reporters: 'Ove Fundin is a natural, and we think he will be better than Nygren and Karlsson by the time he has matured. He uses his head as well as his throttle. But we will not let him come to England on his own yet, he is too young.'

Ove also had a date with the Swedish Army.

'You had to do nine months national service in Sweden, unless you became a sergeant, then you had to do twelve months. I was one of those who had to do twelve months. I became a sergeant, no more. I had so much free time anyway. I'm not one of those who tries to avoid something, and that goes for me in the army. Why should I pretend I'm an idiot when I'm not an idiot? I just can't do it. I know some people did it, quite a lot of people, even some of my friends, they tried every trick in the book to get out of the army. But it's against my nature. And I'm glad I did it. Because I liked the army. It forces you. Same as Boy Scouts, it makes you a man.

'I did resent certain things – being expected to obey without question and being regimented. But in the event of a war, if someone tells you to do something, you do it. If you start arguing, what kind of a way can you fight then? In peacetime it does seem that a lot of things are stupid, a lot of it. But it's practising for a war, and that's what the military is about. In the Swedish army everybody had most – I dare say even every – weekend off. And today, I know from my sons, they had every night off. They would finish at 4.30 p.m. and then they could do what they liked until they had to report to their unit at 8 a.m.'

So Ove went off to do his military duty. But speedway in Britain, though teetering on the brink of an ever-darkening and precipitous chasm, was very soon to experience a bright new prospect whose skill and brilliance over the next decade would illuminate the forthcoming gloom.

FOUR

# IS THAT THE GREATEST RIDER IN THE WORLD?

*'I don't think I've ever known any gay speedway riders… it's not the sort of profession that attracts those sort of people, is it? I had my suspicions… nothing stronger. But you can't prove it anyway.'* – Ove Fundin

Ove's performance in the 1954 World Championship came to the notice of one of the most influential figures in the game, Jack Parker, who had taken speedway touring teams to Australia since the 1930s. And Parker invited Fundin to be a member of his European party for a Test series during the 1954/55 European winter. Parker had been what we now call a superstar virtually since the sport's very beginning in Britain in 1928. A highly skilled motorcyclist and trials expert, he had been a works rider for BSA and was sent to the cradle of English speedway, High Beech, a few weeks after that historic first meeting at the King's Oak in Epping Forest to find out what all the fuss was about. Ever the competitor, Parker stripped his road machine and joined in, and was an immediate master of the broad siding art. He was one of the first to challenge the supremacy of the top Australians in the early days, only to lose to Roger Frogley in the 1929 British Final of the Star Championship – the nearest there was in those days to a World Championship, then split into an Overseas section and a British section because the Australians were considered much too good and far superior to the home riders.

Both Parker and Frogley were members of the English Test side to race in the first official international against Australia in 1930, but Parker endured longer. He became British Champion by beating Australia's best, Vic Huxley, in 1931 and Star Champion in 1934. Following the Second World War he won the British Riders' Championship at Wembley in 1947 and made the British Match Race Championship Golden Helmet practically his sole property from 1946 until Split Waterman finally deprived him of his 'pension' in 1951. The one title Parker was never to win, to his lasting chagrin and regret, was the World Championship. He came nearest in 1949 when he was runner-up to England's first title-holder, Tommy Price. He qualified for seven World Finals, finishing fourth in 1937 and fifth an astonishing fourteen years later, in 1951. Parker, the rider, the powerful personality, the egotist, the sporting diplomat and ambassador, spread the speedway gospel worldwide, to Europe as well as Australia, and it was during one of Jack's visits to Sweden in the early 1950s that Ove Fundin first found himself in close proximity to the great man.

Ove did not meet him, did not even speak to him – he was too much in awe of Jack to do that. But as they were in the same dressing room getting ready to take part in a speedway meeting at Linkoping, Ove was able to observe his hero's demeanour and how he conducted himself.

'I met Jack Parker – well, I say I met him. I didn't talk to him, of course – but I raced with him in Sweden at Linkoping when I first started. Because Jack Parker was the big one, he was a big name then. And I still remember in the dressing room, I saw Jack put his quite dirty feet into these boots without socks. And I thought, "Is that the greatest rider in the world?"

'Even then I don't think I spoke to him. I don't think I spoke to him until I was on the boat going to Australia. Jack travelled first class and we travelled tourist class. But even though he travelled first he spent most of his time with us in tourist, because he would get lonely I suppose.

'It was Parker who invited me to Australia first. He invited me, Ulf Ericsson and Goran Norlen. He wrote to me and asked me if I would be interested in joining him on a tour of Australia. Or he might have done it through the Swedish Motor Federation – I can't remember exactly. He probably asked for me personally because I had appeared in a World Final, and the others weren't so well known. They hadn't raced in England, though Ericsson raced in one World Final.'

The great liners sailing to Australia in those days carried mainly English emigrants on £10 assisted passages going to make a new life on the other side of the world. And, when the European season ended, they transported a large, high-spirited, enthusiastic and often unruly party of speedway riders, who did not normally feel constrained by convention, bound for a few months of sheer enjoyment, part of which – maybe – was some serious speedway racing in between bouts of barbeques and Aussie hospitality.

'It was very hard to get tickets for those boats because there were a lot of migrants going to Australia in those days – half of England migrated, didn't they? There must have been at least twenty speedway riders on that boat. The three of us Swedish boys shared a cabin with Jack, and he was a bit of a ladies' man. He tried everything. One night we were lying there trying to get to sleep and we heard Jack come into the cabin with someone, and we heard a girl's voice say, "Jack, are you quite sure those Swedish boys are asleep?" And Jack whispered, "Yes, yes, yes, of course. Just be quiet. Come on in." And then they got going, of course, having their bit of fun. After a little while, Ulf Ericsson said – not shouted – but he wasn't quite whispering, "Are you going to be finished soon, Jack, so that we can all go to sleep?" Well, everything went quiet for a few seconds – and then we heard Jack and the girl leave the cabin.

'I also recall how good looking Ulf Ericsson was that first year we went to Australia. Dan Forsberg's girlfriend was after him. Dan was very unhappy about it, so much so that later we were all in a meeting in Stockholm and Dan said he was going to run over Ulf and kill him. Ulf was a copy of Errol Flynn, and Errol Flynn was the most hand-some man I think I have ever seen. Ulf seemed almost scared of girls and didn't appear to want anything to do with them. At one time I thought maybe he might be on "the other side", you know, and that he fights with his handbag and all that. But I don't think he did. It just seemed that way to me. And here was red-headed me fighting for the girls. I don't think I've ever known any gay speedway riders... it's not the sort of profession that attracts those sort of people, is it? I had my suspicions, nothing stronger. But you can't prove it anyway.

'But I still remember Jack, at probably one of the last veterans' dinners he went to. He came to me with a letter from a girl and said, "You must read this." I can't remember exactly what it said but it was something like, "It's amazing, a man of your age (Jack would have been in his late seventies then) being able to satisfy a young girl like me the way you did. And it's not like any of the young men I go out with who are finished within minutes − and there you are who can go on almost for hours." Many times he did things like that − even later on after he stopped racing.

'In Australia that winter season he was with us all the time. Of course he arranged things from our side and Frank Arthur, the Australian promoter, arranged it from the other side. We raced at Perth, Adelaide, Melbourne and Brisbane. Frank Arthur ran Brisbane and he also ran the Showground and the Sports ground in Sydney, so we had two meetings a week there. Frank took us around. We had lunch at Sydney Yacht Club − that was something. And he introduced us to Lionel Van Praag and Graham Warren. We weren't paid much, just enough to live on and they took care of all the hotels.'

But for Ove, at least, his racing was a serious business. It didn't take him long to adapt to the Australian tracks, even overshadowing Parker, the man he had been too overawed to speak to. In January 1955, June LeBreton reported: 'Forty thousand packed into the Sydney Royale. I'm sure Ove Fundin's new year resolution must have been to win every race. He was going like a rocket to win four races out of five. In the odd one out Ove finished third. Not a bad effort for any rider, especially as he beat the star of the European team − Goran Norlen − by something like a quarter of a lap. Jack Parker got a second and a third before he had engine trouble, which caused him to pull out for the night. I guess Jack couldn't have felt too bad about not winning when it was one of his own men who beat him.'

In truth, Jack had come to the end of his long and distinguished racing career. The previous winter he had been severely injured while practising in a speed car at Sydney, fracturing his skull and breaking an arm. He did ride again, but his days as a world-class performer were gone and he gave up racing after this final Australian season at the age of forty-six.

A month later, under a heading that announced 'Lawson Stopped An Aussie Rout – Swedes Created Great Impression', LeBreton again reported: 'The best, and I really do mean best, race of the Saturday night was event four of the International Solo Scratch Race. The riders were Ove Fundin (Sweden), Aub Lawson and Lionel Levy (Australia) and Jackie Hart (New Zealand). Ove won by a quarter of a lap from Lawson with Hart third. There are very few riders who can beat Lawson out here when he is riding well, and Aub was certainly doing his darndest in this race. That gives you an idea of how well Fundin must have been going to win by this distance. Believe me, the patrons went wild and Ove deserved every bit of the terrific ovation he got.'

But it didn't always go Ove's way. In the third Test Fundin was involved in a spectacular crash. In heat nine, Lionel Levy ran into Ove's back wheel, bringing him down heavily. Levy stayed on board but, LeBreton reported, 'Fundin seemed to go up in the air with his bike, and while still in mid-air his machine frame snapped into three separate pieces! Ove hurt his leg and was still limping heavily when I saw him days after the meeting.'

Europe won the match by 39 points to Australia's 33. Ove scored 10 and Parker a mere 2. For Australia, Aub Lawson scored 16, almost more than half his side's total. Out of their three meetings in the twelve-heat match, Fundin had beaten Lawson twice. It was the final match of the tour, and Ove's performances must have set Lawson thinking. Tempted out of retirement in 1953 by a woefully under-strength Norwich, who had been promoted from Division Two the previous year, Lawson rejuvenated his own career to the point where he finished third in the Wembley World Final of 1958 at the age of forty-five – the last of the surviving pre-war greats. His leadership worked wonders at the club as well, and he was to go on to become a sort of speedway elder statesman until the early 1960s.

Aub and Ove had become real friends on the boat. When it docked at Sydney, he took Fundin home with him to his farm, and Ove recalled: 'We rode around on horses and had a lot of fun. He was very good to me. I was with him and his family quite a bit. It was like that all the time.' Ove's rapid development over the winter of 1954/55 in Australia convinced Lawson that here was a rider with rich potential for the future, just the sort of talent needed at The Firs. He asked Ove how he felt about riding for Norwich – if he could arrange it.

'Of course I jumped at the chance, even though I had no idea where Norwich was. I was ever so proud. I had been approached once before by Bristol when I rode in Sweden and they came there with a touring team. But nothing came of that. Aub said that if I was interested, he would help me to go and race with him at Norwich.'

He had been noticed once before, without his knowledge, by the wily and experienced Phil 'Tiger' Hart who was manager of a Birmingham team on a Swedish tour. The Tiger had advised Birmingham promoter Les Marshall to sign the young Fundin, but Marshall failed to do so and nothing came of that either. But before Ove was eventually allowed to wear the distinctive gold star on green of Norwich, Aub Lawson was going to have to use all his considerable influence with the speedway bureaucrats. Ove's peers, the Speedway Riders' Association, didn't want him. It was by no means the first, or the last, measure of acrimony that was to be directed at Ove Fundin in Britain – from his side of the safety fence and from the terraces.

'How many kinds of stew can you get into trying to sign a speedway rider? If you want the answer to that one then ask Norwich. They hit every kind of trouble imaginable in their chase for Swede Ove Fundin.'

The conundrum was put before the British speedway public by *Speedway Star* editor Eric Linden in June 1955. Already the speedway season was half over and Norwich, after finishing in the top half of the league table the previous year, were languishing at the foot of Division One. Obviously they needed someone or something to lift them up by their bootstraps. But they still hadn't got the man they were convinced could work the miracle – and that man, according to Aub Lawson, was Ove Fundin.

It was a far from happy time for riders and promoters. The closure of another of London's major circuits, Harringay, had not only reduced the number of tracks in the capital to three – Wimbledon, Wembley and West Ham – but had thrown more riders onto the jobs market, and the jobs market was diminishing. Speedway was in poor shape, so bad that Harringay's team manager, former Stamford Bridge and England star Wal Phillips, who had helped to develop the JAP speedway engine, had gone into print to declare that the sport was dead. So it was not surprising that there was a strong reluctance by the Speedway Riders' Association to allow a team to sign another foreigner when the liveli-hoods of some of their own members were under threat.

The speedway authorities decided that it was a matter of allocation. Of the pick of the Harringay riders, Ron How and Alf Hagon went to Wimbledon, Split Waterman was sent to Belle Vue, refused to go and ended up at West Ham. Danny Dunton was bounced around between Birmingham, Ipswich and Bristol, Jeff Lloyd retired and Allan Quinn went to Southampton. Jack Biggs was allocated to Norwich, and requested that Norwich to pay his air fare over from his home in Australia. Norwich said, 'No.' At least the new manager at The Firs, Gordon Parkins, did. The slim, suave, outwardly sophisticated Parkins, a pre-war grass track rider of note who had served his speedway promotional apprenticeship after the war at Plymouth and Liverpool, had replaced the enigmatic, chunky and meticulous Major Fred Evans. It was Evans who had taken Norwich into the top flight three years before and it was he who had been able to persuade Aub Lawson to resume his career after a year's retirement – a major coup. Lawson was a class act who had held a regular top-four place in the Stenner's Annual World Rankings since 1949.

Now, something equally dramatic was called for at the Norfolk club. The big-time London promotions were already blaming the poor showing of the provincial sides for the capital's shrinking speedway scene, and Norwich had lost 8 of the 11 league matches they had ridden. If Parkins agreed to sign Biggs it would mean a £150 allocation fee to the Speedway Control Board plus the £250 fare from Australia that Biggs was demanding. Parkins didn't think Biggs, an SRA man, was worth it, even though he had come within a point of being World Champion in 1951. He wanted Fundin, though Ove was virtually an unknown quantity when it came to the rigours of racing in what was reputed to be the toughest league in world speedway. Yet Parkins was willing to pay something like £140 in sea and air fares several times for Fundin to commute between Norwich and Sweden, which made him a more expensive proposition than Biggs. But without the say-so of the SRA a labour permit for Fundin to be able to ride in England would not be granted. One way round it was to organise a situation whereby Ove could live and work in England at his own trade, a furrier. Accommodation was no problem, Norwich speedway could see to that. And there would no trouble finding a furrier in the Norfolk area who would be delighted to employ Fundin. So the Mr Fixits down at The Firs made all the preliminary arrangements.

In these modern times, faced with such an expedient necessity, numerous riders have compromised their nationality to ride on a licence of convenience. Pole Tadeusz Teodorowicz rode on an English licence, Englishman Simon Wigg rode on a Dutch licence, Andy Smith, also of England, rode on a Polish licence, and Pole Chris Slabon rode on a Canadian licence. But there was one problem with Ove – an indefinable ingredient called patriotism. When the idea was put to him he turned it down, for the simple reason that he was Swedish. So Norwich put in an official protest against the SRA ruling, and sent Aub Lawson to London to argue their case for Ove at a special committee meeting. Aub used all his diplomatic skills to talk the SRA into reversing their decision not to allow Fundin to sign for Norwich, and spent the following day visiting the appropriate Government offices organising the necessary paperwork. So, in what could have been a storybook ending to the saga, Ove Fundin made his Norwich debut as reserve against Belle Vue on 25 June 1955. Except that it was not quite a storybook ending. Norwich lost to the Aces 49-47.

The Norwich team on that historic day was: Phil Clarke, Harry Edwards, Aub Lawson (captain), Cyril Roger, Billy Bales, Fred Brand and Ove Fundin. Belle Vue: Ken Sharples (captain), Fred Rogers, Ron Johnston, Bob Duckworth, Peter Craven, Peter Williams and Dick Fisher. Belle Vue's team manager was the man who is universally recognised as the father of speedway, Johnnie Hoskins.

Ove made a storybook start, but wasn't able to deliver a Boys' Own finish. His first ride was in heat four partnering Harry Edwards. Their opponents were Fred Rogers and Dick Fisher. Ove won in 73.4 seconds, a trifle slower than the first three heats, but a prelude to the future. 'I got three points straight away,' says Ove. 'I was only in as reserve. I was disappointed that they put me as reserve. They didn't have much faith in me, did they? They should have put me in the team.' He says he remembers little about the meeting, but he does remember he was given extra rides: 'They did kick out poor old Harry Edwards. I took his place. And I took Fred Brand's place as well. Then I was beaten by Peter Craven – nothing to be ashamed of. And then Craven again who had Ron Johnston with him. Billy Bales got 12. Aub got only 8. Phil Clarke – he was good round Norwich – got 6.'

Ove had replaced Edwards for the second time in heat twelve but was on the wrong end of a 5-1 behind Craven and the highly experienced Johnston. Two more third places followed in heat thirteen, when partnering Aub Lawson, and in the final race, heat sixteen. Though 8 points plus 1 bonus might have been viewed as a satisfactory score first time out, the account of the match was less than ecstatic. The almost carping report did not display much in the way of generosity: 'Norwich finally managed to get Swedish star Ove Fundin. Much time and effort went into the work that led up to his riding for the Stars against Belle Vue. But he still failed to make the difference between a winning team and a losing one. The way he rode, there are [sic] obviously a whole bag of points in store from him. But what a storybook debut he could have made. Norwich needed a last-heat maximum to beat the Aces. Out went Fundin [and Phil Clarke], but not even his fast style could peg back in-form Peter Craven. The Manchester lad shot away to win, split the heat points and win the match for Belle Vue.'

It was to be the 'in-form' Peter Craven's first World Championship year. But Ove, whose 'immaculate white-line riding' was likened in the Norwich programme welcoming notes to that of two pre-war greats, Tommy Croombs and H.R. 'Ginger' Lees, was just getting up steam. Almost immediately there were complications in the form of the European Final of the World Championship in Oslo and the Swedish national championship. It wasn't very long before the headlines were screaming, 'They All Want Fundin'.

It looked as though Norwich's hopes of further service from the man described as 'their Swedish flier' were in for something of a set-back when the Swedish Motor Federation informed Gordon Parkins that Ove would be required to fulfil commitments in Austria and Sweden in August, and also that month his Swedish club wanted him for a team tour of Poland.

Though a stranger in a strange land, knowing almost nothing of the language, it didn't seem as though he would be around long enough to get homesick. But he did. Phil Clarke and his wife Margaret took him into their home that first year and tried to make him comfortable. 'The first season I was homesick,' says Ove. 'Phil and Margaret did their best to make me feel at home. I was not sitting in a little room all on my own. I sat there at nights trying to watch television with them because television was something new to me. We didn't have it in Sweden in those days, and England had only one channel, so there wasn't much choice. I bought a television set, and I think I was one of the first in Tranas to have one. But you couldn't really get the signal because the nearest antenna was so far away. You could see a little picture now and then and all your family and neighbours came round to watch.

'I learned the language fairly quickly – and most of it I learned from going to the movies. I went to the movies as often as I could because there I had time to listen to it. And Les Mullins and Aub Lawson for that matter – just all the swear words they used. Les could not say a sentence without swearing – I don't know what he is like today – and Aub was almost as bad. Most of them were. And in Norfolk they have not got the best English in the world, have they? But it didn't take all that long. After the first season I was happy.'

And so were Norwich. From a poor early showing the Stars ended up winning, for the first time in their twenty-four-year history, one of the sport's major competitions, the National Trophy – a knock-out, home and away tournament that was speedway's equivalent then of the FA Cup. In his end-of-season review of the team's performance, Angus Kix wrote that from the moment Norwich were finally given permission to sign Fundin, 'this dashing young man with his love of victory, his complete ignoring of reputations and his hectic, give-it-the-gun style, transformed the side into something more closely resembling a team. They swung into form. They started to move up the league table. They couldn't catch leaders Wimbledon or Belle Vue, but they looked set to steer themselves into grasping distance of third place. Their comeback was as thrilling as Fundin's riding. But it didn't last.'

Fundin, Kix insisted, was the mainspring of their success but Norwich rode their last three home matches without him. They didn't win one of them and they finished up one from the bottom of the table. The spark of Fundin was missing. It was the same in the National Trophy. Norwich swept through the rounds, disposing of opponents, and then came the final against Wembley. 'Wembley,' wrote Kix, 'have never been made to look so bad on their own track as Norwich made them look in the first leg.' Fundin got 16 out of 18 at the Empire Stadium. It was obvious from the start that he loved the place. It would be the scene of four of his five World Championships. He was not there for the second leg at The Firs, nor was Aub Lawson, who had broken a collarbone. The Stars struggled to contain the Lions and hold on to their 21-point lead. They did eventually win on aggregate by 3 points. But they didn't get to be presented with the trophy. Holders Wembley couldn't get it out of the Empire Stadium safe. 'They say that one man doesn't make a team,' wrote Kix. 'I say one man does make a team. And in this case Fundin was the man.'

Fundin rode in only six league matches in 1955, but he scored 73 points plus 3 bonus. His home average was 9.89, and away from The Firs he was marginally better with 10.55, a remarkable record for a newcomer in his first season among the world's best. In Sweden his average was 13.9 for Filbyterna, who finished third in the league. He helped Sweden to a 2-1 win in a Test series against Australasia and was third in the Swedish championship.

For the first time, Continental riders went direct to Wembley from the European Final in Oslo. Ove qualified again with fellow Swedes Olle Nygren and Kjell Carlsson plus Norway's Henry Andersen. Norwich were well represented in the big night line-up with Ove, his landlord Phil Clarke – making his one and only World Final appearance – and Norwich teammates Billy Bales and Cyril Roger. Aub Lawson had qualified but his injury kept him out of the final and Bales took his place. The front runners were Peter Craven, the reigning champion Ronnie Moore and the pretender Barry Briggs. Ove started off well enough, with a second place behind Craven in heat two ahead of Ron Johnston and Nygren. But two third places followed, first behind Jack Young and Brian Crutcher, and then Ronnie Moore and Eric Williams.

As usual, Ove was suffering with big night butterflies. According to Brian Burford's biography, *Peter Craven: The Wizard Of Balance*, Ove and Craven were placed next to each other in the Wembley pits and when Fundin admitted his low score was the result of his nervousness Craven attempted to calm him by offering some friendly words of encouragement. It was a typical example of Peter's generosity of spirit. Though Ove was virtually out of the running for the title, Craven's positive influence may well have had the desired effect. Fundin pulled off a heat fifteen win over Billy Bales, Bradford's Arthur Wright and Henry Andersen – his first World Final race victory – warning the leaders that he could still have a say in who was to wear the crown.

After four rides, Craven had dropped only a single point, Briggs was on 10, Moore and Williams on 9. At the start of the final round, Craven and Crutcher were involved in a tremendous battle, with Craven pulling out all his balancing tricks to try and find a way past the Wembley man. But Crutcher, to the delight of his home crowd, just managed to hold him off. Moore and Williams won heats eighteen and nineteen, putting them on a dozen each. The meeting was set for an incredible climax. Only Briggs could now catch Craven, but to match his 13 points and earn a run-off for the championship, he had to face Fundin in the final heat – and win it.

Heat twenty of the 1955 World Championship Final at Wembley was the prelude to a decade of on-track fierce – often blatantly cut-throat – rivalry between Fundin and Briggs. With the partisan English spectators willing the title to go to little Peter Craven – it had been five years since the home country had been able to acclaim a World Champion – the 'We Hate Ove' section suddenly changed allegiance and this time they wanted to see him pass the chequered flag first. He didn't disappoint them. Ove made one of his masterly starts and for four laps thwarted every effort by the desperate Briggs to take that vital lead. But still the drama was not over. With Craven the new champion – at only twenty-one and a few months younger than Moore had been when he had won the previous year – Moore, Briggs and Williams had to contest a three-man run-off for the minor placings. Moore won comfortably, with Briggs and Williams disputing what was left in his wake. On the final bend they collided and both came down. Briggs righted his machine, started it and rode across the line side-saddle. Williams panicked and failed to rock his bike back on compression. It wouldn't start, and he pushed it past the flag marshal, convinced Briggs would be excluded. He wasn't, and took the third-place tractor ride. For Ove, in sixth position behind Crutcher, one above the fabulous Jack Young and the best of the Continentals – he had even done better than Nygren – it represented major progress from the previous year when he had been bottom of the heap in sixteenth place.

At the end of the season Norwich made it known that they wanted him again for 1956. 'They asked me if I would come back again next year,' he said. 'But I told them that they must supply me with somewhere to live and with a bike – like they had done – because I didn't know anything about the mechanical side, and Les must look after my bike. And it was like that all the time.'

So, Ove Fundin permitted himself to look forward to enjoying a second sunshine winter in Australia before another attempt at his ultimate ambition, the World Championship. But in October he crashed in Sweden and broke a collarbone.

If ever there was a 'gentleman speedway rider' it was Phil Clarke. He began his association with Norwich in 1947 at the age of twenty-four, and is one of those rare riders who stayed with the same club through-out his entire racing career, which spanned twelve years. He was the antithesis of a dirt-track star – very studious-looking off the track with his smart suits and steel-rimmed spectacles. On the track he was a steady and reliable performer, soon becoming one of the club's top riders. He was captain in 1951, made the transition from Division Two to the top league when Norwich were promoted to the National League Division One in 1952, reached the 1955 World Championship Final and represented England in internationals. He rode in a total of 309 matches for Norwich, scoring 2,162 points, both records for the club. Yet he was what journalists of the day were pleased to call 'unfashionable and unsung'. The media spotlight rarely shone upon Phil Clarke, and the word 'sensation' was not one that readily sprang to mind when his name was mentioned. Therefore Phil was, together with his wife Margaret, the perfect choice to become landlord and unofficial chaperone to Ove Fundin during his first season of British speedway. Phil's approach to the sport always seemed to give the impression that, unlike the mercurial Fundin, speedway racing was not the sole purpose of his life. 'You could say that, I suppose,' was his comment. 'I always played by the rules as best I could.'

Of that one appearance at Wembley on World Final night 1955, Phil says: 'You need to have a little bit of an ego to want to win the World Championship in the first place. The road to winning the champion-ship was quite hard really. And you had to be tough because when you got to the European Final stage you were up against some really good boys. I didn't do very much preparation for going to Wembley. I wasn't setting out with any confidence that I would do very well. I think I scraped in through the qualifiers, but it was a good experi-ence. I had never ridden Wembley very well. I didn't like the track, and I never did well on it. I had the riding ability, but I didn't have the mental push to take advantage of it. It was a fantastic experience appearing in that arena on the night. I scored only 2 points. I got one second place, but I certainly wasn't in any mental state to win any races. I don't know why. I think I had a bit of an inferiority complex as regards speedway.

'One thing: wearing spectacles is a big handicap, especially in speedway. Not having particularly good eyesight you've got to wear spectacles – contact lenses had not really been developed much then, and I don't think I would have enjoyed using them anyway. So I normally used Army spectacles with flat sides and triplex glass lenses. I lost a few lenses over the years with stones hitting my goggles and striking the lenses.'

He has what he describes as 'fond memories' of his association with Ove: 'We are still good friends. Margaret and I lived near the stadium and he lived with us for a while. It wasn't easy because he didn't speak much English at the time and I think he was very homesick as well. The stadium used to pay me nominally to cover his food and stuff. He didn't eat very much normally so he wasn't hard to cater for. I think he might have missed his Swedish food. Every country has different dishes and I think he survived anyway on what we had. He was erratic in his domestic ways. Margaret would have a meal on the way and you would suddenly discover Ove was missing. He'd gone off to the pictures or something, or he'd walked into Norwich.

'He had a flashy car – a 1948/49 American-style Ford – so we had a few hectic rides at the time. I used to travel with Ove and Les Mullins, our mechanic. I had a good trailer that his car could pull quite easily. We'd have two or three bikes on the trailer – the track spare and Ove's track spare number two as well. We got on quite well with that arrangement. Ove was a good driver. I think we were all very careful when we were driving. You had to be. I do remember one incident. We'd been away. It was in the middle of the night and we were coming home. I was in the back asleep and I woke up and looked over the dashboard and we were doing just over 100mph with my trailer and three bikes on the back. When I suggested we were going a bit too fast Ove said, "It's OK, we're just testing your trailer – seeing how fast we could go with it."'

But on one occasion Ove was accused of inconsiderate driving following a heated exchange of gestures with the owner of a Mk VIII Jaguar near Norwich. Today it would be called a road rage incident. Ove, in a left-hand drive Mercedes, had overtaken and then, the court was told, suddenly stopped in the middle of the road, forcing the driver of the other car to slam on his brakes, 'throwing his passengers from their seats'. The man was then confronted by Ove 'in a temper' over a perceived gesture and whose manner was, according to one of the passengers, 'arrogant and conceited'. Ove pleaded not guilty by letter but he was fined £5, his licence was endorsed and he was ordered to pay £4 2s costs.

'The travelling was tough,' said Clarke. 'No motorways. Some of the routes you had to follow were very poor. Not developed at all. To get from Norwich to King's Lynn on the A47 used to take a couple of hours or more. There were places where you just couldn't pass. And it's not much better now. If you were going to Manchester to ride at Belle Vue you would have to give yourself about six hours, and six hours back. Coming back wouldn't be too much trouble because there would not be much traffic about. We used to stop at a transport café, which was virtually all you could do in those days, especially at night if you wanted to eat. There were a lot of them open in those days, and some of the things that were offered catered for lorry drivers – beans on toast and bacon – great English fry-ups. Ove would excuse himself and he wouldn't go in.' Trevor Hedge, who in later years also travelled with Fundin a lot, remembered: 'When we used to go away he'd have a bag of apples by the side of him and he'd eat them all the while.'

Ove may have been a tough and uncompromising speedway rider, but he flinched at visiting a dentist. Phil Clarke said: 'There was one thing that did occur with Ove – he often mentions it. He had a bad tooth and it was really playing him up. I don't think he liked the idea very much of going to the dentist, especially in England. I don't think he thought an English dentist would be capable of attending to his tooth. It gradually got worse and it was at a weekend. Eventually I persuaded him to have a slug of whisky, which knocked him out. And then on the Monday I took him to my dentist who fixed it so that he was OK again. But he really had a bad weekend with that tooth.'

Phil was highly experienced when Fundin arrived at Norwich. He'd had eight years of racing in the Second and First Divisions of British speedway. The other members of the side, Aub and Don Lawson, Cyril

Roger, Fred Brand, Harry Edwards, Billy Bales, were not exactly novices. They could, perhaps, have been understandably resentful of the brash newcomer, this very young, very self-possessed foreigner, who turned up and suddenly started shredding established reputations and beating everyone in sight as if of right.

'We were a bit amazed,' said Phil. 'He was different. Very focused on winning – it was vitally important to him right from the very beginning. He was extremely confident in his own ability, without a doubt. He was very much focused on being at the top and he achieved it. He made a very big impression in a very short time that first season he was here. He was a remarkable man. I recognised he had a great ability to ride a speedway bike. He didn't have a particularly good style. He was an awkward rider, but he used to find his way round – and very, very quickly. But as a team man he was a bit of a liability really. He did eventually get a little bit of an idea of team riding but it took a long time. If he didn't win it was very apparent that he was annoyed. He let you know. He didn't hide it.'

Team riding – a heat leader holding off the opposition to help a less able partner – wasn't a Fundin speciality. He confessed to being selfish. 'I didn't think all that much to team riding,' he said, 'I was too much of an individualist I suppose.' He regarded it as his job to score points – lots of them – not to possibly sacrifice them for the sake of a partner who couldn't keep up with him. And it was the same with gate positions. Today they are programmed, then there was a choice.

'If my partner and I were meeting a Ronnie Moore or a Barry Briggs or a Bjorn Knutsson, or someone like that in the race, I would always take the inside position, but if there were other people I would say, "Which gate would you like?" That was not selfish, that was good team tactics, because if I was up against Barry or someone like that I would have to make a good gate. If I won, that was three points, but if I gave away the better position to my partner it could be he would have run a last or got only a point and we would have lost.'

When it came to starting positions, most people did like the inside, says Phil Clarke: 'It did have drawbacks at Norwich. The track would be heavily watered during the day and in the first race there would be puddles lying on the white line. So some people would be quite happy to take the outside position. Aub Lawson was always happy to take the outside, and I was to a certain extent. But normally on small tracks every rider would prefer to be on the number one gate.

'There was a good team spirit at Norwich, though we didn't get together much other than on race days or when we had an overnight stay. We had a few characters: Cyril Roger was a character, Ove was a character, Aub was a character. If you were working late on your bikes, which we often did, Aub would suddenly disappear for a few minutes and come back with a crate of beer on his shoulder. Whether he had paid for it or just taken if from the bar I'm not sure, but that management didn't give much away. There was not a lot of free beer about so he had probably paid for it. They were good guys. We helped each other out and did things for one another.'

So instead of being resentful of Ove's obvious outstanding ability, his teammates were ready to accept somebody like that. 'He was obviously a great rider,' said Clarke. 'Unfortunately he was a little bit temperamental, to put it mildly, and we all learned to adapt ourselves to him and hope we could keep up with him some of the time – which wasn't easy. He was never arrogant and he was never other than a nice fellow inside, but he just had the ability to – not exactly blow his top – but if things didn't go his way he would let you know. He would mumble a few words in Swedish probably and retreat into his shell. He was very determined right from the start and he would get the power on at the right time. He used to straighten the bike up and then go. He was a little bit prone to this problem of diving through on the inside and there wasn't always quite enough room for him, which was somewhat disruptive. Overtaking on the outside was a little bit dangerous. You could get jammed on the fence fairly easily. But sometimes you could get away with it. The Norwich track was a beautiful shape, big and a full 425 yards round the line. You could use the whole of it. So sometimes you could get round the outside. There were plenty of racing lines. You could make use of the track, the surface was excellent, and usually the track was very, very good at Norwich. We had an extremely fine trackman who would get the water on in good time on race days so that it soaked in and gave a nice surface.

'Ove had what we termed a strong right wrist and he used to turn it on mostly at the right time. And when he did turn it on he'd go because he used to get straightened up quickly, his wheels in line and all the traction.' Ove says that his technique from the start to the first corner was 'always to have just enough lift. Lifting a fraction is ideal, because when you had a little bit more lift you had to shut off. At Norwich they used to say that they saw me reaching the first corner with my front wheel still standing still. It was hanging like that all the way to the corner.'

Clarke says: 'He used to get rather keyed up before important meetings. I think he used to get – I know I've used the expression before – focused. It is an ability that sportsmen either have or don't have, and to a certain extent it's the main thing that sportsmen need. To focus on that task in hand and be determined that nothing is going to stop you. That counts for everything.'

Ronnie Moore recounted an incident some years after Fundin had really given up regular competitive speedway: 'Before a race you couldn't speak to Ove. He could often be found sitting on a toolbox for an hour before a big meeting, holding his head in his hands and working himself up to beat the world. In 1969 he came to New Zealand determined to show that there was still some life in the old dog. And he succeeded. At Templeton he was lined up against Ivan Mauger, who was then World Champion, and me in a series of races labelled a Champion-of-Champions contest. Before racing started we were all introduced to the crowd over the speaker system. Ove told everybody he was really retired and they were not to expect too much. What he didn't tell them was that for an hour beforehand he had been marching up and down the pits, talking to no one and mentally preparing himself for battle.'

Ove beat Ivan and Ronnie in three straight races, and before the end of the series had not only broken the lap record but set a new four-lap record as well.

# FIVE

# CAN YOU COPE?

*'Poor Les, he must have had hell to put up with, with me and my temper.'*
– Ove Fundin

Throughout speedway history there have been many memorable rider/mechanic partnerships: Vic Huxley and Dick Dendy, Ron Johnson and Alf Coles, Harold 'Tiger' Stevenson and Alec Moseley, Vic Duggan and Jack Scott, Lionel Van Praag and Leslie Dymond, Tommy Price and Cyril Spinks, Graham Warren and Vic Scales, Peter Craven and Harold Jackson, Ivan Mauger and Guy Allott. But there has perhaps never been one quite like the partnership that grew up between Ove Fundin and Les Mullins at Norwich. For the decade it endured during Fundin's British and international career, it was blindingly successful. To opponents it must have seemed deadly. For the two men involved, who became so intimately and closely associated, it was – given the white-hot and stressful atmosphere in which it was compelled to flourish – many times turbulent out of necessity. And because of the diverse and volatile temperaments of the principals, it also proved on occasions explosive.

Les Mullins really wanted to be a speedway rider. He learned the basics with His Majesty's Forces in Egypt. 'I would rather have been a rider than a mechanic,' he says. He did try to further his ambition just after the war with such youthful wannabees as Billy Bales and Reg Morgan and the many other youngsters who were farmed out by Norwich to the club's nursery track at nearby Yarmouth: 'We used to train at Yarmouth and Norwich. I had second-half rides at both places. Unfortunately I had a bit of an accident at Yarmouth. The bike turned over at the starting gate. It was a concrete starting area at the time and I damaged my back. I didn't realise how badly damaged it was at the time until years later.'

And that was the end of Les's track career: 'After that I couldn't get into it any more because my back was playing me up so much. Then Dicky Wise left Norwich and Major Fred Evans replaced him. They wanted another mechanic and I had the opportunity to join. Wilf Lucy, the chief mechanic, was then recovering from a bad road accident so he needed a bit of help. Norwich had track workshops then. We had a proper speedway stores and everything. Among the riders, Paddy Mills used to use the workshops, and Bob Leverenz, Alec Hunter and Bert Spencer were all still there.

'Just before the start of the 1953 season I was waiting for Wilf Lucy to return, but he never showed up. Fred Evans told me Wilf wasn't going to come any more. They didn't want him any more, and he said to me, "Can you cope?" Just like that. He asked would I get things mobile? It was what I loved doing and I thought I'd give it a go. So I said okay. A lot of people think I was Fundin's mechanic solely. I wasn't, I was the team mechanic. Then Aub Lawson joined us. He was a terrific team man. He had a workshop in the pits. His half-brother Don was there at the time and he used to do his engines. Later on Don left and Aub asked me to do his engines. That meant taking sole responsibility for everything that went into the motor. Strip the engine down, check the balancing. We used to have a firm that did the reboring for us, but the rest we used to do in the workshops. We used to grind all the heads and the valves. Aub would like different compressions and valve timings depending where he was riding but it was all pretty standard. I never tried to lighten engines or do any of the gimmicks you hear about today. What they did as individuals I wouldn't know. I used to set up an engine how I thought would be good enough.

'I used to do Billy Bales' engines right from the early days at Yarmouth. Billy was in the stable with me right from the start. In 1955

Gordon Parkins, who took over as manager when Fred left, said we had this Swede coming who Aubie had recommended, Ove Fundin. We were a little bit prejudiced about foreign riders coming in and taking the bread and butter from our own riders then. It was a sore point at times. It was quite restrictive. We'd had several foreign riders at Norwich but they weren't any better than the ones we'd got.'

Les had first seen Ove when he came over for the 1954 World Championship qualifiers at Norwich and West Ham, and said: 'Little did I know what was coming. I was the team mechanic and Ove was part of my team. He got no special treatment, though obviously when we were going in for the World Championship I made absolutely certain. But I did all bikes the same. I did Ove's engines, Billy Bales' complete bike, Aub Lawson's engines, Harry Edwards' engines, Reg Trott's.

'Ove always used to bring his own bike over from Sweden for Wembley finals, but he always used to ride Track Spare number two. One year, 1957 I think it was, the bike was standard, the engine was standard, before we started to play around with cams. Around 1959-1960 everybody started to play around with cams. In this particular race he just flew, but he came in and said the bike wasn't going fast enough. Then it was announced that he'd knocked two seconds off the track record, which had stood for I don't know how many years. And I just looked at him and said, "I can't help you." He said, "What do you mean?" I said, "Well if that isn't good enough for you I don't know what I can do to help you. If that isn't going fast enough for you, you'd better look elsewhere."'

Les had to learn to live with this hugely demanding personality, and now puts it down to the fact that Ove came from a reasonably well-off background. 'His people in Sweden were furriers,' said Les, 'and when you went to his home town of Tranas almost every sign was Fundin, Fundin, Fundin – the names of his father and uncles. When Ove came into speedway it was all good money and he could be very temperamental. I coped with it with a lot of patience. He always commanded attention whenever he walked in somewhere. I won't say he was big-headed or anything, but he would come into the workshop and think he could take over. I wouldn't wear it. I used to tell him

straight: "Don't try that with me. We either work together as a team
or forget it." Of course, the fans made him that way.

'I was in Sweden with him once, and he was going to a funeral
– one of his uncles. He wanted his wife, Mona, to go with him, and
she wouldn't. I don't know what the reason was. Anyway, I heard my
name mentioned, and he slammed out and left her there. When I
asked Mona what it was all about she said, "He told me there's only
one person who can argue with me and that's Les." I was the only
one he would listen to. And that was our relationship. If it was going
to work it was because we had respect for each other, and the record
speaks for itself.'

Yet despite his fierce determination to remain his own man, Les
was also protective of Ove's racing interests. In 1957 Ove was World
Champion, and the British Speedway Control Board could hardly
ignore any longer his claim to be allowed to challenge for the British
Match Race Championship, a major competition at the time that
had pulled huge crowds through the turnstiles. Traditionally, the first
challenger of the new season was always the World Champion. Not
only that, but Ove had also topped the poll in the world rankings.
But Ove was a foreigner, and foreigners were banned from taking a
tilt at the Golden Helmet until then – not just because there was
prejudice against foreigners, though there very well may have been
because the SRA was very touchy about them at the time – but,
because of overseas commitments, foreigners could not guarantee to
be available each month to defend the Golden Helmet, should they
win it.

The problem did not rest solely with the British authorities, however. It was reported that Sweden had not given clearance for Ove to
compete. Barry Briggs, who had been placed sixth in the World Final
and fifth in the world rankings behind Ove, Ronnie Moore, Brian
Crutcher and Golden Helmet holder Peter Craven, was nominated as
the first challenger. Crutcher had apparently been asked, and had said
he was not interested. Ronnie Moore had quit speedway temporarily
to race cars. Craven beat Briggs to retain the title and the rules were
changed to allow Fundin to enter the competition. Crutcher must

have had second thoughts because he and Ove met in an eliminator at Ipswich and, though Crutcher was in devastating form at the time, Ove beat him in two straight races, which set up Fundin to become Craven's next challenger in July. 'I think he was just confident that he could take the Golden Helmet,' said Les. 'It was part of his dominating personality.'

According to Brian Burford's biography, *Peter Craven: The Wizard of Balance*, 'Peter had a thing about Ove Fundin. He had the beating of Briggs and Ronnie Moore, but for some reason he found it harder getting the better of Fundin. Of course he did beat him, but he was his biggest rival.'

Some people believed that Craven was intimidated by Fundin. One of Craven's teammates at Belle Vue, Peter Williams, said Craven disliked being at the tapes with Ove, who would not keep still. Williams recalled: 'I can remember Craven getting ready for a Match Race with Fundin and turning back to the pit gates, getting off his bike and saying: "I'm not going to race until he stops messing about." Fundin was a great one for rolling at the gate, looking behind. Craven used to come to the gate and stop. He was as honest as that. Fundin must have known why Craven had turned back, but it was Ove's way of psyching him up a bit.' If there were any mind games going on in the first leg of Fundin's July challenge they didn't work. A home track advantage brought a 2-0 win for Craven at Belle Vue. Ove's motor let him down in the first heat but he led into turn one in the second only for Craven to sweep past for a win. The return leg at Norwich went to Fundin 2-1 to force a decider at Southampton.

Les recalled: 'I went down there and Wilf Lucy, who was then at Belle Vue, arrived with Little Pete and Harold Jackson. Wilf saw me and the bike in the pits and said, "Come on, let's go and have a cup of tea." So I said, "Well, there's nobody else here, I want to stay with the bike." "That'll be all right," he said. I said, "No way. I've done too many hours' work on it to walk away and leave it unattended." I was afraid someone would come along and tamper with it. That's the way my mind was working.' But Craven kept the title that time, beating Ove 2-0.

Les's unease may not have been entirely misplaced. A possible attempt at sabotage took place two years later at Norwich on 29 August, just before the first leg of another Match Race with Craven. Reporter Bill Cooper wrote: 'There were real panic stations in the Norwich pits when Fundin's machine refused to start. But some fast work by Les Mullins brought his motor roaring to life just as the meeting was due to start. Gordon Parkins told me afterwards that the tension lead [which carried the electric current to the spark plug] showed a definite cut as though wire cutters had been at work. With the problem sorted out Fundin was able to line up for the first heat to meet Craven, and what a heat it was. A real thriller scrap that saw Craven in front until the last lap. Then Fundin blasted his way under him to hold the lead on the last turn, but on the run-in, with Fundin's machine up on the rear wheel, Craven just nipped in front to win by about half a wheel.' In the next heat, Fundin was the complete master, winning by about forty yards, and in the decider he went past Craven round the line on the first turn to build up a good lead and win by about thirty yards.

Ove recalled the incident: 'I know everybody thought it might have been sabotage. It could have been one of Peter's supporters or someone not liking me. I'm sure Craven had nothing to do with it.' And though Fundin had won that first leg 2-1, he lost the return leg at Belle Vue and eventually the title went back to Craven by default because Ove was forbidden to take part in the decider at Oxford by SVEMO, the Swedish speedway governing body.

Fundin says of Craven: 'We had a lot of tough races together. We were two of a kind because we were both there to win speedway races. He was such an outstanding rider, there is no question about that. He was always nice and friendly, but I'm not too sure I was all that nice and friendly. He was a very clean rider, which you could not always say about some others. But you could always trust Peter. He wasn't one of those riders who would try and fence you.'

Ove was not to get his hands on the Golden Helmet for the first time until the beginning of the 1958 season, when once more he was chosen to challenge Craven. Again their match went to a decider, with Ove finally winning at Poole. After that it was a nightmare, says Les Mullins.

'It was every month. My work load was going up and up and up. Ove used to get wound up and so did I. I used to get terrible stomach pains sometimes. You would see that the next one was Barry Briggs or Ronnie Moore or Ron How and I used to wonder whether I could keep this going. I had all the Norwich riders' engines to look after as well. I used to be at the workshop until two o'clock in the morning.'

Les's wife Doris now says, memorably, that the situation was rather like Diana Princess of Wales's famous remark when interviewed about the relationship between her, Prince Charles and Camilla Parker-Bowles. Doris said, 'There were three people in the marriage... and one of them was Ove Fundin.' But was Ove aware of the mounting demands that were being made on Les?

'I don't think he realised my workload,' said Les. 'I think all he was interested in was the next meeting. Like when I first went to Sweden, he said to me, "Put the bike in the car. Here are your ferry tickets." He got a map out and drew a red line across the North Sea to Esbjerg, told me what ferries to get and said, "Don't be late." He flew. Those were all the instructions I got. I had no idea where I was going or what I was going to find at the other end. I found my way across Denmark, had a meal on the first ferry because I knew I wouldn't get any food on the next one, and when I got to Sweden there was a terrific thunderstorm – you couldn't see your hand in front of your face. I was in the middle of woods, didn't know where the hell I was. I just pulled over in the end and curled up in the car and had a sleep. When I woke up the sun was shining. I found out where he was – I was only about ten miles away. The greeting I got was, "Where the hell have you been? Look at my car. Covered in mud!" I'd been on all these dirt roads, and all you could see of the car was a bit of clear windscreen and the rest was caked in mud. In those days the roads were a bit of asphalt, a bit of dirt, a bit of asphalt, a bit of dirt... and that was how it was. Another time I knew where I was going and I got to the Swedish customs – I don't know what made me do it, but before I went I got a bit of tape and put it over the Norwich Track Spare No. 2 nameplate on the bike and put the name Ove Fundin on it. The customs officers went through everything. They opened the boot and said, "What's that?" "It's a motorcyle," I said. "Yes, we can see that. Whose is it?" I said, "The name is on the name plate. It's Ove Fundin's. From Tranas." They thought it was this important bike. Then they took the tape off and I tried to explain that the bike was the one he used at Norwich and that the nameplate was a kind of lucky charm. I told them that the best thing they could do was to ring him. They did, from the customs office, and the officer said, "He wants to talk to you." Ove said, "What the hell are you doing there? Tell them to get stuffed and come on." I said, "I can't tell them that or I'll be here for the rest of the week. They want a lot of money to let me go and you gave me only enough to get me to Sweden." They did release me in the end. They gave me a docket to fill in and said they wanted to see the bike when I went out again.'

When it came to World Championship Finals Les's preparations were meticulous: 'I used to start preparing in June for the World Championship in September by saving engine parts. I would race them, once or twice – whatever I thought they needed. Then I would label them with what they had done and place them in the stores. Then I'd replace them and race another barrel and piston. I'd even race chains – hang them up. That's Wembley, that's Wembley. Mark 'em all. I'd put the engine together and the frame. And when I'd put the bike together I used to think, "Well, that's up to him now. I've done my bit." And it used to work. If something wasn't right he would tell me. He couldn't tell me what was wrong, he'd just say, "That doesn't feel right." And it was up to me to find out what didn't feel right. That's how we did it. I'd make sure everything was as near perfect as I could get it. Set everything up. Get everything ready and then take the two bikes to Wembley. He always took his Swedish bike, and I'd say to him: "Which one are you going to ride?" And he'd say: "We're going to go on the No.2." There was so much inferior stuff coming to me in those days, cam followers, conrods, crank pins and big end cages. It was a complete battle to keep on top of engines, to keep them running as they should. When we got a new engine from the factory it was no good racing it. We used to have to strip it completely and I would spend as much as £50 [the equivalent of £750 today] on it to get it as I wanted it.

'The night that Little Pete lost his World Championship, when his motor stopped on the pit bend in his second ride of the 1956 final, I went to Harold Jackson and Wilf Lucy – not to gloat – but said, "What went wrong, Wilf?" He said, "The bloody rocker arm broke." And straight away, that made alarm bells ring for me. So I always checked rocker arms very carefully. I was doing Aub Lawson's one day and I saw just a faint line and thought, "There's one going there." I stripped it all out and went and saw Aub and showed him what I'd found. And he said, "How the hell did you find that?" I said, "Well I've got a suspicion about these things now and I'm always looking." So we had a purge on finding the old rocker boxes with the beautifully made rocker levers – because when the new rocker levers came out they were horrible things, they didn't look as though they had been ground properly. So we found all the old motors we could and used them. And we eliminated that problem.

'Ove used to have a book at the stadium, like an invoice book, in which he would record everything. He would enter everything in it and then pass it through to the office and they would log it in their book. Then as he raced they would take the cost of the spares off his pay cheque. All the spares were covered by the stadium. And then they would deduct the amount. If they thought one account was getting a bit high they would consult me and ask me if it was necessary. And I would say yes and it would be okay. That was the way they helped the riders to maintain their equipment. Not every track did it that way – some asked riders to pay a certain amount of money – but Norwich always did it that way.

'When we had match races at Norwich we used to have Reg Trott's bike as a spare because Ove could ride that one as well as his own. So Reg's bike was always ready. This one night Reg went out and had the best night he'd had at Norwich for some time. I think he scored 10 points. He was really going well and he was so happy when he came

in that he had scored a few points. Then Ray Cresp said he wanted
Reg's engine checked because he thought it must be oversized. He
said, "Engines can't go that fast. He passed me as if I was standing
still." I looked at Reg, and he was so despondent. "Don't worry," I
said. "I know that engine isn't oversized." I said to Cresp, "All right.
Put your money where your mouth is." But he backed down. Reg
said: "Well, I don't know. For once I have a really good night... and
get called a cheat."

'But Ove was accused of riding an oversized engine after one World
Final. The machine examiners who measure the engines, they are
floating about all the while in the background, they are watching you
constantly, keeping their eye on you to see who is in the running for
first, second and third. As soon as the meeting is over they are on you.
They ask you to strip down the engine so that they can measure it.
And you had to take the head off. The one who was doing it at that
particular time – I can't be exact about which year it was, but it must
have been the second time Ove won it, probably 1960 – he came to
measure the engine and I stripped it all out. He put all his gear in
and said, "This engine is oversized." So I stood back for a second and
took a deep breath. I was on a high, and I went from up there to
down there. I said, "You must be joking. I don't know where you got
our measurements from. I suggest you measure it again. You've made a
mistake somewhere in your calculations." At first he said no, then eventually he did it again and said, "I must apologise to you. Everything is
all right. It was my fault. I miscalculated." I went to the dressing rooms
and told Ove there was a bit of a hiccup, the machine examiner had
said the engine was oversized. He thought I was winding him up. "No,
he genuinely thought it was oversized," I said. I thought I would let
Ove know that it was not all as easy as he might have thought it was,
so that he didn't take it all for granted. You can imagine how I felt. I
was mesmerised for a little while.'

Les recalled one incident that occurred after Ove had been to
Southampton for a Match Race against Bjorn Knutsson in August
1961. Ove was the Golden Helmet holder and Knutsson the challenger – the first all-Swedish clash in the history of the competition.

'Knutsson won the first race and in the second – I couldn't quite see from where I was – I don't know whether Ove tried to go round Knutsson or Knutty went across him, but they collided in the first turn. Knutty got away and the next thing I saw was Ove's bike go up in the air. And I thought that's the frame up the shoot.' Ove borrowed Jack Scott's bike for the re-run, and lost again. I dragged the bike back, and of course Ove and Knutty were at loggerheads. I looked at the bike and thought, "I can't do anything with it." The frame had gone. We'd got this bike ready for the European Championship in Vienna. We were at Southampton Tuesday, on the boat Thursday and I think it was Vienna Saturday night. Ove said, "What are we going to do? This bike was all ready." I said, "I'm the one who's got to worry, not you." Alec Jackson kept a supply of Rotrax frames at his premises in London, and we thought that if we could find a chap named Harry, who used to work for Jackson, we'd ask him if he would come with us to the shop to get a new frame. We got to London about midnight and banged on Harry's door and we drove down the Harrow Road to the shop. Harry went in and turned on all the lights. And there in Alec Jackson's front window was a bike, with a Rotrax frame, all made up with a dummy sitting on it in leathers and crash hat. So we said, "What about that one, Harry? After all, we are using Ove's name to sell the frames." He said, "We can't take that one. The guv'nor comes up here every morning, that's his pride and joy." We were desperate. So while Harry was thinking about it, I got the dummy off the bike and laid it flat on the floor. By that time it was one o'clock in the morning, and three policemen walked past the window where we were taking this bike to pieces, but they never took a scrap of notice. They looked in the window. I had taken the engine out, there were wheels and handlebars all laid out on the floor. I stripped it completely. We took the frame and left all the bits laid out on the floor in the window. We had to get back to Norwich and rebuild the bike, check the engine over, and then get to Vienna.

'I saw Harry at Wimbledon some time later and said, "What happened, Harry?" He said, 'Well, Alec walked past the window, looked in and saw all the bits lying on the floor, walked away and then suddenly stopped. Then he came back for another look at the chaos but he didn't ask anything at all." And we never heard any more about it.' And it was all worthwhile, because Ove won the European Championship in Vienna with a 15-point maximum, beating Bjorn Knutsson into second place.

But back in England their Golden Helmet match turned out to be an incident-packed second leg on Ove's home track at Norwich. Asked by the EsO factory in Czechoslovakia to test their new speedway machines, Ove was riding one of the bikes that were later to become the highly successful JAWA. Ove was never happy on an EsO and promptly lost the first race. The second was a shambles. Ove was put on two minutes but did not appear. When he eventually did the race was started with the red lights still showing, and Knutsson's machine failed on the second bend. It was ruled 'no race', and when they got going again, Knutsson won to take the title that Ove had held for a year. But he was to reclaim it from Knutsson later.

The relationship between Les and Ove on occasions reached flashpoint. 'Many a time we've had a squabble in the workshops,' said Les. 'I'm normally placid. I can take so much, but when I flip, I flip. He said something to me in the workshop one night, and I just blew. I got my hammer out and said, "I'll do you! As sure as anything, I'll do you!" Then two of the Norwich directors happened to come in and I said, "And you can get out as well, or I'll do you too!"

'Ove used to push me. He sometimes used to go on about Englishmen, just to wind me up – and he used to wind up other people too. We were going through a military cemetery in France one day. I was getting so wound up, I thought to myself, "I've had enough of this," so I pulled up right in the centre of the cemetery, stopped the car and took the keys out of the ignition. He said, "What have you taken the keys out for?" I said, "I know what you are, you'd leave me standing here and just drive off. If I've got the keys so you can't do it. Come with me," I said. "I want to show you something." He'll probably deny all this, but as far as the eye could see there were all these crosses – it was a British cemetery – I said, "When you talk about Englishmen, look and see how many Englishmen and Commonwealth soldiers are lying out there. You Swedes never came into the bloody war. These people gave their lives. Don't you come to me and say that Englishmen are a load of twits. There is a load of twits lying out there, and because of them you can go and earn the money that you do in England." I was so angry. I couldn't stop, I was like a machine. He said, "You've made your point, let's go." That is the sort of thing that used to happen.

'I think we were both our own men, really. We had a lot of respect for each other. It was a funny relationship in a sense. It was give and take. At one time there were a lot of people he was with who would jump when he used to shout. That never happened with me because I wouldn't let it. And that's where the mutual respect came in. It was just a partnership. I can't explain it really – it was more a love-hate relationship. We had some terrific arguments sometimes. He will tell you that himself. He didn't have much patience then and he is still the same. When we used to go to away meetings he would jump in the back of the car and pull a coat over his head. I would turn the radio on and we would be driving along and he'd say, "Must you keep driving on the bloody cats' eyes?"

'I have watched a lot of brilliant riders at different times – Jack Young, Freddie Williams, Barry Briggs – but Ove was so consistent. One of his secrets was when he went into a turn, the thing he was looking for was to get his wheels in line very quickly. That's where he used to get a lot of his speed from. And when they brought in handicapping, he had to give some riders up to twenty yards' start. But before he went down the back straight he was in front. He just used to fly past them. We were very close, there is no doubt about that. I trusted him and he trusted me. But it all went a bit sour towards the end.'

At the close of the 1964 season, speedway was terminated at The Firs. Effectively, so was Ove Fundin's serious speedway career – and he and Les had an argument and fell out. For sixteen years they didn't speak. The row was over finances.

'I enjoyed what we did,' said Les, 'but it came to an abrupt end, and when that happened he spoiled it for me. When Norwich closed he more or less said, "That's it." We had a bit of an argument and I told him to get stuffed and I never spoke to him for sixteen years. That's the way the relationship was. The particular night it happened I thought, "What have I been doing this last ten years with him?" My whole life was centred around Ove Fundin. I wasn't his personal mechanic, though I was to an extent. He wasn't the only rider I was dealing with, there were four or five other riders who were all my responsibility. I had to fit him in. And when he was going to all the other international and open meetings, The Laurels and that, he used to say, "You will come with me?" Well, I didn't have to go. And I didn't get paid for it. I was on a wage from the stadium and he more or less took it as read I would go. The workload and the travelling – what with the match races and preparing for World Finals – I mean, it was enormous. He just expected me to go with him. I thought he would have had a bit more respect for me and what we had achieved together. And it was an achievement, no matter how people looked at it. He was never off the World Championship podium for ten years. But we are all right now and let's just leave it at that. I never felt the same towards him as I did. I'd like to elaborate it a bit more, but I think it best to let sleeping dogs lie.'

Ove was also reluctant to go into detail about the falling out and would say only: 'He expected me to look after him financially, which I did in a way. He always had ten per cent of the Match Race winnings, but he also wanted it from the World Final. I think I gave it to him once, but there was no "arrangement". It's the same as giving people a tip. They are employed by someone else, but they provide good service for you, so you must give them a tip. I'm pretty sure I was the only one in the Norwich team to do that.'

When Norwich closed Les had an all-expenses-paid offer to go to Wimbledon and he considered it seriously. 'But I thought, "I've had sixteen years of this,"' he said, '"and I don't think I can take any more."'

It was the end of Les Mullins' speedway career too.

# SIX

# NORWICH TRACK SPARE NO. 2

*'The myth grew up. It was a little bit off-putting for people who went out for a race and there was a guy riding Track Spare No. 2 who duffed them up quite comfortably.'* – Phil Clarke

The offer Aub Lawson made to Ove Fundin was one he couldn't refuse. Lawson took Ove to one side during that Australian tour of 1954/55 and asked him if he would like to ride in England. 'I said it would be my dream,' says Ove. 'And Aub said, "If you are interested, I will help you to come and race with me at Norwich." He must have written to them because on the boat on the way back he came to me and said, "It's fixed. But you cannot take that old shitty bike that you have. I arranged a bike for you as well."'

The bike that Aub arranged was eventually to become one of the most famous – perhaps notorious – speedway machines in the sport's history: Norwich Track Spare No. 2.

'They gave me this track spare, and right from the word go I went very good,' says Ove. It carried him to four of his five World Championships and with him in the saddle carved a glittering path across the world stage. It is equally as prominent in the sport's folklore as Ivan Mauger's famed Gold Bike presented to him following his unique three-in-a-row World titles in 1968, 1969 and 1970.

Ove says: 'Les Mullins was the Norwich team mechanic. I suppose he was told by Gordon Parkins, who was the manager, to "look after Fundin. See he is happy." You know how it is with somebody who is fairly good.' Les Mullins remembered: 'Gordon Parkins came to me and said Aubie had recommended that Ove should come to Norwich and he told me, "I want you to build him a bike." So I said, "A new one?" "Oh, no," he said. "You've got plenty of bits hanging round the workshop, just build him a bike out of what you have there."'

But that wasn't the real beginning of the exploits of Norwich Track Spare No. 2. Phil Clarke, who joined Norwich in 1947, spent his twelve-year career with the club and became the fledgling Fundin's landlord during Ove's first year at The Firs, knew all about the bike. 'Well, it's an interesting story,' he said. 'That bike was used by Bob Leverenz when he came over and didn't bring a machine.' Leverenz was probably one of the most underrated Australians. He had joined Norwich in 1949 and in 1951, with an average of more than 10 points a match, helped the Stars to gain promotion to the First Division, proving himself world class by qualifying for that year's World Final as a Second Division rider. In the top league in 1952, he again managed a 10-point average, matching major stars such as Jack Young and Ronnie Moore.

Phil Clarke recalled: 'There were not too many Rotrax bikes in use at the time. They brought in the new frame and I'm not sure if Les was actually chief mechanic then or whether Wilf Lucy was. I think Les was probably acting as assistant to Wilf, and they both built the bike. I think Wilf probably did the engine. Bob had a terrific season on that bike. But he didn't complete the season – he had a problem at home and he went back to Australia halfway through the year. Up to then he had done really well. He'd had a lot of extra bookings in second halves, at Wembley and places like that. When he went home he left the bike. A lot of people used to do that. The normal thing was the club would buy the bike and the rider would pay for it out of his earnings. A lot of the Continentals, Australians and New Zealanders did it. As a matter of fact it was a fairly essential procedure. So anyway,

Bob went off and the bike was left. I'm not absolutely sure of the sequence but I think it was immediately designated as the second track spare. Bob Oakley came to Norwich from Wembley in 1954 and he had the bike for a while and did quite well with it. It wasn't built specially for Ove, it had been around for a while. I'm not sure, but when Bill Gilbert came in 1952 and they had to put a bike under him, I think Bill used it.

'Ove came over and brought a bike with him, which was a monstrosity... it was absolutely hopeless. They gave him the track spare to use and he rode it very well. That bike must have had something about it, whatever it was. It was just a standard Rotrax – chromed of course. Then the myth grew up. It was a little bit off-putting for people who went out for a race and there was a guy riding track spare number two who duffed them up quite comfortably. A funny incident happened over that. Cyril Roger decided he wanted that bike after Ove had done very well on it. I think he wanted the engine, and I think he did get it. Either Les or Wilf put in another engine that was equally as good. I don't think Ove worried about it at all. It was just a bike underneath him and it was going well and he just took advantage of it.'

Ove remembers that particular episode very well: 'Cyril Roger wanted the bike they built up for me. He was not nice to me at all then. "Those foreign bastards come over here and take our jobs and we sit on the fence" – there was a lot of that going on at the time, and directed to me. Cyril said something to my face, I can't remember exactly what. But he was very nice to me later on.'

Clarke said: 'I think Cyril got the engine and used it probably for a season. But Cyril was always fiddling with his bikes. He was either using nitro-methane or a big cam or something. They were playing around with nitro in those days; Barry Briggs and Ronnie Moore were playing around with it. Nobody had a great deal of success with it. It was terrible stuff to get right. The problem was carburation. It was either too weak or too rich. Or too much nitro. It used to burn things up. Those people like Moore and Briggs, and various other people, they used to get you going with tales about nitro. I mean they were good riders. All they needed was standard equipment. They used to

sort of let it be known that they were using nitro. They may never
have been near nitro, but it made you very concerned that you were
not going to go as quick as they were going. I am surprised that the
Swedes weren't conversant with it, because a lot of Swedish riders were
very technically advanced. I would imagine that if there was some
advantage to be gained, those Continental people would have gained
it. But I am sure that when Les said he used only standard equipment
he was telling the truth.

'The JAP engines were hopeless. Les used to take down and reas-
semble even brand new ones. He was very methodical when it came to
Ove's engines. He would try different magnetos, different compression
ratios, different pistons in the period building up to a World Final, and
if he had something going really well he would keep it to one side.
Then he would transfer all the good things to that engine and gradually improve it. He would have Ove use it for the qualifying rounds
and if it was still going well he would keep it back for the World Final.
That was a big plus. There were so many things that could have an
effect on the performance of an engine that if you could combine all
the good things together you were gaining an advantage. The cylinder
head could be very critical, and Les was very good at cleaning out
the ports and streamlining the tracts so that he would gradually get
that engine to a perfect pitch – it could be very like tuning a musi-
cal instrument or a concert orchestra. And of course, on the night,
all the other contestants would also have good engines as well, but I
think Ove had some good equipment during his career because of
his association with Les. I didn't expect the same treatment. Les could
physically do only so much. Ove was his baby and Les gained a lot
of kudos because of the association. It was well known that Les was
looking after Ove's bike. He was well known in later years as the man
behind Ove.'

Ove is insistent that, after he was ordered to ditch his big red
'monster' of a home-made bike, he never actually owned a speedway
machine throughout his entire career – but he did, a Norwich Track
Spare No. 2 'ghost'. It was a replica of the one Les built for him at
Norwich, which he raced in Sweden. He said: 'They were almost the

same. A JAP engine with a Rotrax frame, made to look as near the same as possible with identical handlebars and saddles. When I joined Norwich, not even for the first meeting did I have a bike of my own. I had their bikes all the time. And anywhere else I went I rode their bikes. Except in Sweden. I had the bike in Sweden. But I never had more than one – not at the time. I had only one brand new engine in my life – except for the EsO, which I hardly used in Engand. I used it elsewhere. That's why the people at the EsO factory were not too happy with me. They supplied me with everything. And when I won that last championship in 1967 riding for Belle Vue, just the frame was an EsO/JAWA and the engine was a JAP. It was well hidden in the frame and not many people noticed it.

'Les was a very good mechanic. But he was not really a tuner, because he never experimented with anything. And if you look back on all the World Finals I did, not once did I have an engine that stopped. I probably never had the fastest engine, but I had a reliable one. Les would live only for the World Final. Early in the season he would see something that was good. A magneto for instance. He would put it aside for Wembley. He worked up everything just for Wembley – we didn't think it was the World Final in those days unless it was Wembley. I'm afraid I must admit that Les spent probably more than half his time on my bike and the rest on the others. Which... well, that's the way it goes, I suppose. Aub did his own bikes – mostly anyway. Don, his half-brother, helped him and some of the others. They more or less did their own. But Les was the one who oversaw everything. Together with Aub, Cyril Roger was the best one at Norwich. Phil Clarke was very steady and good for a few points, but he was one of those who was really too nice and too kind to be a speedway rider.'

Mullins remembers Aub Lawson telling him that Fundin was on his way to Norwich: 'Aubie said he was going to be very good. He came and spent the rest of the season at Norwich and they said they'd signed him to come back. Then they said build him a new bike with everything brand spanking new – so we had two Norwich Track Spares No. 2. I said to Ove, "You had better have a nameplate on it." But he wouldn't have the Norwich Track Spare

No. 2 taken off because he reckoned that was a good omen. But only that nameplate survived from the original bike. I know I went to Wembley one year, took the bike off the trailer and pushed it into the pits and I heard one of the Norwich supporters say, "Oh, my God. He's got the Norwich number two track spare, he isn't going to do anything tonight." He always used to bring his Swedish bike over for Wembley finals, but he always used to ride Norwich Track Spare No. 2.'

Olle Nygren, who was able to study closely the relationship Ove and Les 'enjoyed', observed that it was not always sweetness and light between them: 'Ove was not very friendly because he was not that kind of rider. It was concentration all the time. And he'd chuck things at Les Mullins. I felt more sorry for Les. Ove was more narked at him than anybody else. If he came second, he'd come in and: Bang! Crash! Spanners everywhere!'

Phil Clarke also vividly recollects the histrionics that would erupt in the Fundin section of the pits: 'Mechanically Ove left everything to Les. But, if it wasn't going quite as well as he thought it ought to be, he would go into one of his modes and play up hell with Les. Les had a lot of bad times with him. He couldn't tell Les what was wrong, he would just say it was not going fast enough, he couldn't give Les any mechanical advice. Les was a very competent, painstaking character and he kept good motors under Ove all the time. It was all very hard work for him. He looked after my motors for a long time and he put in terrifically long hours. Les used to pull Ove up sharply if he became too troublesome. Les could handle him. He was in a good position, actually. He couldn't have turned out such good motors if things hadn't gone right between them. But Ove used to lead Les a dance on the big occasions. Les had to put up with quite a bit, but he was quite capable of coping with it.'

Ove was extremely upset when Norwich was closed down at the end of the 1964 season, the stadium sold and Norwich Track Spare No. 2 not given to him. The bike was put up for public auction, so he sent Eddie Franklyn to the sale with instructions to buy Norwich Track Spare No. 2 for him – because he considered himself its rightful owner.

'I had to pay a lot, a lot more than I was really expecting to pay,' says Ove. 'I don't remember how much it cost me exactly. I think we paid £500 [the equivalent in today's values of £6,290]. That was only because there was one man who kept raising the price all the time. You know, because he had set his mind that he had got to have it. His name was Albert Collins and he was one of the directors. He was the best of all the directors, apart from Jack Thompson. He used to run all the buses around Norfolk. So money was no object for him. I must have collected it, but when I can't remember.'

Ove eventually gave the bike to Barry Briggs for the short-lived speedway museum he opened at Donington Park race track. The museum had to be closed down, and Barry still has Norwich Track Spare No. 2.

Somewhere.

1. The man who 'discovered' Ove, his father Arvid, and brother Torsten. Ove is on the left.

2. *Left:* The class of '46: Ove at school – he is second from the right on the front row.

3. *Below left:* A family send-off before the 1968 World Championship. From left: Ove's mother Ruth, Mona's mother, Ove's niece (Elsie's girl) Annelie, Madeleine (six), Paul (five), Eric (eight), Michael (nine), Mona, Ove with Niclas (two). It is a Swedish custom to say, 'Hold up your thumb for luck!' and they are all giving the thumbs-up sign. But it didn't work: Ove was ninth that year.

4. *Above:* Master class – a lesson from the expert: Ove teaching Madeleine and Eric to ride speedway at Malmo.

5. The house in the country, and Mona. Life with Ove, she says, was sometimes like living near a volcano.

6. Ove with Catharina. They 'lived happily ever after for ten years', then they split up.

7. Mr and Mrs Fundin. Ioanna with the gentleman who took her out. That's Ove's Czech golden helmet they are holding.

8. *Right:* Introducing the new boy: the first picture of Ove to appear in the Norwich match programme when he joined the team in 1955.

9. *Far right:* The unpolished product: Ove pictured in London during 1955, his first season with Norwich.

10. Ove's first year with Norwich. The 1955 team, from left: Don Lawson, Billy Bales, Cyril Roger, Gordon Parkins, Aub Lawson, Ove, Fred Brand, Phil Clarke, Harry Edwards.

11. The master craftsman: the style that had his faithful fans believing 'that this was the most fantastic rider who ever lived'. (Alf Weedon)

12. Murdering England: Ove on his way to an 18-point Test maximum at Wembley in the first senior international between England and Sweden in 1956. Brian Crutcher is the rider in his wake. (Alf Weedon)

13. The beginning at Wembley in 1954. Ove shakes the hand of Ronnie Moore before going out for heat thirteen. Ronnie won and Ove was last. They were also to finish at opposite ends of the meeting – Ronnie rode unbeaten to win his first World Championship and Ove came last with a meagre 2 points. But it was the start of an era.

14. Swedish invasion: Peo Soderman, Ove, Olle Andersson and the man who put a dampener on Jack Parker's amorous adventures, the very good-looking Ulf Ericsson, line up in the pits before the 1956 World Final at Wembley.

15. That's ours! World Champion at last in 1956. Ove is presented with the *Sunday Dispatch* trophy by editor Charles Eade. (Alf Weedon)

16. Homecoming: Ove was given a hero's welcome by the townspeople of Tranas when he won his first World title in 1956, and they all turned out to see him demonstrate his technique at the local recreation ground.

17. Just champion. A supporter took this study of Ove at Western Springs
Speedway, Auckland, New Zealand in January 1957.

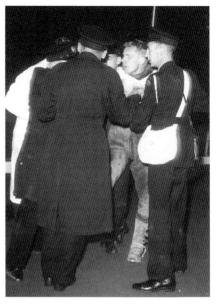

18. *Above left:* Fallen idol: Ove is attended by ambulance men after crashing out of the run-off with Barry Briggs at the 1957 World Final. Briggs halted his lap of honour to make sure Ove was all right.

19. *Above right:* No excuses, no accusations: Ove is on his feet, but the pain and the anguish are plain to see.

20. The victor and the vanquished: after their sensational run-off clash, Briggs shows off the championship trophy, with Ove and Peter Craven on the traditional Wembley tractor ride.

21. *Above:* For some reason, Peter Craven 'found it hard to get the better of Fundin', but he's ahead this time.

22. *Left:* Little Pete, and big Ove. There was mutual respect, but Craven was not impressed by Fundin's starting technique.

23. *Below:* Another second place. Commiserations for Ove in 1958 from land and water speed expert, the late Donald Campbell.

24. *Above:* For the first time the World Final is not held at Wembley, and it proves a clean sweep for Sweden. Ove celebrates his third win at Malmo in 1961 with Bjorn Knutsson and Gote Nordin.

25. *Below:* Craven crown: Little Pete wins his second World title in 1962 while Ove (third) and Barry Briggs (second) put him through the hoop.

26. A smart turn-out at The Firs. From left to right, back row: Harry Edwards, Fred Brand, Gordon Parkins, Cyril Roger, Phil Clarke, Malcolm Flood. Front row: Don Lawson, Aub Lawson, Ove, Billy Bales.

27. Ove's Australasian pals invade Tranas. From left to right: Ronnie Moore, Ove, Trevor Redmond, Aub Lawson, Geoff Mardon, Ron Johnston. Kneeling: Barry Briggs.

28. The invaders hard at work on their bikes outside Ove's house.

29. *Top:* There were no luxury facilities in the Harringay pits and, typical of the Fundin turnout, Ove's right boot is held together by elastic bands.

30. *Above:* Captain Ove introduces his Swedish teammate Olle Nygren to Southampton promoter Charlie Knott, the man to whom he promised £25 if he didn't lower the track record. (Alf Weedon)

31. *Left:* They didn't get on too well, as the body language shows: Bjorn Knutsson and Ove.

32. *Top left:* Internationale prize: Ove won three years running, and Norwich would buy the engines from him.

33. *Top right:* A member of the Norwich Speedway family. Ove is standing second from the left, Les Mullins sitting third from the right. Other teammates include Phil Clarke, Geoff Pymar, Aub Lawson, Harry Edwards, Billy Bales, Reg Trott and manager Gordon Parkins. (Alf Weedon)

34. *Above left:* The great dictator: Ove is all smiles with Arne Bergstrom on the pre-meeting parade at Wembley for the 1970 World Team Cup Final.

35. *Above right:* One of the few trophies Ove has kept and displays in his home.

36. Your call! Ove and Barry Briggs consider the toss of the coin for starting positions before one of their many Match Race Championship contests. (Alf Weedon)

37. *Left:* Let's get the show on the road. The riders before another Match Race duel at Oxford, accompanied by their 'seconds', Ted Flanagan (centre left) and Bert Croucher. (Alf Weedon)

38. *Below left:* The old firm: Fundin and Briggs, the best of rivals.

39. *Below right:* Taking the sponsor for a ride: in the driving seat wearing Ove's Golden Helmet is *Sunday Mirror* sports editor George Casey.

40. *Above left:* Speedway is a great way to meet girls – and there was no shortage. (Alf Weedon)

41. *Above right:* On the threshold of a technical revolution. Ove being shown the way round the Czechoslovakian EsO machine, the bike they threatened to ban.

42. *Right:* Sweden's Sportsman of the Year 1963. Ove is being decorated by Prince Bertil.

43. The night of the speedway 'Oscars'. Ove, centre, flanked by Peter Craven (left), Gordon Parkins and Ronnie Moore, but there is no sign of Stan Stevens. Far right is *Sunday Mirror* speedway columnist Don Clarke, and behind Peter Craven is Mona.

44. Ove astride the beautifully chromed Internationale prize bike, but it was no match for his real prize mount, Norwich Track Spare No. 2, in the background.

45. A star line-up at the Wembley practice session before the 1959 World Final. From left to right, back row: Barry Briggs, Cyril Roger, Ronnie Moore, Peter Craven and Ove. Front row: Mieczslaw Polukard, Arne Carlsson, Josef Hofmeister and Rune Sormander. Ronnie won, Ove was second for the third time and Barry was third.

# SEVEN

# PASSION AND PRIVILEGE

*'I used to get pissed off with him. I remember one night taking him by the throat and chucking him across the pits and throwing him into his workshop.'*
– Barry Briggs

'In World Championships and other big meetings down the years, nobody has given me more trouble than Ove Fundin.'

That is how Barry Briggs, Ove's great track rival – and now respected friend – began chapter sixteen of his book *Briggo: Barry Briggs Speedway Champion: His Own Story*. Barry, with four World Championships – only one less than Fundin – followed up with: 'Just about the most controversial rider of recent times, Ove certainly knew how to get people to react to him. Fans loved him or hated him in more or less equal proportions.'

From observing them together, and researching their careers when they were racing opponents, they seem to have enjoyed – even revelled in – a 'love-hate' relationship that in later years America's Bruce Penhall and England's Kenny Carter and Denmark's Hans Nielsen and Erik Gundersen would mirror. They would spark off each other in a similar way to the Fundin-Briggs rivalry, forcing standards in the sport ever upwards and their personal abilities to even greater heights. The Briggs-Fundin era, the twin decades between the early 1950s until the later 1960s, was probably tougher, because it was the time of an elite of riders of outstanding ability, the so-called 'Big Five' who, as well as Ove and Barry, included England's Peter Craven, Sweden's Bjorn Knutsson and New Zealand's Ronnie Moore.

'When two blokes want to do the same thing and there's only position for one, then someone's got to give a bit,' says Briggs. 'Both of us were probably unforgiving. I think I harnessed my feelings a bit better than Ove did. Ove showed he was pissed off, and that's why he got booed. I didn't really let my feelings show too much. We weren't really pulling strokes on each other. We raced each other. I used to get pissed off with him. I remember one night taking him by the throat – I can't remember why – and chucking him across the pits and throwing him into his workshop. And he then had to come and ask me if he could come back with me to London, because he used to stay with me. It didn't worry me: "Sure, no problem Ove."'

That was almost certainly the night at Norwich when, Briggs claims, Ove and Aub Lawson went out on the track and stirred up the crowd against him. Barry says: 'The fans at The Firs idolised Fundin like a god, and anybody who tried to put one over on him was not popular.' This particular night, says Barry, Ove put on a bit of an act and gave the supporters the idea that Briggs was using unfair tactics to beat him. 'Some irresponsible fans tossed rubbish at me from the terraces, and being bombarded with apple cores and rolls when you are travelling at 75-80mph along the straight isn't very funny.'

Ove says: 'Could well have been. I don't remember. But I don't think they ever threw anything at him there. Coming down the straight at 70mph they would have to aim fifty yards in front of him to hit him. And maybe Gordon Parkins had arranged with Barry for him to get me back to London. I never arranged how to get to and from the airport – Norwich always did that. Often I had my car there and I took it to London airport. In the earlier days it was quite easy. You could get away with parking by the freight office and leaving the car. It would still be sitting there when you came back.'

'It's a long time ago,' concedes Barry. 'And if you were passionate about something, you can look back at things you have done wrong. It means different things to you. Ove came from a privileged background compared with what we did. You look now and everybody tots up. I was never really a totter-up. I would probably have been a ten-times World Champion if I'd moved to Wembley when I had the opportunity once. It would have been a home track. It was a bit of a joke but I didn't even think that way. The World Finals I ballsed up were just down to me, nobody else. One year I went to Earl's Court for an exhibition, because I had a stand there. And I stood at Earl's Court until about two o'clock in the afternoon – and I'm racing in a World Final at night. You look back now and think, "What the f— am I doing here?" with something as important as that.

'With most sports you get on and practise. With speedway there is no warm-up, nothing. It's tough. Before another World Final I went to Swindon to practise and blew up the bloody bike that I was riding at Wembley. And Newbury races were on and I got caught up in traffic on the way to London. I wasn't going to make it, but then a copper got me out of trouble and zapped me through. It was that kind of shit but that's life. Most of it was brought on my own head. And my weight – I'm one of the heaviest blokes and that's a disadvantage, because you have the same bikes pulling someone heavy, like me, and someone light, like say Craven. He could have got away with half a bike. I liked lightweight bikes – no bits hanging off them – because I was giving away a couple of stone, and if the same engine is pulling both of you from the start to the first corner, if you have the right traction and the right throttle control, the lighter bloke is going to beat you. Simple. Not so much on the smaller tracks, but certainly on the larger tracks.

'It's a fact of life. I had a bad situation with bikes. That probably did me a lot of harm, although everything I did was by my own hands. The ones I won I won by myself, and the ones I lost I lost by myself, so there were no recriminations. Whereas Ove went to Norwich and his mechanic Les Mullins was the perfect foil for him. It was perfect because Ove didn't care for all the mechanical problems and that kind of crap – and that's something less in your head you've got to worry about. He was a certain type.'

It has become well known that Ove professed to know nothing about the mechanical side of speedway racing and that he just turned up and rode. And Fundin readily admits that, at best, he knew very little. Trevor Hedge was a junior just breaking into the Norwich team at the start of his career during the last few years of speedway at The Firs. He later went on to become an English international and World Finalist. Trevor says, 'I think Ove had his work cut out to remove a spark plug and put it back in. And that's one of the reasons why he was so good – he knew nothing about the thing mechanically. So psychologically he would not be worrying about the engine, just concentrating on winning the races.'

Olle Nygren remembered that Ove's lack of mechanical knowledge once cost him a big Continental meeting: 'We weren't too good as mechanics, Ove and me. This time he didn't have Les Mullins with him. He was going to do something to his bike – take the cylinder head off and put it all back again – then the rocker box. But the rocker box didn't get tightened up again. That evening, the meeting was a big one with Peter Craven, Ove would have won if he had known enough to tighten that rocker box. He was swearing his head off, but he had no one to blame but himself.'

Briggs believes that, when it came to the mechanics, Ove 'didn't want to know, did he? He wasn't that type.' Barry was a regular member of an Australasian side that used to make an annual tour of Scandinavia. It included Ronnie Moore, Trevor Redmond, Ron Johnston, Aub Lawson, Jack Geran, Neil Street, Peter Moore and Jack Biggs. Briggs recalled: 'When we first went there Ove couldn't speak English. He led us all the way to Norway and we were stopping for cups of tea and Cokes, and we were getting really late and he was getting nervous. He still does a lot of things by himself. I rang his home in France one day and asked where he was and was told he'd gone to Sweden. I said, "What, is he flying?" And they said, "No, he's gone on a pushbike!" He's different. And that's why he was such a good speedway rider.'

Briggs once commented that Fundin was 'too intelligent to be a speedway rider'. 'He's got an intelligent mind,' says Briggs. 'I don't think the rest of us were dumb. We were kind of pushed towards the sporting things, rather than the intellectual things and museums. Great. I think Ove was pushed that way more. I don't really know or understand why. When we were young we never really worried about it, never really talked about it. We were all young and we rode speedway because we were enjoying ourselves. We used to go to Rye House on a Sunday nearly every weekend, going in the rowing boats, playing cricket... we were just a bunch of kids having a good time and getting paid for it. We used to travel everywhere together. We were a young team at Wimbledon and we did it because we enjoyed it. That was the type of stuff that Ove never really had the fun of. He never thought why he was different from me, he was concerned more about his health. It was an important thing to him.

'I had to start off with the bikes. I didn't know anything about bikes. Well, only a little bit because I'd tinkered around with them in New Zealand, but suddenly I was pushed in at the deep end and my bikes were crap. I think I was too honest with myself, thinking, "Ah well, this is me." I was in and out of the Wimbledon teams and in the end we had to take the bike away from Wimbledon. Trevor Redmond, who was riding for Wembley at the time, started doing my bike. He did it when it was raining, outside with a coat over him. That was the alternative because my bike wasn't getting done – it was about seventh in line. One night I lent it to Ronnie because Ronnie's bike broke down. He had about an 11-point average at the time, and he came a bad third on it. He came in and went nuts. Then I had a couple of bad tuners and in the end I had to learn to do it myself.

'You can't be a proper speedway rider, I don't think, by doing your own bikes all the time, by spending all your bloody time doing it. And now when I look back I wonder how the hell I ever did it, because I was one of the first blokes on the Continent grass tracking, sand tracking and all that stuff. And my brother Murray didn't have transport, so I used to take him to the grass track meetings. I finished up riding over there as well.'

Ove's obsession with winning frequently produced dramatic histrionics – sometimes publicly, sometimes privately. Briggs recalled a public display of temperament by Fundin at a long track meeting at Pfafenhoffen, Germany, when, after making a dream start, he found his path blocked at the end of the first lap: 'Fundin reckoned that I had cheated at the start and demanded that the race should be run again and, to strengthen the point, had parked his bike across the track.' Not for the first time – or the last – there was a public shouting match.

'I got quite friendly with him when he first came over to England,' says Barry. 'He got into terrible trouble, knocking people off all over the place. I had been through all that and I sympathised with him. He was the hardest rider you could imagine. Running into Ove was like colliding with a brick wall. But at least he would run over you with class. He dished out plenty of rough treatment to any rider who got in his way, and not surprisingly got some given back.'

The night they met in a Golden Helmet Match Race at New Cross in July 1960, Barry enlisted the aid of Jack Young to go to work on Ove and try to unsettle him psychologically before they went out on the track. Fundin was always a bag of nerves anyway and, after Young had wound him right up, Barry could tell Ove was having a real attack of the jitters. Barry recalled: 'Although I tried really hard, running over his left foot a few times – once his steel shoe almost came off and he went down the straight kicking it back on – Ove would not shut the throttle. He took more than half a second off the track record that night, so Youngie and I decided that wasn't the way to tackle Ove. If he was in the right mental state he was like a racehorse. The more excited he got, the faster he went.' Briggs' assessment was more than borne out when Ove went on to win the main event that evening, a Southern Riders' Championship qualifying round, with a 15-point maximum.

'That was probably my best meeting ever,' says Ove, 'when I went to New Cross for a Golden Helmet Match Race with Barry Briggs in 1960. I beat him in two straight runs and I lowered my own track record. I loved that little track.'

He certainly did. The previous month, in a National Trophy encounter between New Cross and Norwich, Fundin had been in top form, with 16 points out of 18. But his temperament was showing again: 'Controversial Swede Ove Fundin reckoned that he started off the wrong grid in heat five [he had finished third behind Barry Briggs and Leo McAuliffe] and his protest held the meeting up by fifteen minutes. A section of the crowd booed Fundin, but he soon silenced his detractors by proving himself the greatest rider in the world on present form.

In heat seven he set new track-record figures of 57.8. In heat nine he reduced that to 57.6, then in heat twelve again clocked 57.8. Fundin dominated the Norwich scoring.' Norwich lost the match 46-61, but won on aggregate 113-102.

He says now of his performances at New Cross: 'I think I would have got on well with the small tracks of today, because I never did like Norwich. And I hated Belle Vue. I did like Wembley. Okay, it was almost as big, but Wembley was pear shaped. The first corner was very sharp and quite tricky – the same as on a small track. Belle Vue was so bloody big, it was like ice racing – all you had to do was go round and round. I didn't particularly like big tracks – they were too easy. Norwich was big, but not quite the same. I liked the Belle Vue stadium, the funfair and the zoo – but I did feel sorry for the animals, because it was more or less 100 years behind the times. They kept those poor animals in cages – where today they are more or less free.'

At that time, says Briggs, the Swedes were the best nation. 'It's a hard sport. And if you don't want contact or you don't want to race, you might as well go and play tennis. It was better in those days because you could out-think blokes and do stuff like convince them you were going to do something and then go the other way and pass them and beat them. And if you were behind blokes you had to hustle. I'd hate to be riding now, if you didn't trap and got behind – and that goes for Ronnie, me or even Ove – and Ove was a trapper. But can you pass now? It's like getting a weight on the end of a piece of string and circulating it, if you can keep up that circulation how can you get past it? You know, in the old days the tracks were shitty and we had big wheels and it was hard to go flat out.

'Ove did a completely different corner from me. I used to go flat out. I had to be a lot more precise than he did because if I f——ed up I'd shoot off in the wrong direction. But he did it a different way, and on a lot of tracks it was the best way if you're in front. Blokes sometimes f——ed me up and, instead of reacting there and then, sometimes you'd think, "F—— me, you deserve one." And it might be a month later. Because I've seen too many blokes in speedway go out and try and clear up grudges and hurt themselves – and others – badly. I remember one particular rider who said he was going to fix someone. He did... he killed him! People just don't quite realise that you are riding right on the edge.

'I remember one night I closed the gap on Jimmy Gooch at West Ham. Now I liked Goochie, he was a paratrooper. But on this particular occasion we didn't have room and I got him halfway down the straight. If you do hit someone, or something goes wrong, you can hurt them – seriously. I was kind of a boy racer when I came to England in 1952 following Ronnie to Wimbledon. Ernie Roccio was killed at West Ham, and I was supposed to be in that race. Ronnie Greene told me that if we got a 4-2 in the race before I could ride in it, if we didn't get it I'd be pulled out. Well, we didn't get it and they put Cyril Maidment in instead of me. Maido ran into the back of Ernie and Ernie got killed and it was horrible.

'Lots of things in life take a swing to your advantage. It's a serious sport. Years later, when I did that Hall of Fame at Donington Park, I had a Lest We Forget section that included the names of all the speedway riders who had been killed racing. There were a hundred and something names of boys who had died and I knew sixty per cent of them. Tommy Jansson, Ernie Rawlings and Johnny Thomson... you can never, ever forget that. And some blokes did. Lots of times blokes get killed when it looks a simple one, rather than a horrendous one that you think they'll never get up from.'

Fundin professed to be shocked when he learned that in the 1959 World Final both Briggs and Moore had used nitro-methane in their machines, a fuel that was later banned. 'That's bloody well cheating, isn't it?' he said. It wasn't at the time. 'I'm surprised – and disappointed, because Ronnie has been my big favourite all along. He was the only one I ever looked up to.'

The title went to Moore that year, Ronnie's second. Ove was runner-up – frustratingly for the third successive season – while Barry, after being seeded direct to the final because he was the previous year's champion and there had been a stand-off with his promoter over his return fare from New Zealand, won a third place run-off against Olle Nygren and Aub Lawson. Ronnie revealed his use of nitro like this: 'The main worry as the World Championship final drew near was fuel, or the lack of it. Nitro-methane was becoming the fashion and I decided that if I was to stand a chance of winning I would have to use this mixed with my fuel. Everybody else was going to be tanked up on it.'

The main advantage of using the nitro-assisted fuel mixture was that it gave riders a better drive from the start and, in a World Final especially, making a good gate ahead of rivals could be a decisive factor in the cut-throat competition for points. The downside of using nitro was that, according to some, there was a danger that the motor could run so hot it could melt a hole in the piston and wreck a highly tuned engine. Not so, says Briggs: 'Nitro was a form of tuning that allowed parts to be older. It was cheap. It would cost you maybe £1 a meeting. The pistons didn't have to be quite as good. If you had a mechanic who pulled your motor down after every meeting and did the valves it was probably just the same as that. It didn't give you an unfair advantage, that's for sure. All the blokes had it. It was the blokes who had it when it was banned – that's when it was wrong. There were a few of them around. There wasn't a danger of it burning pistons. No different. You had to know how to tune with it.'

Moore said: 'Nitro-methane was between £7 and £8 a gallon, if you could get it. I'd hardly used it at all before the championship and had no regular source of supply, but in years gone by I'd been a keen aero modeller and I recalled that the tiny diesel aeroplane engines ran on nitro. I knew that model shops would have it in stock, so in the fortnight before the World Final I visited just about every model shop in London – and there were quite a few – and in each shop all I could get was a few cubic centimetres at a time.' He ended up with about a pint. It was just enough, he calculated, to allow him to have a brief practice and take part in his five races. But his calculation was out. When it came to his final, vital ride, heat nineteen against Brian Crutcher, Aub Lawson and Peter Moore, he had only enough nitro for about two laps of the four-lap race. Barry was also using nitro. His fifth ride had put him into an extra race run-off – there would barely be enough fuel for both of them. Ronnie's machine was set up for nitro, there was no time to alter the engine to take conventional methanol. But Barry offered to let him have what nitro there was in his tank, and Ronnie finished the night on a 15-point maximum. They then tipped back the remaining fuel into Barry's bike and, after he had won the run-off to put him in third place, they found there was hardly enough fuel for another lap.

Briggs said that his great American friend Jack Milne, the 1937 World Champion, always told him that he had a bike and he never touched it, and that if he made the start, he knew why he'd made the start. 'One week I'd have a carburettor with a 40mm,' said Barry, 'then I'd have twin bowls on it. The next I'd have a different cam. No matter how good a motorcyclist you are, it takes you time to adjust. In the 1962 World Final all my bikes were crap and I hired a bike from Josef Hofmeister, because we were mates, and I did one race at Southampton on it and went to the World Final at Wembley, got beat in my first race and then won all my others because I'd adjusted to it.'

Fundin insists that his engines were what he describes as 'very normal'. He said: 'I never had anything but a very plain, very normal engine. Because Les Mullins wasn't one of those who experimented. We just had a good engine. I wanted to experiment a couple of times with camshafts, but when I brought one over once he tried it and he didn't like it so he didn't use it. He wanted just a good, reliable engine. Just about the time that Ivan Mauger came into the game they started experimenting with nitro, though it had probably been around a long time before then. Nitro was used by the Norwegian Basse Hveem. Olle Nygren bought an engine from him once for the long track, because Basse's favourite was the long track. He was outstanding. Straight after Hveem had won an important meeting, Olle said to him, "I'll buy your engine but I want you to take it out now." Olle didn't want anything done to it or altered on it. But it was useless when Olle rode it because it had been set up for nitro, and he did not use nitro – but he didn't know at the time. I was a good gater without nitro. But, you know, today they won't even let you bring your own methanol to a big meeting.'

Briggs says: 'Fundin knows how to ride a speedway bike. He always rode the right part of the track. Millions of times you'd come roaring right up to the corner behind him and he'd stop! And you think, "Yeah! Got him!" And just as you'd make your move, that's when he'd done his move and you got covered in shit... and he'd got perfect traction. And there was no way to counteract it.'

At the special meeting to celebrate British speedway's seventy-fifth anniversary at Rye House in 2003, Ove, at the age of seventy, took part in a special Match Race against Mark Loram, the 2000 World Champion. Loram was riding an 'old fashioned' JAP, Ove was on a modern bike and was winning until it died on him on the final corner. Barry said, 'All around the youngsters were saying, "Cor, Ove's tough, isn't he?" They don't really know what day of the week it is. You hear a lot about how tough these kids are, but I wonder whether they really know what's happening.' Afterwards Ove said, 'I was waiting for him. I was going inside and outside and waiting for him to catch me up.'

'Of course,' says Barry, 'these four valves are much easier to ride than the old bikes. You had an apprenticeship to serve on the old bikes, and blokes these days don't do it. You can see a fifteen-year-old kid going round without shutting the throttle. We had them at the Golden Greats. We had Mark Loram when he was World Champion on his home track, and Peter Collins and Michael Lee beat him twice by the length of the straight. Because Mark did one corner wide. If I'd done that it would be: "Shit, that's wrong!" I'd go right round the grass, but Mark kept doing the same kind of thing and that killed him. I'm not saying that PC and Mike were any better, but riders now have 70-something horsepower, so they don't care whether they go round the fence. With 50 horsepower it is okay until you are about halfway out as you have enough speed, but if you go wide you're slow.

'My theory about speedway was that the fastest one round the line should be the winner, because it's the hardest to do and hardest to keep up the speed. It was normally all the lunatics who went round the fence, but sometimes you'd be forced to do it because you were going to get beaten. And you thought, "It's not really what I want." But look at how Ryan Sullivan rides a track like Peterborough today.

'These days Ove and I get on well. I think he has mellowed a bit, and I think we have a respect for each other, but you just have to try and contain it.'

Ove Fundin was in despair. He was sitting in the Wembley pits with his head in his hands. He had just dropped two vital points in his opening ride, heat one of the 1956 World Championship Final, to his two biggest rivals, Peter Craven and Ronnie Moore. It was Saturday 22 September, the first time that a World Final had not been held on Wembley's regular race night – Thursday. The switch was introduced partly to encourage more fans to travel from outside London and partly because spectator levels for the most important meeting of the speedway year had been steadily falling, along with the number of tracks. The 1956 Empire Stadium crowd was down to 65,000 from the 90,000-plus of earlier years, even though the speedway prints were claiming that 'World Championship fever is sweeping the speedway fraternity.'

Ove had been widely tipped as one of the favourites after a brilliant season for Norwich and Sweden. He had played a significant role in the Swedes beating England home and away in a Test series. Craven had been seeded direct to Wembley – the first time a reigning champion was not required to battle through the qualifying rounds. Moore was at the top of his form. There was, reportedly, what was described as an 'unbearably tense atmosphere' in the pits before heat one because three of the main contenders were in the race. If there was indeed an 'unbearably tense atmosphere', then not one of the participants was remotely conscious of it.

Ronnie Moore recalls: 'I was not aware of any tension, I looked at World Finals as just another meeting. If you missed out in your first ride you just hoped whoever won that race missed out in a later race.'

Ove says: 'I'm really surprised, because I have no memory whatsoever. I may have been tense – probably because of nerves. But, you know, I always kept to myself.'

He had reached Wembley from the Continental Final at Oslo where, despite being unable to practise because the Norwegian archery championships were taking place the same morning, he led the European qualifiers with a 15-point maximum. And Craven had not seemed unduly troubled at all. When the riders finally went to the tapes, eighteen minutes after the scheduled start time, it was Craven, in the blue helmet, off grid two, who rocketed away from the line. Fundin, in yellow/black off the outside grid, tried to come across Moore, in white on grid three, as he sought to reach his favourite position on the inside line. But Moore took him wide on turn one, which let in the fourth man, Ove's fellow Swede Peo Soderman, in red off grid one.

Craven's spectacularly precarious balancing style had the crowd gasping because he looked in danger of coming down at every turn. But he flashed past the chequered flag a full ten lengths clear of Moore in the fastest time of the night by nearly two full seconds. It was a warning to the others who were after his crown that he was not going to give it up easily. Ove, who had recovered enough to snatch third place – and a single point – from Soderman, rode into his favoured spot in the Wembley pits, the stone steps on the right as you look down the tunnel, and slumped down dejected. The four-leafed clover lucky charm given to him by one of his nephews before the meeting didn't seem to be working. He confessed later that he had lost it. Les Mullins, aware of the despondent Fundin, says: 'I knew what he was going through. He would always get nervous before a final anyway. He used to find a place where he could get out of the way of everyone. Only occasionally would he come to me and say, "Is everything all right?"'

Out on the track in heat two, other dreams were being crushed. The much-fancied Wembley hero Brian Crutcher, his concentration apparently ruined by Belle Vue Ace Dick Fisher's machine standing on it's rear wheel next to him at the start, also dropped two points to Bradford's Arthur 'Black Prince' Forrest and Ken McKinlay of Second Division Leicester.

After preparing Norwich Track Spare No. 2 for Fundin's second ride in heat eight, Les Mullins decided to climb the stone steps to the St John Ambulance platform and take a look at the racing. It was heat six and, before his eyes, more drama unfolded. Three race winners lined up for heat six, Craven, Birmingham's Alan Hunt and Barry Briggs, together with Crutcher. Craven snatched an early lead from Crutcher with Briggs in third place after Hunt had pulled out with engine problems. On the last bend Craven also hit motor trouble and stopped but, to the crowd's sympathetic encouragement, pushed his dead machine to the finishing line for one point.

'I just happened to go up top to see what was going on,' said Les. 'And little Pete stopped right on the pits bend. And I thought, "That's ours!"'

He meant the World Championship. What he had seen convinced him that the title was going to be Ove's for the first time.

'Of course,' says Les. 'Ove was despondent. He was on a low. I had to pick him up again. I went back and told him. I said, "Little Pete's just stopped. He's your main worry. All you've got to do is just go for it."'

Had anyone in the speedway world doubted that Ove Fundin was on his way to great things, 1956 put them wise. He eased in with an early season tour of six of the seven British Second Division tracks, guesting for Swedish club Monakerna, of Stockholm, but had to give way to the greater experience and higher profile of Olle Nygren when it came to topping the score chart. Olle's masterly performance in the six-match tour produced 80 points out of 90. Ove's 7 points on 30 March at Southampton, which Monakerna lost 54-42, was an opening-match blip, but three successive maximums at Swindon, Coventry and Oxford, plus a round dozen at Leicester, put the Swedes on a four-match winning run. Another 12 in the final match at Rayleigh brought Ove within 4 points of Olle but couldn't prevent a 46-50 defeat. *Speedway News* columnist Barney Bamford had already been moved to write, 'It's pretty safe to say that "F for Fireworks" Fundin has made a greater impression on the British public than did his fellow-countryman Olle Nygren. Certainly in his own country he has ousted Olle from the position of number one public favourite, and currently Ove heads the points chart as well as the popularity poll in Sweden. The Swedish speedway and sports press are wondering whether the Filbyterna Firework can do what Olle Nygren has failed to accomplish – take the World Championship back to the Land of the Lakes.'

Jumping on the Fundin bandwagon, a *Speedway Star & News* caption writer commented: 'For a number of years Olle Nygren has been top dog in Sweden. Now he's had to move over to make way for the red-headed flier, twenty-three-year-old Ove Fundin. Ove is an extremely robust rider – throttle taps wide open at the corners is his maxim.' 'Robust' was a mild assessment of the Fundin philosophy – on and off the track. Nowadays he would be described as someone 'with attitude'. He was involved in several incidents that can only be described as being of a petulant nature, which did not endear him to either the British speedway public – especially at Wimbledon – or the British speedway press. And it was almost certainly these that were at the root of the rough and frequently openly hostile receptions that all too often greeted Fundin whenever he appeared at Plough Lane.

It was the first year that Sweden and England met in an official series of senior internationals, confirming how far and how rapidly the Swedes had progressed in only eight years of properly organised speedway. The headline after the first encounter at Wembley proclaimed, 'FUNDIN MURDERS ENGLAND'. He did it with an 18-point maximum. In a special Test report after a shaken England had suffered a virtual rout, Eric Linden wrote: 'England didn't know what hit them when the Swedes started making mincemeat of them. Led in scoring ability by Ove Fundin, they murdered the country that has long been the cradle of world speedway. Don't let the 10-point margin they won by fool you – the Swedes were twice as good as that 59-49 victory suggests.'

The one excuse England had was that they were riding on unfamiliar rear tyres. A new, narrower tyre had been compulsorily introduced in Britain and it had taken some time for riders to adapt. Unfortunately, the Swedes were not bound by British tyre rules, and elected to race on the 'old' tyre, forcing the England riders to swap back again and putting them at a considerable disadvantage. As proof, World Champion Peter Craven, alone among the English riders, had ridden a race on one of the new tyres and had been last – by fifty yards. The trouble was, wrote Linden, 'Riders can't just make such a change and take up where they left off. Before a wheel was turned, England were on the defensive. The Swedes were full of confidence. They weren't going to lose and they knew it.' For England it was a virtual one-man crusade by Brian Crutcher against the rampaging Swedes with a score of 14. Alan Hunt, wrote Linden, was 'fighting like a demon all the way through'. Unfortunately super-patriot Hunt – 'the greatest honour any man can have in this game is riding for England' – allowed his nationalism to get the better of him to the point where he antagonised even the home Wembley crowd. They took exception to his tactics in his first ride against Olle Nygren, which brought England's only heat win in the entire first half of the match. Split Waterman was well in the lead with Nygren and Hunt going at it 'hammer and tongs' behind him. Linden reported: 'This was a needle race all right. To put it mildly I'd say that neither rider particularly likes the other! On the pits bend Hunt went inside Nygren in a space that wasn't there. At the top bend Nygren attempted to blast round the outside, while Hunt drifted towards the fence.'

It looked, wrote Linden, as though they hit shoulder to shoulder, and Nygren bounced down the straight along the fence. On the last bend Nygren made 'a suicide dive to pass Hunt, clouted him good and proper' and finished up in the Wembley dirt. Before he hit the track the steward (referee) had excluded him. It was a 5-1 for England and it looked as though it might have been the inspiration needed to save the match. Instead, the crowd let Hunt know how much they disapproved of his riding by booing him. Hunt was obviously determined to live up to his nickname of 'Whacker', which he earned as a wild Cradley novice.

The matter of questionable tactics was put to Ove, and he said there were some riders who were unfair or 'just unscrupulous, but it wouldn't be nice to name anyone'. Pressed to be specific, because there were some who were well known and were people to avoid, he said: 'I'll give you one name because he is no longer alive. Alan Hunt. I saw him take people off to the fence. I could name Ray Wilson because he once took me out – that was a really bad ride. I don't care if he is still around. Any rider knows, they all know it, we all know it. We knew the people to avoid trying to go round. Just the same they also knew riders like myself, Peter Moore and Dick Bradley, who they thought could only pass on the inside – which was wrong of course.'

Hunt was at it again in the second Test at Wimbledon, a much closer match with the Swedes again winning, but by a single point, 53-52. This time Whacker was head-to-head with Fundin. There had been what was described as 'a skirmish' in heat nine between Hunt and Swedish veteran Kjell Carlsson. The pair had locked together and Carlsson was thrown over his handlebars and rushed to hospital with severe concussion and a skull injury. It was Carlsson's last ride. He never recovered sufficiently to race again. The match was incident-packed. From a racing point of view it was outstanding, with thrills galore, plenty of close finishes and ending in an extraordinarily climactic last-heat decider, with Fundin and Hunt involved controversially in the action. Early on, the tension had been stoked up when the starting tapes began to rise unevenly, giving the riders on the outside gates a clear advantage. Some of the Swedes, Ove among them, refused to ride again until the fault was fixed. The incident brought condemnation from Angus Kix, who questioned the Swedes' sportsmanship: 'My favourite Swede, Ove Fundin, was right slap in the middle of the rumpus and stating that he wasn't riding again. Now this is stupid. I like Fundin as a rider, but he's a big boy now. He should leave that kind of temperament to ballet dancers. He did go out and race again, but what a fit of the sulks.'

By heat sixteen – two heats from the end – Sweden had a 2-point lead, the first time they had been ahead in the entire meeting. Ken McKinlay and Brian Crutcher slammed in a 5-1 in heat seventeen, leaving England needing to draw the final heat for victory. The fiery Hunt and partner Dick Bradley were determined to get it. They combined brilliantly to keep Fundin back in third place. Then, sensationally, Ove rode into Bradley and they both came down. Fundin was excluded and there was a furious public shouting match between him and Hunt before he finally left the track. Bradley, too shaken to ride in the re-run, was replaced by George White. So it was Hunt and White against the Swedish reserve Birger Forsberg. When Forsberg slipped between the fast-gating English pair, Hunt and White stayed together to make sure of the safe minor places. But White's engine failed. His bike stopped, trapping his close-riding partner against the fence, and Hunt fell. White gallantly began the enormous task of pushing his bike two full circuits of the 343-yard Plough Lane track, but Forsberg lapped him. So the Swede was the only finisher and won the match – and the series – for his ecstatic teammates. In the third Test, at Norwich, nothing went right for the Swedes. They lost 42-66 and were plagued by mechanical problems. At the end they were down to their last bike and were borrowing machines from the English riders. Ove, on his 'home' track, top scored for Sweden with 15.

Later in July Fundin was at Wimbledon again with Norwich, and having to ride 'heel first' to avoid putting unnecessary weight on a poisoned left foot. It may have been the pain from the foot that made him bad tempered, but he was involved in yet another stormy incident when he was excluded from heat eleven following a tangle with Cyril Maidment, which pitched him into the fence. He obviously felt that Maidment was to blame and an argument developed between the two of them, which was resolved when Wimbledon promoter Ronnie Greene stepped between the squabbling pair and ordered Maidment away.

A 14-point score in Gothenburg gave Ove the Swedish national championship, the first of nine, and with the Continental title in Oslo he was set up nicely for the World Final at Wembley. The pundits were openly asking 'Is This Fundin's Year?' One forecast that it would be a 'gater's' World Final and pointed out that Ove was an exceptionally quick gater. As he had won fourteen out of fifteen starts at Wembley so far during the season the result, it was predicted, was practically a foregone conclusion. Until the fateful heat one.

To have any kind of a chance Ove could afford no more lapses, and his second ride would determine whether he and Les had succeeded in repairing the psychological damage caused by the disaster of that first race. Ove went to the tapes this time wearing the red helmet cover and in the favoured starting position on the inside. Next to him was McKinlay, then fellow Swede Olle Andersson II and Norwich team-mate Gerald Hussey. Hussey leapt from the gate and crossed the paths of the other three. But Andersson and Fundin swept past him at the pits bend and so did McKinlay. From then on Ove took command and, even though McKinlay put in a desperate challenge on the final bend, it was Fundin's race. Four heats later another 3 points went onto his scoresheet and after three rides he was the joint leader on 7 points alongside Crutcher and McKinlay.

Heat sixteen was the crunch one with Crutcher. Ove led Australian Peter Moore and fellow Swede Ulf Ericsson out of the first bend with Crutcher in last place correcting an overslide. By the pits turn Crutcher had moved up to second and was challenging Fundin hard. At the end of the back straight next time round Crutcher dived reck-lessly underneath Fundin to take the lead, only to crash in a spectacular somersault. He jumped to his feet and stamped on the track in fury and disappointment. The race was stopped and Wembley's golden boy excluded, his bid for the title over.

Now it was between Fundin and McKinlay on 10 points each, with Moore, Forrest and Briggs hovering on 9 with one ride to go. But McKinlay crashed out in heat seventeen and Moore took his total to 12 in heat nineteen with a win over the luckless Crutcher. With 10 points from his first four rides and the title to all intents and purposes in his pocket, Fundin was just four laps away from being World Champion. As he prepared for heat twenty a pale-looking Ove said he didn't feel well.

'That was because I was nervous,' he says. 'I don't know who wrote that. It was probably when I was sitting in the stairway with my head down. It was probably someone who thought I didn't feel well. I don't think they spoke to me because even if they had spoken to me I wouldn't have said, "I don't feel well." I don't think I would have even answered.'

In heat twenty he had to face Briggs, Forrest and also-ran Eric Boothroyd of England and Birmingham. A Forrest win would mean a tie with Moore. A Briggs win would mean a tie with Moore. A second place for Fundin would also mean a tie with Moore. Out on the track, if Ove had not been feeling well, he soon forgot about it. From the tapes he streaked into the lead, but a fierce duel developed between him and Forrest, both sensing they were seconds from greatness. Forrest battled past Fundin into the lead, but Ove forced a way through again and, as the chequered flag dropped, he rode into speedway history by taking the World Championship to Sweden for the first time. Briggs was third. Second-placed Forrest had the consolation of beating Craven in the run-off for the third spot on the rostrum.

The incredibly tense climax to the meeting moved Eric Linden to describe it as 'the best final I have ever seen. Ove Fundin is the new champion, a worthy champion. Never lose sight of that fact.' It was all too much for some of Fundin's female fans from Norwich, who actually fainted during his winning last ride. As for Fundin himself, being World Champion did feel, he said, 'a trifle overwhelming'. Asked how he had felt after his disastrous first ride, he said, 'I felt very relieved being third... because before I was so nervous and I thought I had a very good chance of winning, but then I thought, "This is it and now I'll just do my best. There is nothing else I can do." So it was good for me I guess, but at least I suppose I was lucky that 13 points were enough to win it.'

As he had crossed the winning line in heat twenty the other Swedish riders and pressmen had gone wild with delight. But the men running British speedway did not share their enthusiasm. A foreigner winning the sport's biggest prize meant the very real threat that they would be forced to kiss the season's main money-spinner goodbye. The day surely could not be far off when they would be unable to keep it an exclusively Wembley affair. The Swedish authorities had that objective in mind and had been pressing Olle Nygren to make another serious attempt at the world title. Olle says: 'I was the top rider in the league with Rune Sormander. He was my biggest competitor. Then Fundin came up and got better and better. Then we came to these World Finals. I was third and he was last, then suddenly he won it. Before he won the first one in England, I was doing more road racing. And they said to me, "Why don't you try and win the World Final?" Suddenly Fundin won the bloody thing. I couldn't even guess he would win the World Final, because they put the World Final so high up. It was only for the English guys, not for the Swedes. That's why we felt it was so hard to think we could win it. But when Fundin won it, that was unbelievable and it also put Sweden on the map – it was like Ingemar Johansson. You would never have thought a Swedish boxer could win the boxing World Heavyweight Championship. Everyone remembers that. It had the same effect. Not with the journalists, because they didn't like anyone riding a bike. They said that it was not a sport because you had an engine helping you. So therefore not every paper reported it. But Ove put Sweden on the map and that's why England lost the World Finals.'

For the time being, though, England was safe. The Swedes were not quite ready. There was the real possibility that the World Championship's main sponsor, the *Sunday Dispatch* newspaper, would ditch its interest if the final went to another country, and speedway's world governing body, the Federation Internationale Motorcyclisme (FIM), would hardly have been thrilled about that. But the Swedes let it be known that they could not afford to stage a World Final, at least in the immediate future, and the reaction of the new champion was: 'We haven't a stadium big enough, although there may be one ready by 1958. Anyway, next year I'd like to defend the title on the same track where I won it.'

After his lap of honour at the front of the Wembley tractor, Fundin went back to the pits to gaze at the machine that had carried him to the top of the speedway world. But one man who took quiet pride in the achievement was Les Mullins, who'd had a plan all along that paid off brilliantly. 'I had a sort of scheme in my own mind,' he said. 'I had built the engine up as I thought. I didn't go through the sequence as I did in later years, because that first time I didn't know whether Ove had a dog's chance of winning or not. The plan was to give him a fresh tyre for every race so he got the maximum grip out there all the time. And that worked.' It was a precaution that Tommy Price had also taken in the 1949 World Final and he always swore it had enabled him to become the first Englishman to win the title.

When it came to the presentation of the prizes, Ove says that though others before and after him were allowed to take the magnificent *Sunday Dispatch* World Championship trophy away with them, he was not. Perhaps it was because he was a foreigner, which had also excluded him from being nominated as a challenger for the British Match Race Championship Golden Helmet. 'A big Swedish departmental store, a sort of Harrods of Stockholm, borrowed the trophy to have it on display there,' he said. 'I still remember they had to pay a very hefty insurance fee to the *Sunday Dispatch* to borrow it. The last time it was raced for, Barry Briggs won it and he still has it! It belongs as much to me as to him. It was very beautiful. Then the *Sunday Mirror* big winged wheel came in. And Ivan Mauger has that.'

There was, perhaps, some consolation in the pay packet for his night's work – £575 10s. In today's money its value is equivalent to £8,920.25. Another perk winning the World Championship was a sponsorship from Astorias cigarettes, a popular brand at the time. 'They used to do that for everybody after a World Final,' says Ove. 'I don't smoke, though they didn't seem to care about that. But Les Mullins, he used to smoke like a chimney. They paid me in cigarettes, not money. Free cigarettes while I was champion. Anyway, Les was happy because he received a hell of a lot of cigarettes.'

One person who was more delighted than anyone about Ove's winning performance, apart from his sister Elsie and mother Ruth, who saw it all on television, was the young woman who rushed into the pits and gave him a huge congratulatory kiss. She was Mona Forsberg – no relation to either Dan or Birger – Ove's Swedish girl-friend. Both of them were soon to realise the punishing schedule that went with being World Champion. The morning after the Wembley triumph he left London by car, travelling via Dover, Calais, Belgium, Germany and Denmark to his home in Tranas – a journey of 1,300 miles – which he reached on the Tuesday afternoon. By 4 a.m. the next day he was on his way back to Norwich to keep a promise to ride at The Firs on the Wednesday night, arriving an hour before the start of the meeting. In his first ride his forks snapped. It could so easily have happened in that vital last race at Wembley. Ove missed only five league matches for Norwich in 1956, but raised his average to an overall 10.34. As in the previous year, he did better away – 10.58 – than at The Firs – 10.05 – and Norwich, next to bottom in the league the season before, finished fourth.

They wanted the new World Champion in New Zealand that winter and when the invitation came, Ove asked Mona to go with him. 'I was on top of the world,' said Ove. 'When I said to her would she like to come, she said, "Sure I'll go with you… if we get married." Because people didn't live together unless they were married – not even in Sweden – though it was no problem if you didn't do it openly. Of course, I had brought her to England once or twice, but then we had to have separate rooms because we had separate passports, and in those days you always had to present your passports. We had to have separate rooms. So we got married, quick. It was quite a big white wedding in Tranas. There were a lot of people. I had to take a Saturday off to get married, but I still had to ride on the Sunday in Sweden.'

At Norwich's 20 October meeting a message from Ove was broad-cast to the supporters. It was, 'Just married and very happy.' And in December, when the 1956 world rankings were published, Ove Fundin's name topped the list.

# EIGHT

# MONA... IN HER OWN WRITE

*'The more successful Ove became as a speedway rider, the more success he had with girls.'* − Mona Forsberg-Fundin

Mona Forsberg-Fundin was married to Ove for fourteen turbulent years. Ironically those years measured the span of his World Championship career. They had seven children, and another child each from other relationships. Mona and I have never met, though I have seen pictures of her, read about her and we have corresponded. Among her many attributes, she is a highly competent journalist with, as you will see, strong and individual views on life and the living of it. When I approached her and told her I was writing a book on Ove's life she unhesitatingly agreed to answer a number of questions I put to her. Not only that, she allowed me to see numerous newspaper cuttings about herself, Ove and their family, kindly translating many of them for me. The result of her generosity is what you see here − a moving and searing account, in her own words, of her life with a highly talented, complex and volatile personality, adjectives that would not be misplaced in describing her as well as Ove. For, make no mistake, there is much, much more to them both than a mere association with speedway racing.

Because of the strength of their combined personalities, it was perhaps inevitable that eventually they would go their separate ways. Yet
they are inextricably bound together by their children, Eric, Michael,
Paul, Madeleine, Niclas, Annika and Monica. Both are now in their
seventies, though age has not diminished either's forthright views
on the human condition. After many years without contact, Mona
received an invitation to Ove's seventieth birthday 'grand celebration',
which she accepted.

Soon after Mona had graciously answered my questions, I was
surprised – and very pleased – to receive another letter from her that
she entitled 'My Husband the World Champion'. It is a unique docu-
ment and, once again, it is Mona in her own words.

*I was seventeen years old when Ove and I met, and Ove was nineteen. At that
time I was going to senior school. The summer holidays are quite long in Sweden,
so I said to my father, 'I wish I could find a job during the summer.'*

*'Well,' he said, 'I know this lady who has a restaurant on the west coast.
I could ask her if you could work for her.' And so he did. It was quite a long
way for me to go there by train as we lived in the middle of southern Sweden.
I enjoyed my job, which consisted of making salads, cakes and coffee etc. I felt
free and independent. I proved to myself that I could make my own living. The
lady I worked for, Mrs Svensson, was divorced, but she had a partner – not only
in business, as I found out. Her partner was Ove's uncle Axel. That summer,
Mrs Svensson celebrated her fiftieth birthday and among her many guests were
my parents as well as Axel's sister-in-law, Ove's mother Ruth. Ove's father,
Arvid, had died only a couple of months before, and I remember that Ove wore
a mourning band on his jacket the first time I saw him. People hardly wear
those bands any more. Ove was there as his mother's chauffeur.*

*There was another girl working in the restaurant, Ove's cousin Britt-Louise, called
Bissis. When the party was in full swing, she came up to me and said, 'Haven't
you heard of my cousin, Ove Fundin? He is quite famous you know. They
have written about him in the newspapers. He is already a star in speedway.'*

*I had to confess that I didn't follow what was going on in sports, nor had
I read the sports pages in the papers. Consequently I had never heard of him.*

She insisted, 'He has his own car. Why don't you come along tonight and we will go for a ride? There will be four of us because he has brought a friend too. You've got to meet Ove, he's so nice. He used to be a Boy Scout, and do you know what? Sometimes he'll pack a rucksack with a pan, plate and spoon, food and stuff, and go into the woods camping on his own. And he likes children too. He'll babysit for his sister's little girl. He is really something special.'

You would think she was in love with him herself, or was she a matchmaker?

Anyway, we went out that night, the four of us, Ove and me sitting in the front seat with him driving. He didn't say much, in fact he seemed very shy, casting quick glances at me at times and smiling. I noticed that he had beautiful blue eyes. His silence encouraged me to talk. That summer I really felt that even I was somebody too, after having grown up in the shadow of a very domineering sister. I think I blossomed out as a young woman, and became more self confident. I guess I had become quite a charming person, and that's why Ove fell in love with me. But I was also flattered by the attention of other boys, and wouldn't have him as the only possible boyfriend. So I flirted a little with other lads as well.

After my summer work I took the train back at Tranas, Ove's home town, which is about twenty miles from the village where I lived. Ove was there at the station to meet me. I had not told him when I was arriving, so he must have found that out himself. He took my suitcase and said, 'Why don't you come home with me and say hello to my mother?'

'Oh, no,' I thought. 'Only couples who are going steady do that – get introduced to mum and all. So I said, 'I've got a bus to catch, so I'm sorry I can't do that.'

'No problem,' he said. 'I'll drive you home later.'

Soon I was sitting in his mother's living room chatting with her. I found out that she was a very nice lady with a great sense of humour. Afterwards Ove told me that I made a very good impression. His mother had said, 'That's a girl I wish you could go on seeing.' I think that created a special bond between Ove and me, being recognised by his mother and everything. But we were young and kept on seeing other friends of the opposite sex. Mind you, at that time teenagers didn't have sexual relationships very easily. What it was mostly all about was kissing and hugging and perhaps some petting. 'Nice' girls didn't go any further. A young girl could very easily get 'a bad reputation'. You might get that even if you didn't go 'all the way'. Sweden got a reputation in the 1950s *through Anita Ekberg, the film star, of having a very free and open attitude to sex, but that simply was not true.*

*After finishing school at the age of nineteen I felt I had to go on with some kind of higher education with the idea of eventually getting a good job. So messing around with boys, risking pregnancy, was not included in my future plans. After having tried training at a nursing school and a secretary school, and finding out that neither was for me, I was lucky to find work as an apprentice at a newspaper in Boras, a town some miles east of Gothenburg. I enjoyed that, although it meant being alone in a new town and I missed Ove quite a lot then.*

*That was in 1956. It was the year he became World Champion for the first time. He told me he had been invited to race in Australia and New Zealand that winter and asked me if I would like to go along with him. I was thrilled. I was really in love with him, so I said I would go with him, on one condition though – that we married first. I knew that, in those days, the British were quite prudish and we would not be able to share a room in a hotel unless we were married.*

*'No problem,' Ove said. 'Let's get married!'*

*So my parents organised a very nice wedding just in time for the departure. We started from Southampton at the end of October 1956. The ship was an old vessel from the war and it was quite crowded. Ove and I could not get a cabin of our own. He shared with Ronnie Moore and Trevor Redmond and another speedway rider whose name I forget. And I had to share my cabin with three other ladies who were total strangers to me.*

*We were on our way for several weeks! It could be quite boring at times, but we made a couple of stops on the way. The first one was Curacao, a former Dutch colony in the Caribbean. I remember we had a terrible storm just before we arrived there, but somebody said to me, 'Have a glass of brandy. That helps against seasickness.' And it did too. I recommend that. Going through the Panama Canal was quite a thrill. The ship made a stop at Panama City where young Indian children tried to sell beautiful hand-made souvenirs to us. We also made a stop at the Pitcairn Islands in the Pacific where the Mutiny on the Bounty took place.*

*I remember the time spent in New Zealand as one of the best in my life. What a wonderful land. The climate, the nature and the people – everything was superb, except for the feeling of isolation. It felt so far away from civilisation, from Europe. I thought it would be a very nice country to live in, but it also* felt like once there you're stuck. It was too expensive to go anywhere outside the country unless you were very rich. Of course, a lot must have changed in the years since then. In those days the roads outside the towns were terrible, for example. There were not even dirt roads, like we still have a lot of in Sweden, they were roads covered with coarse gravel.

Many Swedish companies were generous in giving 'gifts' to the new World Champion. Of course, they also wanted Ove to publicise their products. One factory in Sweden, Monark, which made both ordinary bicycles and motorcycles, presented Ove with a small motorbike. We took it with us all the way to New Zealand and used it to get around the towns. In Auckland we rented a small flat, consisting of a kitchen and a bedroom. We had promised a Swedish paper, Tranas Trading, to send them reports from abroad. Ove encouraged me in writing and in those days we felt we were equals.

I had noticed of course that Ove was an intelligent guy. Although I had studied more than he had, I found out that he had a good general knowledge of a lot of things, and he liked to read a lot. He was also health-conscious – he neither drank alcohol nor did he smoke. I was attracted to him, and I felt we could develop a love together.

After some time in Australia we flew back home because I didn't want to go on a long sea journey again. We spent a day in Hawaii and went on to Los Angeles where Ove's cousin, Bissis (the matchmaker, remember?) was working at Disneyland, and then to my sister in Chicago. She had gone through an unhappy love affair with a guy who later married Ove's sister. To get away from it all she emigrated to America. At the time she was really enjoying the American lifestyle and tried to persuade Ove and me to stay and live there. She said she would fix jobs for us. Ove was very tempted, and if it hadn't been for me he would have stayed. And there wouldn't have been any more World Championships on his part.

When I was young I was quite a romantic person. Once married I thought it was for ever. Even though you had your ups and downs and disagreements at times, I thought you should talk and work out your problems. And you should of course be faithful to one another. I was fully aware that you might be attracted to another person of the opposite sex, and you might even give yourself permission to flirt a little. But there were limits to be set – you shouldn't be sexually unfaithful. I still hold that opinion.

*At that time I felt that Ove loved me, and he sent me a lot of letters that confirmed that. I answered every single letter in which I assured him of my love. Therefore I was quite jealous when Ove got a letter from a former girlfriend in which she proposed they meet in London during her stay there. 'There's nothing to it,' Ove assured me. 'We could spend some time together, the three of us.' 'Well, all right then,' I said. We decided she could go to Norwich where Ove and I had a rented furnished house. But then Ove had to fly to Sweden for a speedway meeting, and there I was, on my own, having to entertain this girl over the weekend. Once I heard her mutter, 'If I'd known Ove wouldn't be here, I never would have come.'*

*That was before we had any children. I had also noticed by that time that the more successful Ove became as a speedway rider, the more success he had with girls. When Michael, our first child, was due to be born in Norwich in 1959 we had brought a young girl with us as a kind of au pair, as company and help for me, since Ove was away so much racing. My labour started while he was away, and I was alone with this sixteen-year-old girl. It all went through and I had a wonderful little boy. But of course Ove fell in love with this au pair girl. I would soon find out that Ove flirted a little too much with other girls, at least to my taste. I called these incidents his 'little love stories'. But he would always assure me after every one that it was me he really loved, and he would give me jewellery and roses to confirm it. And I believed him. When we were apart, we kept on writing wonderful love letters. In fact, being apart so much from each other even intensified our love. At least I felt so. And we had more children.*

*Speedway itself also put a strain on the relationship, because Ove had to concentrate so hard when racing. Before a speedway meeting he had to build up energy, both mentally and physically. If people around him irritated him he would burst out screaming and yelling and sometimes even hurting and scaring the ones he loved. I tried to be diplomatic and understanding, sometimes acting as a shield between him and others. I don't think it was any good for either me or the children to always take into consideration his needs and to tolerate his outbursts. It was scary, and how can you have a close relationship with someone you are afraid of? It was like living near Etna, the volcano. I knew he had a good heart, and I still loved him, but many people – not just me – found it hard to cope with his temper.*

*Of course, when he was racing I was scared at times that he might get hurt, and he did hurt himself many times. I remember injured knees and even* broken legs. But that didn't stop him from racing. He even almost won a World Championship with one leg in plaster. I admired his fighting spirit and trusted his skill to avoid serious accidents. He used to be a very fast driver on the roads as well, and that scared me too. I often thought that the guardian angels were merciful to him, and half joking I used to say, 'Don't overstrain your father on the Other Side.' I thought he would help protect him.

I didn't spend a lot of time in England when Ove was racing. For a couple of seasons we had furnished houses where we spent time together. That was before we had any children, and when we had only two sons. But when we had another daughter and a son Ove had a flat in Norwich for the season, and I visited him only now and then. I found it easier to take care of the children at home in Sweden. We lived in the same house as Ove's mother – she had one flat and we had another with two bedrooms, a kitchen and a living room. Four children in four years – that was quite compact living, both mentally and physically, especially for me. I also preferred the weather in Sweden. In the summers we used to go swimming in the little lake where my parents had a nice summer house. The children loved that, and my parents really loved their grandchildren.

I missed the close relationship I had with Ove when in England. I remember in the summertime we used to spend wonderful days by the sea at Great Yarmouth. But after having more children I couldn't bring them all over to England, and that was partly because of Ove's nerves before a speedway meeting. He was so strung up that it was as though his nerves were really lying on the outside of his skin. Sometimes I would go to England on my own to see Ove. He said that I had a calming influence over him. Then, especially, my parents took care of the children, for which I am still very grateful. I wish they can feel that in their heaven. That made it possible for me to watch all those immensely exciting speedway World Championships Ove rode in at Wembley Stadium.

I have always felt that I wanted to develop my own special gifts, as I think unless you do you won't be happy. I was always interested in society and what's going on in the world, and since I enjoyed writing I thought that was one way to fulfil myself. When I was very young I may have thought that being in love and having children with the man you love should be enough. But I soon found out that wasn't so for me. I wanted to be a good mother and wife, and be able to work at a newspaper as well. In the 1960s it was quite easy to get girls to *help you with the children, so I decided I'd work part-time, which meant four hours a day at the local newspaper called* Tranas-Posten.

*I may have been modern and radical at the time, for many of my friends just gave up their professional plans after having children, even more so in Britian, I noticed. I just couldn't understand that. I remember Trevor Redmond's wife. She used to study medicine and she had only one term left before she was due to qualify as a doctor. Then she married Trevor and gave up her professional plans completely. She said, 'I shall either concentrate on my marriage or my work, and I've decided it'll be our marriage.' I thought it should be possible to combine marriage and a career. I even feared that giving up work would decrease your awareness of society and the world, that being 'only' a housewife and mother — although very important — would make a woman a kind of narrow-minded and dull person.*

*I was building up my career on the newspaper before I married Ove, and my editors encouraged me. Therefore I felt pretty self-confident about being a journalist without having to use Ove's name and celebrity — as John Lennon put it, 'In my own write.' Ove has said that we grew apart because he was away racing a lot of the time. And that is true in a way, I think because the children and I had to build a life of our own. When Ove came home, mostly for short periods of time, everything seemed quite hectic. There were so many things to be done, giving gifts to the children, playing with them, working and seeing friends.*

*I think he tried to fulfil his dreams of how he saw a happy childhood. That was having a dog — he bought one without asking me, and I wasn't used to dogs. Having horses too — he bought two, and I wasn't used to horses either. He even bought a goat with horns. And, you might guess, nor was I used to goats. Then he would be off racing and the children and I would be left to take care of everything. We also had a cat, but that was my choice. During the last years of marriage we lived in the country in a big old house. Quite a lot of mice ran about, so I thought a cat would be very useful.*

*Ove had asked a neighbour who was a plumber to help with the horses, but he had time only occasionally. That ended up with his wife being jealous of me because I invited him for a cup of coffee now and then after he had helped us. But, from a material point of view, I had nothing to complain about really. The surroundings were beautiful, we were not short of money. And of course the children were lovely — but I missed my husband. I remember once the sports writers published a story that Ove spent only four or five days in a whole year at home. If he wasn't in England racing he was riding on the Continent, and in the winter he went to Australia to ride speedway. But all the time I was getting these lovely love letters from him. They kept me burning.*

*I had my suspicions, of course. And eventually they were confirmed. He had girlfriends all over the place, and had a lot of correspondence with them too. He was a Mick Jagger-type. He just couldn't resist the temptations of girls hanging around. It was only about five years ago that I discovered he had fathered a daughter in England who was born within two days of me giving birth to a baby girl in Sweden. His English daughter, Karen, was adopted by a nice English couple. Later, Karen wanted to know about her biological parents and found Ove when he was living in Belgium with his third wife. She is very much like our daughter, Annika. Now, I understand, Ove and Karen have a good relationship. She is a very nice girl. I have met her because she has been to Sweden. I have nothing against her, for of course she can't help being born. Had I known about her at the time of her birth, though, my marriage to Ove might have ended then, and our four other children may never have been born.*

*Now, I think, there is no such thing as coincidence – what is meant to happen will happen. When I was eighteen a man looked at my palms and foretold my future. I remember him saying that I was an intense person (I am a Scorpio) and would fall deeply in love, but still I would have some trouble with men. I only giggled, because I hardly believed him, and asked him, 'Will I have any children?' He said, 'I don't want to scare you, but you will have plenty.'*

*Ove and I have four boys and three girls. Our attraction to one another lasted that long. I remember that, at the end of our marriage, I got a postcard from him with Romeo and Juliet on it on which he had written something like, 'We are like them, aren't we?' 'Bullshit!' I thought, because I had just found out at that time that he was having a hot love affair with a Yugoslavian woman in Malmo who was divorced with three daughters. I felt then, deep in my heart, that our love was over. The other day I saw an old English documentary about John Lennon's life. His first wife, Cynthia, was interviewed about the time The Beatles went to India. They were all going by train up to the mountains to see a guru, but the train was crowded and she couldn't get on it, and it pulled out leaving her standing there crying on the platform. She said that at that moment she had this firm intuitive feeling that it was the end of her and John's life together. Now, so many years after my marriage to Ove ended, I could identify with her and recognise the feeling. 'That was fate,' she said. And I agree with her. Even before Ove and I had our last baby, Monica, during my pregnancy I felt that our life together was over.*

*After the break-up the difference in my life wasn't so great as before. Neither I nor the children had seen much of him. We were used to living on our own. But what really hurt them – especially the older ones – was that I decided to move, and they blamed me for that much later in life. I didn't want to live out in the countryside any longer, however idyllic it may have looked, our big, red-painted house with white corners, as is the custom in Sweden, and a large garden.*

*I had been very depressed and cried a lot when I discovered Ove's affair with the Yugoslavian woman. I met this young student, Bo, and eventually the local gossip about me became unbearable. It all started the summer before our break-up. A Finnish girl came to us as an au pair, primarily to learn Swedish. She noticed that Ove was away a lot, so one day she said that I should let Ove live his life and I should live my life. If I wanted to go out and enjoy myself, she would babysit. Bo was nine years younger than me. I didn't really think we had a future, what with me being a mother with seven children, but he persisted. I moved to a bigger house in Linkoping where all seven children and I could live together. Bo never moved in with us. He had studied law and had a small flat of his own. We met in the evenings though, and at the weekends. He used to say that having a baby together would be as glue to our relationship, it would strengthen it. Well I agreed and we had son, Karl, who is now twenty-eight.*

*Bo became a minister of the Church of Sweden and we got married and moved to a vicarage in the country. During all these years I kept writing articles for small newspapers. I also taught adults English, German and French at evening schools. Bo and I were married for about ten years, until I felt I was kind of trapped in my role as 'the vicar's wife'. I had been on my own for so many years and was accustomed to running my own life, so I didn't feel very comfortable in my marriage. Furthermore I felt that the distance between me and Ove's children increased through my marriage. Of course they were welcome to visit whenever they liked, but I think they felt like strangers in my new surroundings.*

*Now I live on my own and do whatever I like whenever I like. I bought an old house in the neighbourhood where I lived as a child and I keep busy interviewing and writing about the elderly, which may be a book eventually. I also work for the local Red Cross and am the manager of their second-hand shop. My relationship with Ove since the marriage ended has not been very close, if you ask me. He avoided me, and it has been only in the last two years or so that he has spoken to me. But then I was invited to his seventieth birthday party, which I appreciated very much. After all, we did have seven nice children together, and we have wonderful grandchildren.*

*Ove's seventieth birthday party was a grand celebration. Two men from Tranas City Council were there, and they said that a statue of him is being put up in the town to honour him. We all went aboard an old steamship and had a wonderful trip on the lake of Sommen, one of the largest in Sweden. Yes, it was a day to remember.*

*Looking back, I think I have led a rich life, and Ove has been an important part of it.*

## MY HUSBAND THE WORLD CHAMPION

### By Mona Forsberg-Fundin

WHAT does it take to become a World Champion?

Lennard Hyland, one of Sweden's most famous radio and television commentators, asked this question of my husband, Ove Fundin, on 16 September 1967 in London after he had won his fifth World title in speedway. I have given the question a lot of thought and tried to research material nearest to me, in other words, the man at my side – the man I was married to for fourteen years. I came to the conclusion that a winner and champion has to be able to mobilise all the strength he has and to be able to release this power at the right moment. On top of this he has to have talent and technique. This is essential.

With Ove the process of mobilising his strength could start a couple of weeks before a big meeting, when he knew he would be up against rivals as good as himself. I noticed that this preparation for Ove made him very absent minded, and with a wish to be let alone. He worked, like a concert pianist, with his fingers to make them soft and flexible. It was important to let go of the clutch lever like lightening at the starting gate.

He became less and less interested in what was around him. It may have seemed snobbish and unfriendly to people who did not know the reason. As an example, I can tell you about a visit my mother and sister-in-law made a couple of weeks before a World Final. We were talking about my father's sickness that was very worrying. Ove was also at the table but did not take part in the conversation. He was complaining of a headache – another symptom of his preparation – and seemed uninterested. I was surprised at his total lack of interest in the health of his father-in-law. Ove is at heart a very kind and caring person. I was given proof of this after the World Final was over, when he was again happy and relaxed. 'What are you saying? Is your father not well? In that case we must visit him,' he said.

During his preparation he was not easy to live with. The smallest incident could make him explode, then it was up to me to eliminate the problem, as when the children were lively and made too much noise. But I knew him and seldom got angry, not even when he took it out on me. I knew that he was the happiest and world's most charming man *after* the races, especially if it went well for him. And it did, most of the time...

I realised quite soon after I met him that he was a very sensitive man. He was totally focused on whatever he was doing, and he is very talented in many ways. All of this made me fall in love with him. I want you to know that he was very intensive in his courting. He used to send me flowers at least once a week ever since I first met him when I was seventeen. I thought it was very romantic and it impressed me, as well as my girl friends. It was not common that young boys tried to win a girl's heart that way.

Specialists in any field tend to be narrow minded, but not Ove. For instance, we very seldom talked about speedway. He had so many interests besides his sport, and his business when he ran a fleet of trucks. He read a lot, mostly in English – a language he mastered. The thicker the books the better he liked them, preferably American bestsellers.

As you can understand, he is not an 'old man'. It is not often that an 'old man' wins a World title. He also raced bobsleigh and Formula V cars. He took up parachuting. He did a lot of flying in single engine planes as well. I would rather have seen him do something less dangerous – such as collecting stamps.

# NINE

# MARRIAGE

Ove Fundin has had three wives, Mona, Catharina and Ioanna. There were other relationships too, from time to time and – because he was an itinerant speedway rider – in different parts of the world.

Ove and Mona, whom he married after his first really big success when he became World Champion in 1956, have seven children and were divorced in 1970. There are no children from his other marriages, but he has a daughter, Karen, from a relationship with an English nurse. Karen, who lives in London, was able to trace her father but has never been able to find her mother.

## MONA

'She is the mother of all my kids, except Karen. She was a journalist. Still is. My uncle Axel, the car dealer, also owned a couple of hotels, one of them on the west coast of Sweden, and we went down there with my mother and a couple of friends. Mona happened to work there. It was her summer job while she was at university. It would be the summer of 1956. I went down there for the weekend because I was busy racing all the time. We got married in 1956 only about a week before I was going to New Zealand. Barry Briggs, Ronnie Moore and Peter Craven all got married around the same time, more or less.

'Mona was a local journalist at the time, working at smaller newspapers. She covered everything that happened. She still does that. We are still in touch. She sent an article to me less than a week ago. She gave it up when we went off to New Zealand. After we got back from New Zealand, for the whole first summer in Norwich, Mona was there all the time. But towards the end of that season she went home to Sweden because she didn't want to give up her work. I went to South Africa for the winter. And then June Briggs stayed with Mona for a few months that winter while Barry and I were racing. We weren't together.

'After that I lived in a flat at Boundary Garage in Norwich at the time when Mona went back to work and we couldn't be together. So I used to be there on my own. My friend Eddie Franklyn knew a lot of the local Americans and he could buy everything from their PX stores. Mona would come over, but not to stay – only maybe for a week or a few days. And that's why so many people ask me how come we have so many kids. I wasn't home too often, so when I was home it was pretty hot I suppose.

'Mona is quite a strong character, and so am I. Maybe that's why we split up. We were married for fourteen years and we have seven children. When I came home to stay after I retired from speedway we weren't the same any more. We had gone different ways. She had been to university and got a good education. She was interested in more intelligent things than I am. Also – maybe this was a little bit to do with it as well – for some time she was studying to convert to become a Catholic, which is not very common in Sweden. But she never did become a Catholic.

'And I was flirting around all the time. You know, I wasn't all that good. And she found someone as well. He was a law student who later became a priest. And eventually they married, then she had another child by him. But they also were divorced, and she has been living on her own for quite a long time. I tried to mend my marriage to Mona with a trip across America from California to Florida – but all that happened was that our seventh child was conceived.

'I don't think I was flirting around all that much, but you know you are a man after all and, being away for months, there are always some willing girls hanging around you. Being a speedway rider is a good way to meet girls. Being good at any sport is a good way to meet girls. And girls are obviously attracted to successful men. There may have been groupies at the speedway tracks, but I didn't have the time to hang around. I often had to skip the second half at Norwich. I rode in the match but very often I had to miss the scratch races – not every time – to travel to a Continental meeting, so I didn't have time to hang around with girls.

'I have been accused of being in the habit of having a quick sex session with some willing local girl before every Norwich meeting. That is not true. I even avoided having sex with my wife before speedway.

'Every now and then I did have a little bit of spare time, and not least when I went away overseas. During the Australian season maybe we rode only once or twice a week, so you had all the time in the world. And I don't think there were so many good-looking, and shall we say willing, girls as in Eastern Europe – but probably half of them there were looking for marriage to get out of the country.

'It was Mona who wanted the divorce, and afterwards I went to live at Malmo. When I retired from racing full time I started a trucking business delivering oil for domestic heating and the company was based there. I didn't want to live in Tranas after the divorce. I wanted to live in the country and have horses. So I bought three horses for the kids to ride and pull a sledge in the winter.'

## CATHARINA

'She came and babysat for me as a young girl. She and a friend used to come and babysit. After my divorce from Mona I was living in Malmo and I met her there with her mother. She was seventeen and she asked if she could hitch-hike up to Tranas in one of my trucks because she was homesick. I said 'Sure, no problem,' and I started seeing her. Then she moved in with me and of course we were married. We lived 'happily ever after', as they say, for ten years, then we split up.

'The relationship went wrong. It had a lot to do with her being so much younger – she was twenty-two years younger than me – and had different interests. Partly because she liked nightclubbing and I liked to go to bed fairly early when I was home and not stay up. But she would say she would want to go out much more than I did. It didn't work out. But there again it was she who asked for a divorce. Thinking about it now, I wonder what her parents thought. Bloody terrible, isn't it?

'That's when I decided to sell my business. I would have kept it, it was a very good business. I made very good money. I wouldn't be living here in France if I hadn't made that money. Certainly I would not have made enough money to be able to retire at fifty-five and come and live here on the money I made from speedway. That was gone anyway – my divorces took part of it. I've been divorced twice, and another girl I lived with for three or four years also received her bit. I bought her a house and everything. She was a Yugoslav girl. She was too bloody beautiful, that was the trouble with her. She was the one before Catharina. She was so beautiful that everyone was after her. That didn't work out either. And I was too protective, I suppose. Jealous, yes.

'I bought Catharina a dress shop, a boutique, and she shipped in designs from Italy and Berlin. But when Sweden devalued the krone in 1982 the items cost more to buy and eventually the business closed. The devaluation also hit me hard financially. The divorces cost me a lot of money, too. But the one who cost the least money was Mona. Of course I never paid a penny for Karen... not a penny.'

## KAREN

'I first met Karen's mother in Italy. Her name was Diana Maclean – like the toothpaste. She was a nurse. I was with my brother. She was English. I went to see her in England. She looked a bit like Karen. We met probably half a dozen times, but I have never seen her since. It must have been near Epsom, she used to live at Epsom. She had told me she was pregnant, and then she said, "Don't you worry about that because I am taking care of everything. You don't have to do anything." It turned out that she'd had another baby before – the very same thing, so she knew what to do. She arranged for the baby to be adopted. She called me from the maternity hospital and asked me to go there to sign the papers to say that I was the father. I'm glad that I did because when I look at Karen there is no doubt. And that is how Karen tracked me down.'

Karen says: 'I always knew I was adopted. When you are eighteen you can start looking for your natural parents, but I kept putting it off. Eventually I went to the children's home in Southwark, south London, from where I was adopted and there they had a file which mentioned Ove.

'At the time I was working at the *News of the World* newspaper, so I went to their library and found various cuttings on him. The Veteran Speedway Riders' Association gave me his address and from that we arranged to meet. I went along with various pictures of him. It was very emotional for both of us. Naturally I was concerned for my adoptive parents and when I told them they were very upset. But later, when they eventually met Ove, they got on well with him. My father particularly was very wary at first, but now it's "my friend Ove". They're mates. Ove and I see each other when we can – when he comes to England. Going to see him in France is not so easy for me. I go when I have the time and money.

'I knew about speedway of course, and I was always keen on motorcycles. It was wonderful when I realised he was somebody interesting. When I learned what he had achieved, and that he was quite famous, it was terrific. One thing that hit me was that I have no English blood. My mother was half Irish and half French. Ove showed me a picture of her in a Swedish book. She was lovely – a bit like Audrey Hepburn. Ove and I have some similarities. We both have short tempers, but there are things we don't have in common, like his flying. I'm terrified of flying. But recently I qualified as a scuba diver and when he found out he was quite cross. "It's dangerous," he said.

'I have done everything I can to find my mother, but seem to have run out of leads. When I have time I'll probably try again. So really, for now it's the end of the road. We're taking it as it comes. Everyone lives happily ever after and, because of me, Ove has another grandchild, Amelia, and they adore each other.'

# IOANNA

'I met Ioanna when I was still married to Catharina, when she came as a guest to us, but there was no kind of romance or anything then. None whatsoever. I had lost my driving licence – I was banned from driving for a year. I had one of the best lawyers in Sweden to try to defend me. He couldn't do it, but it didn't stop me from driving. Once, though, I went on a train to Tranas to collect a truck. That was in the days when I had my business. I had made good money and I travelled first class. And Ioanna was in the carriage – there were just the two of us. I got talking to her. She had got on at Malmo, the same as me. I had flown from Bucharest to Berlin and taken a train from there because there was no airline that flew direct from Bucharest to Stockholm. And we got talking. We talked about everything – we spoke in English – and I said, "On your way back give us a call and you could have a break and you can stay with us a night – myself and Catharina – and we can have some drinks and continue to talk."

'She said, "Thanks very much." And when she did come down there she didn't want to stay the night because she was booked on a late train, but we spent a few hours together, went out to a nice restaurant and talked. And all of us enjoyed it. A few weeks after – maybe a month – Catharina and I split up. I think Ioanna wrote to me because she had seen an article or something on television about me and she recognised me. She thought, "Christ, that's the gentlemen who took me out." In Romania she was a very well-known film and theatre actress and they still show some of her pictures on Romanian television. We have a property in Bucharest and now when we go there people stop her in the street. She is far more famous than me.

'Anyway, I wrote back to her – no, telephoned her because I was too lazy to write – and asked her what she was doing. She said, "I'm here in Sweden. I've left Romania because I couldn't stand it any more and I'm living in Stockholm." She asked the normal things, how I was and how Catharina was. I told her that Catharina was gone. "What do you mean, she's gone?" she said. "She's gone," I said. "We are getting a divorce. She has moved away." "Oh, poor you," she said. So I said that maybe the next time I come to Stockholm we could meet up and she said she would like that. Well, I didn't have any reason to go to Stockholm right then, but I phoned back and said, "I'm coming up." So I went there and we went to a nice restaurant, talked and I went back home. She phoned first to say thank you and I phoned later, and suddenly I was there again. I don't think we met anymore. I think we decided that it was no good her living in Stockholm and me living on my own, so she should come down and join me. I went to Stockholm and collected her and we lived together for quite some time until we decided to get married.

'After I sold the business I had to sign a contract to stay with the firm and help run it for two years. I wasn't happy. I was used to taking all the decisions, being a bloody dictator. But suddenly I was an employed person, a managing director, which I didn't like. Some time before I had already started another trucking firm in Belgium to operate within the Common Market. Someone had to build up the business in Belgium, so Ioanna and I lived there for almost two years, the two years I promised to stay with the company. But before that time was up we bought a plot of land in the south of France and built the house on it where we now live. I never actually finished that business because all this other trouble came in between.'

'This other trouble' was cancer.

TEN

# THE CANCER

*'I felt very sorry for myself when I learned about the cancer. I didn't expect to live until I was sixty. So every year now I consider I have lived on overtime.'* – Ove Fundin

Just before the start of The Laurels meeting in 1957, reporter Rick Eldon was observing the usual highly charged activity taking place in the cavernous area beneath the stands that was the speedway pits at Wimbledon's Plough Lane stadium. As the riders prepared themselves for the evening's racing, above them the atmosphere on the terraces quickened: mechanics fired up the high-powered machines, the roar of the engines and its accompanying vibration transmitting itself like an electric current through to the feet of the spectators waiting impatiently above for the thrills to begin.

The palpable tension in the pits immediately before the commencement of racing at any event, let alone one as important as Wimbledon's traditional all-star occasion, is unique in sport. It is a private – almost sacred – world inhabited by special men and special motors, a restricted area of intense concentration, bustle and noise, full of the unspoken knowledge that these special men will soon be entering an arena which their presence will turn into a cauldron of emotion, of adoration and, yes, of animosity, plus the inevitability of danger. Highly strung riders disguise their nervousness by being overtly calm and casual. Mechanics hide theirs by giving extravagant attention to coaxing the finest performances from the delicate machinery entrusted to their care. Officials with their clipboards appear oblivious as they carry out their tasks.

It is virtually impossible to communicate directly because of the decibel level of the exhausts. From them a heady aroma permeates the air – it is a unique and infinitely intoxicating combination of internally combusted methanol racing fuel and castor oil. All of these ingredients amount to a tingling sense of breathless anticipation – among spectators and competitors – of being part of a carefully choreographed scenario, with the merest suggestion of latent hysteria lurking just below the surface; of blue touchpaper just waiting to be ignited. It can be encapsulated in one word: excitement!

Amid all the activity, Eldon saw one of the last competitors to arrive, his friend Ove Fundin, one of the stars the eager crowd had paid their money to see. And, wrote Eldon, 'When I watched him come into the pits he walked as though he knew he had a body and wished he had left it at home. I know that Ove is in a little bit of agony, is having a bit of private hell.'

Ove, with his distinctive red hair and pale Scandinavian skin, was indeed in acute discomfort. People with his colouring are susceptible to the infrared and ultraviolet rays emitted by the sun. Ove was suffering from severe sunburn. 'Overhead shines the villain of the piece,' wrote Eldon. 'The glaring sun, which has fried our Fundin to a frazzle. Ove is raw red. It is agonising every time his leathers touch his skin. Bad enough walking, but he has to ride too. It is enough to put him sufficiently off form to drop a lot of points in such distinguished company. Spectators cannot understand – and some are frankly delighted – why the reigning World Champion cannot win a race.' The reigning World Champion scored only 7 points. His fellow Swede, Per Olaf Soderman, won the meeting.

Thirty years later, in 1987, a mole appeared on Ove's shoulder. 'It grew and grew and grew,' Ove says. 'I wondered what it was. It started off as quite a little thing that itched. I went to my ordinary doctor who looked at it and he sent me, the very same day, to a big university hospital at Lund in Sweden. They took a little look at it. The doctor said, "We'll operate today." It was a big thing. They carved quite a big piece out of it and I had to take it steady for a while. They put me out and I was in hospital for the night. Then they said they would let me know what it was. Some days later I went to my local doctor. He said, "I'm sorry to have to tell you that it is a melanoma." I didn't know what the hell a melanoma is.'

A melanoma is a malignant tumour in the skin, often a result of excessive exposure to sunlight.

'There, again, he said it was a bad kind. I was devastated,' says Ove. 'I was thinking, "This is it!" He told me I shouldn't worry all that much. He'd seen those things before and the doctors who had operated were very good.'

But that wasn't the end of it.

'Then another one came on my back and I couldn't even see it. In between I had one on one of my hands, you can still see a scar there. They had to take a bit out of that, which was much worse because the skin on your hand is so thin – there is nothing there. They said that it's not so good, we'll take as much out as we can. Then another one came on the other hand. And then a big one came on my back. I felt very sorry for myself when I learned about the cancer and I didn't expect to live until I was sixty. I only ever told my son, Eric, but later on I know the other children got to know about it. I wanted Eric to know what I wanted done if I died. You have to tell someone. Ioanna knew as well. She knew straight away because she was there. So every year now I consider I have lived on overtime.

'Since I've been living in France I've had a few on my arm. I have a doctor I go and see every six months. The people here don't cut them out, they just burn them away with a kind of laser. I'm sure they know what to do because they have a lot of it here because of all the sunshine. But I'm not so worried anymore because it's gone over ten years now. The doctor I see here, he's a friend of mine, so he is honest with me. He says there is no reason why I shouldn't be around for another twenty years. So don't worry.'

Two years after the cancer was discovered, Ove finally sold his business and, with Ioanna, moved to the south of France to live. The business had been a huge success. 'I knew I would have to have something to live on when I stopped riding,' says Ove. 'I had very little education, and you couldn't make any real money in speedway, could you? I had been riding every day and I'd had no time to train for anything. I began to think: what can I do off-season, instead of going to Australia and New Zealand? So I bought a truck. First I painted the truck and learned to drive it, then I went to Falkenberg on the west coast of Sweden, and there I bought fuel oil for houses. People in Sweden need an awful lot of that. I brought it home, sold it and then went back for more.

'I knew nearly all the people in Tranas, but then it became too small, so I had to improve things. And I had a bit of help. I had a few people who sold for me – they got a few krone for every cubic metre of oil they sold. I didn't have any money to pay for it. I had an arrangement with the company I got the oil from – because they didn't trust me at first. I paid them with a cheque every time I picked up a load, but that cheque was postdated about ten days and I expected to get the money in by the time the cheque was due to be cleared at the bank.

'It didn't take all that long before I had enough money. I used to drive at night, deliver during the day. My mother took all the orders over the phone, but I had to do all the invoices – and there was always lots to do. It was 1968, and I knew at the time that my speedway could not go on much longer. Being restless, I was never able to sit still at home. I wanted to do something where I could travel. Because now I had learned to drive a truck I thought maybe I should start a trucking business between Sweden and the rest of the Continent, which I did. I bought one to start off with. And then I didn't have time to drive myself, so someone who used to help me with the speedway bike took that job. A cousin of mine drove the tanker and then I took him in as a partner and he stayed until I sold out.

'You could earn good money on the Continent, but you had to have permits – and to get those permits they were so strict, so I looked around and I bought another two trucks and then I bought a business which had a dozen trucks. It took quite a bit of money, so in part payment I had a villa in Spain that I'd bought from an uncle,

but I never had the time to go down there. I threw that in, and I also
had a big plot of land in front of it. I never wanted to go to the bank
to borrow money. I had a little tiny office, but as the business became
bigger I had to have my own yard and garage. That was the only time
I borrowed money, but I didn't borrow it off the bank. I borrowed it
off an insurance company. I never drew wages from my company.

'When I bought my first brand-new truck, I remember that at the
time I was riding somewhere not all that far from Tranas. I bought
the truck from an agent there, and the salesman came to see me with
the contract. In between races I had to sign and give him a cheque
for all sorts of things. I could see he was worried, maybe he thought
that a speedway rider was not good for his money. He was like my
first father-in-law, he didn't trust me at all – I was somebody with no
education, nothing. But when Mona and I got married in 1956, just
after I won the World title, I think he trusted me after that.'

The cancer diagnosis made him decide to sell the trucking business.

'First I wanted one of my children to take over. I thought Erik would
have done it because he was working in the office with me all the time.
Michael was driving so he wouldn't have been interested. Madeleine
also drove and she was the only one who showed any sign that she
wanted it, but it was too much for her. So I contacted a business lawyer
who played golf with me in Malmo and asked him what to do. He
said he thought he knew someone already who might be interested,
quite a big firm in Sweden that had numerous interests. They were
interested, but they had a big board of directors and it took so long
for them to come to any decision. One of the directors approached
me and asked would I mind selling to him? He lived in Switzerland,
in Geneva. He said, "If I fly into Malmo could we talk?" So I met
him at the airport and before I had driven him to his hotel – because
he wanted to go to the hotel before he came out and saw my place
– he had bought the firm. It was all done on a handshake, without
seeing anything – he had only read the papers about the company's
performance of course, which showed that it was a good business. It
was making very good money. There were about seventy-five trucks
and it employed about 150 people. We did a deal in the car. He said,

"Would that satisfy you?" He offered me much more than I expected, and a lawyer friend drew up a contract. What he offered me was very substantial – otherwise I would not have been able to afford to retire here to the south of France.

'I had lost a hell of a lot of money through poor investments. I had very bad advice from a financial company in Sweden and they lost me about a million quid. Honest. I was told by my lawyer to take them to court to see what could be done, and I received about £100,000 in damages. The lawyer said I should take it otherwise I might get nothing and luckily I took it because, this investment firm, about a year later they went broke. But that was a lot of money to lose.

'My business was eventually amalgamated with a shipping company, then it was sold off again to Poland. They couldn't make money. They kept losing money. The managing director kept a house in Stockholm; he also had a flat in Malmo and flew back to Stockholm every weekend. They employed a lot of people and had big wages, of course. The first years after I started the business I didn't have any wages at all. It all went back into the company. I didn't have any wages to speak of until I sold it.

'Now I have no worries. I've still got money left. I'm still living. I haven't had a penny in income since. And even so, in any case, you know how the markets have gone down everywhere, not just in Sweden. I've lost a hell of a lot of money again. For instance I lost on Ericsson – you know the electronics company – just on that one firm, what have I lost? More than £100,000, and then I also lost money when the Swedish krone was devalued in 1982.

'But I definitely wasn't worried because I didn't expect to live very long. When I sold the firm I thought while I'm still alive and the kids can think something good about me, I'll give them something. So I gave every one of the seven, about £30,000 each. They were still in school and that was quite a lot of money for them. I expected every one of them to come screaming to me, you know, thankful, and that didn't really happen. But that's the way kids are, I suppose. Well, some of them did, but I guess they thought I had caused them much sadness and disappointment by leaving the family, because they stayed with

Mum and that way she could tell them her version of everything, which wasn't my version, for sure. And of course they understood afterwards. I have very good relations with all of them, which proves that I wasn't all that bad. And now two of them are already divorced themselves – Madeleine and Paul. So they understand it much better. They understand what it's all about which they probably didn't at the time.'

# ELEVEN

# MURDEROUS MOMENTS

*'We came down that back straight and I'm absolutely beside him and the corner is coming up. I had no doubt in my mind that I was legal. I just went into the corner. Ove had put his arm over my throttle hand. Tough shit Ove.'*
– Barry Briggs

When Ove Fundin became World Champion at Wembley at around 10 p.m. on the evening of Saturday 22 September 1956, he put not only Sweden on the speedway map, he put the modest country town of Tranas on the map as well. The townspeople considered what he had done an almost unimaginable achievement, and when he returned home in triumph virtually the entire place turned out to acclaim him. Tranas gave him a hero's welcome back to the streets where he had grown up. The huge crowd of well-wishers then assembled at the local recreation ground.

'First they rode me round the city. They took me in an open car, drove me down the one big main street and up to the sports ground, where there was a running track round the football pitch maybe two metres wide. I rode my speedway bike round there so that people could see. Lots of people came to watch. And then they presented me with a trophy.'

After that there was the pressing matter of the wedding to Mona and some outstanding racing commitments in Sweden, which in October included a three-match international series against a visiting England side, including the man with whom Ove had exchanged heated words at the earlier Wimbledon Test, Alan Hunt, the England captain. Hunt was quoted as saying, 'We'll do our darndest to turn the tables on those slick Swedes who made monkeys out of the Old Country this season.' An expressed confidence that 'our lads' would return with the 'Union Jack flying high' above their shoulders was misplaced. Our lads lost all three, those slick Swedes running out winners 65-43 at Kumla, 71-37 at Stockholm and 69-39 at Linkoping, Ove scoring 17, 16 and 14 respectively.

Soon afterwards, the new World Champion and his bride were on their way to New Zealand. But, aboard ship, all was not plain sailing for the newlyweds. Prevented by the prim and proper rules of the times in Britain from sharing a room without the evidence of a wedding certificate, their voyage upon the high seas proved to be anything but smooth, and the path of true love took a decided drift towards the farcical!

'Not only were Mona and I on board, Ronnie Moore had just got married and Jill was on board, Dick Campbell and his wife were also on board – and we were all separated. I had to share a cabin with Ronnie Moore, Dick Campbell, and someone else – it was a four-berth cabin but I can't remember who the other person was. [According to Mona, it was Trevor Redmond.] The girls had to share another cabin.'

But then Aub Lawson – Gentleman Aub – observing their predicament, came to their rescue.

'Aub was friendly with the representative of Thomas Cook and Aub said, "We are going to give him twenty quid or something and he will get you a cabin for Mona as well." So what happened was that one couple got the cabin for two hours between 10 and 12, another couple got it between 12 and 2, and so on. The other guy in the cabin, he hadn't got a girl, so he could never use the cabin, only at night to sleep. He had to stay outside in the day! What a set-up.'

Ronnie Moore's colourful recollection of the hilarious situation was this: 'There were four fellas sharing the cabin. Every afternoon they got locked out by Ove because he was doing "you know what" with his wife.'

In New Zealand Alan Clark, who enjoyed a track career on both sides of the fence, was in the privileged position of being able to observe Fundin from the best possible viewpoint, right there in the racing pits. Clark's career embraced solos, sidecars and speedway administration. He is now a renowned historian, journalist and photographer of the sport. At the time he was competing in his homeland and also sending reports of the racing to the British speedway press. Clark says: 'Ove took racing in New Zealand very seriously. I think the last night he appeared there in the 1956/57 season he fell off at one corner. He was most upset because they tried to carry him off the track. But he said, "No, no, no! I'm here for the crowd." And he got back on the bike and finished the race rather than let them carry him off.

'He was such a friendly guy and always got on well with everyone. He went to one or two country meetings, and – before or after – I have never, ever seen what he did at Rotorua. It was a 480-yard track, a lovely little country track. It was good to ride on because the surface was a type of pumice produced by the volcanic activity around there. But this pumice used to break up. It was a lumpy material – or it looked lumpy – and you would ride round and see this lump in front of you and think, "I'm not going to ride over that." But if you did, it would disintegrate – it would just fall apart. Once you got used to that idea, it was a fabulous track to ride. We had mixed meetings with top-line riders as well as juniors. Ove raced off a 300-yard handicap. I was just a young beginner in those days and to see him, from three-quarters of a lap behind, catch the guys and win a four-lap race, well – my eyes bugged out.'

Clark's contemporary report, under the headline 'Champ Makes Up 300 Yards', recorded: 'On New Year's Day, 1 January, Ove Fundin was booked in to ride at Rotorua Speedway. In the first race the handicaps were Fundin 300 yards, John Henderson 20 yards, and Scottie McPherson off the gate. After two laps it was Fundin all the way in 87 seconds.' In the second race Ove was against three local riders, one of whom started 100 yards in front of the gate. He passed the lot of them on lap three. But one of his opponents, Gordon Anderson, broke a chain and hit the fence. 'After crossing the line,' reported Clark,

'Fundin turned round and went back for Anderson and gave him a ride to the pits. The crowd had never seen this happen before and gave Ove a big ovation for the gesture.' In the third handicap Fundin again made the front on lap three and won easily, and in a fourth, with rain falling, Clark reported: 'Once more Fundin was an easy winner but tried to make a race of it.'

'The thing that impressed me,' says Clark, 'was that I went up to meet him in the pits afterwards. I'd met him casually before at Western Springs, but he greeted me like an old mate – like he still does today. For years I might not see him, but you see him again and it's: "Hello, how are you?" He always remembers who you are. He's a fantastic guy.'

At the Western Springs meeting, also reported by Clark, this time before a 10,000 crowd, visiting former Wembley star Eric Williams had stolen some of Fundin's thunder in a handicap race, but Ove got his revenge in the Big Four Scratch Race, beating Williams and Ronnie Moore. It was at Western Springs, too, that Ove tried his hand at sidecar racing. He turned out as driver Joe Williams's passenger in two races, but said afterwards, 'A very nice experience, but I think I like two wheels better.'

On his way back to Europe with Mona, Ove raced in Australia at Melbourne, Brisbane and Adelaide. In Brisbane Jim Geran, brother of top Australian international Jack Geran, reported that the sport there had 'received its best shot in the arm for many a long day thanks to the appearance – for one meeting only – of the reigning world Champion, Ove Fundin'. Riding a borrowed machine he won the scratch race final from local big names Keith Gurtner, Keith Cox and Lionel Levy, his performance fully justifying his rating as the World number one, according to Geran, 'and this was accentuated by the fact that he was riding under extreme difficulty with a broken bone in his right foot'. The injury was the result of an earlier collision with Jack Scott at Melbourne, where he had to give best to Ken McKinlay and Jack Young twice in a Champions Match Race series.

Ove may have put on a show of geniality for the country crowds, but he wasn't greatly enamoured of the handicap system. In an interview given to Swedish journalists Goran Norlen [it was not made clear whether this was Goran Norlen the former Swedish Champion speedway rider, with whom Ove had toured Australia in the 1954/55 season] and Ingemar Antvall he told them he didn't like the frequent handicap races. 'It would be all right,' he said, 'if all the riders were old hands in the game. But there were also some inexperienced riders in these races and they create some dangerous situations.' He remembers now: 'I took it very seriously. Handicapping was not just New Zealand, it was more so in Australia. I remember when I first came across handicap racing at Claremont – I'm sure I had to give 300 yards, maybe more – I thought it was quite dangerous, because when you came to pass those front people they rode very slowly, so therefore I was always a bit scared. What happens when he can hear me? Should I go inside him or should I go round him, or what? I always went inside because I didn't trust them.'

The comments carry more than a touch of irony in view of the situation in which Ove was to find himself in 1962 when, as one of the 'Big Five', he had to endure the handicap system in every National League match in Britain.

He and Mona flew home via America, calling on Mona's sister in Chicago, where speedway's new World Champion resisted the temptation to hitch his future wagon to the Stars & Stripes. Ove didn't stay long in Sweden. He was back in Norwich on a cold, blustery and showery April night for the opening of the new British season at The Firs for the Malcolm Flood Memorial meeting – and was pipped by a point for the trophy by his mentor, Aub Lawson.

According to Peter Morrish, 1957 'was one of the unhappiest years for speedway as the sport struggled against innumerable obstacles'. Petrol rationing was one, so the start of league racing was delayed until Whitsun. The man who had begun to be something of a minor nemesis for Ove, Birmingham captain Alan Hunt, was killed racing in South Africa, and members of his touring party, who included some of his Midlands teammates, were fined and suspended for riding on unlicensed tracks, an action that precipitated the closure of Birmingham. And – probably worst of all – on a liner cruising off the Canary Islands, Wembley boss Sir Arthur Elvin also died. Soon afterwards, on the eve of the new season, it was announced that the jewel in speedway's crown, Wembley, was to close to regular weekly racing. Elvin, who had been a champion of the sport from almost the very beginning, had kept his Lions going at the highly prestigious Empire Stadium long after they had ceased to be a strictly profitable proposition.

With Wembley, which came to be claimed as the spiritual home of speedway, and Birmingham gone and Poole and Odsal soon following, speedway was plunging towards its rock bottom in spite of the removal of the financially draining Entertainment Tax. There was only one major league of eleven teams and a Southern Area league of four minor clubs. But for Ove Fundin it just got better and better. The crowds turned up in their thousands to see him at The Firs. He rode in fifteen league matches and six cup matches, scoring a total of 283 points for an average of a phenomenal 13.47 points a match. Here it should be explained that there are two ways of calculating a rider's average. The first is to divide the total points scored by the number of rides and then multiply by four, which is the usual number of rides taken in a match. The result is a rider's official Calculated Match Average, his CMA used to evaluate his ability. But often, riders of Ove's calibre would be given extra races as tactical substitutes. When the total number of points is divided by the number of matches ridden, the result of this is a mathematically accurate match average – which resulted in the 13.47 figures.

Ove was Swedish Champion for the second time and, as he was World Champion, the British speedway authorities could no longer realistically exclude him from the Golden Helmet match races. They scrapped the 'no foreigners' rule, but Ove's first tilt at the title, against holder Peter Craven, ended in defeat in the decider at Southampton a month before the World Final. It seemed the only setback to a sensational first year as World Champion.

This time, to reach Wembley, Ove did not have to go through the mill of all the Continental rounds, which were formidable, because as reigning champion he was seeded direct to the final. But for the Swedes, particularly, it was an arduous route. They had to contest one Swedish qualifying round, a Nordic qualifier, then a Nordic Final, then a Continental Final and a European Final. And it was Peo Soderman, Rune Sormander and Dan Forsberg who managed to battle their way through.

With the demise of league racing at the Empire Stadium earlier in the year, the approaching Wembley final was lauded by the critics as the first to be held on a truly neutral track. There had always been those who, in the past, had pointed to the so-called home track advantage supposedly enjoyed by Lionel Van Praag in 1936, Tommy Price in 1946 and 1949 and Fred Williams in 1950 and 1953. They had all won their titles as Wembley riders at Wembley. Now there could be no more doubts, excuses or 'unfair' complaints.

Fundin was only second choice for the title when the pre-final pundits put forward their fancies. They said that the edge seemed to have gone off his riding slightly in the weeks immediately before the final, and they cited his failure to relieve Craven of the Golden Helmet as proof. Little Pete was top favourite. He was considered 'a certain winner' by some, partly, it could be surmised, because of patriotic wishful thinking, partly because of his so-called bad luck the previous year when his machine had let him down in the crucial heat six and partly, of course, because he was in superb form. It was pointed out that Fundin was the only man to get to the final without riding in the preliminary rounds. Nevertheless, magnanimously, it was conceded that he still had an excellent chance because his rides were beautifully spaced in heats one, eight, twelve, sixteen and twenty. Rated as danger men were Ken McKinlay, Barry Briggs and Aub Lawson, whose scoring for Norwich was slightly ahead of Ove's and who, it was predicted, was about to have his best final for years.

It promised to be one of the most fascinating World Finals, and as the near-60,000 crowd brought speedway at Wembley once more to vibrant, expectant life on the evening of Saturday 21 September, they were about to witness one of the most explosive and controversial climaxes to a World Championship ever seen in the annals of sporting history at the stadium.

This time there was no time for nerves to get the better of Ove. He was out in heat one with two of the favourites, Peter Craven and Ken

McKinlay, plus fellow Swede Rune Sormander. Craven missed the gate. Ove didn't. Sormander was third. McKinlay, after choosing the wrong gear, was last and realistically out of the running already. But for Ove it was the best possible start. The extra-long wait between Ove's first race and his second in heat eight, which some experts thought might upset him, didn't bother him at all. A second win over Ron How, Ian Williams and George White set him nicely on course to retain his title. Craven dropped two more points in heat six to Australian Jack Geran, who surprisingly kept Briggs behind him in second place. So, after two rides, Ove was unbeaten on 6 points and being challenged by his 'teacher' Aub Lawson, living up to expectations also on two wins. The two New Zealanders, Briggs and Ron Johnston, were next on 5.

Craven opened the title race up in heat ten by winning it with Aub Lawson third. The crunch was going to come two races later when Fundin lined up against Johnston and Briggs, and Barry's other friend, Germany's Josef Hofmeister. This time it was Briggs who made a dream start with Fundin last into the first corner behind Johnston and Hofmeister. With Briggs away and Johnston not far behind, it took Fundin time and distance before he was able to find a way past Hofmeister, who had fallen off in both his first two races. Now it was Johnston's turn to make things difficult for Ove. It took three laps to catch him and the best part of another lap to get by into second place. The dropped point meant that Ove and Barry were joint leaders, level on 8 points each. Both had difficult rides to come, facing veteran Aub Lawson who, with Rune Sormander, was only one point behind them and still in the running on 7.

Barry eased ahead in heat fifteen, but only after a re-run. Barry saw it like this: 'My Wimbledon mate Ron How came off and broke a wrist. In the re-run Aub Lawson, the oldest man in the field, led most of the way. I took a death-or-glory dive on the last turn to squeeze past for another win.' Eric Linden saw it like this: 'In a wonderful heat fifteen that yanked the 50,000-plus crowd screaming to its feet, Briggs whipped past Lawson on the last turn.' Fundin saw it like this: 'Barry was way back behind everyone and Ron How fell off and stayed on the track and lay there until he managed to get a re-run, and Barry won the re-run.' But Ove won the next heat so they were still both level on 11 each. Then Briggs set the seal on his night in the very next race with a comfortable win to finish on 14 and put all the pressure on Fundin in heat twenty.

It was, reported Linden, the 'worst race of the night, when the hitherto flying Fundin suddenly started feeling his way nervously around'. Behind him Lawson, who had ridden a forceful final up to then, was proceeding with even more care. 'I thought this one would never end,' wrote Linden. But end it did, with Barry and Ove on 14 points each and the huge Wembley crowd breathlessly anticipating the electrifying prospect of two deciding run-offs. Craven, Lawson and Sormander were all tied on 11 points and had to race for the minor place, Barry and Ove for the highest prize in the game.

Briggs was soon out on the track and ready to race. Fundin took his time. Observers concluded that he was playing a game of nerves and trying to unsettle Barry. In spite of track staff calling him out several times, he stayed talking to fellow Swedes Sormander, Dan Forsberg and Peo Soderman, even finding time to have a word or two with former World Champion Fred Williams, who was in his brother Ian's pit crew. Briggs was approached by Johnston who warned him, 'You look out for him. Don't let him pull anything on you.'

When the pair of them finally came to the tapes, Fundin on the outside, Briggs on the inside, the majestic Empire Stadium's packed terraces fell silent. Everyone in the pits craned to see the drama about to unfold under the brilliance of the floodlights. Then the place erupted as the two riders roared away from the starting gate. Ove, with one of his lightning starts, had the all-important first-turn advantage – which should have been decisive. But instead of trying to get as far ahead of Barry as he could, it looked as though he had decided to rely on track-craft tactics. Briggs stayed close behind, stalking him. Barry remembered, 'Fundin was choosing precisely the line he wanted. He was never the easiest man to pass and twice he took me out to the fence and twice I had to knock off and wait for the next opening.' Then, coming out of the second corner on the third lap Ove left just a little bit of room on the inside.

It was the chance Barry had been waiting for, and he was up beside Ove in a flash. With the sound from the vast crowd reaching a crescendo, they hurtled side by side down the back straight towards the pit corner. As Briggs laid his machine over to take the turn, Fundin appeared to go straight on, lose control, bail out and disappear under the fence. All Briggs had to do was ride a formal lap to take away Ove's World crown. The Wembley thousands had been witness to one of the most controversial speedway races in the sport's history, one that is still discussed, argued about and relived to this day. As Barry passed the crash site for the final time he could see ambulance men, officials and photographers crowding round the defeated champion and, after taking the chequered flag, he sacrificed the usual congratulatory reception by the fans – an equal number of whom seemed to be booing him as cheering his victory anyway – to stop his bike and find out if Ove was all right. High up in the Wembley grandstand, an irate Ove Fundin supporter climbed over seats to get to Barry's wife, June, and slap her across the face – which reduced her to tears at the greatest moment of her husband's speedway career, his first World title.

Ove denies now that he decided to ride a 'defensive' race. 'No,' he says. 'With Barry Briggs behind you? Of course not. Then you go for your life. It would have made more sense if I had overshot the corner – I was coming in faster than I should have done – than I should ride defensively. You can't stop him anyway. No. I went as good as I could, I'm quite sure. I'm quite sure that we were coming down into the corner – it was the round corner, not the difficult corner. But I knew we had reached a point where you have to shut off, but he didn't shut off, he just went straight on, he went straight into me.'

Those who were in the pits and watching in line with the back straight at Wembley that night, and I was one of them, insist that Ove placed his elbow over Barry's throttle hand as they were about to enter the corner.

'You mean it was a desperate move when I saw him come at me? Probably. But I shouldn't think so because if I did anything I used to stick my leg out – and stop people that way. But not my elbow. You must remember I rode with my handlebars up like that, so it might have looked as though I put my elbow over his hand, but if you look at any picture my elbows were always up because I had my handlebars so high.'

Barry says: 'I was quicker than him. He was good at blocking. I was riding really good that night. You know we came down that back straight and I'm absolutely beside him and the corner is coming up, and Ove does this – puts his elbow over my throttle hand. There is only one answer to that. If I'd taken him on past the corner I could have been excluded. But if I kept my line, which I did – I just dropped on the line – Ove just flew off. But he has said that had it been reversed he'd have done the same. Because you had to hustle. You've got yourself in an uncompromising situation and the smart thing is to know when to let go. I had no doubt in my mind that I was legal. I just went into the corner. Ove had put his arm over my throttle hand. Tough shit Ove. He would have done the same to me.'

Ove remembered: 'There was nothing to lose. If both of us had fallen off, we couldn't have been worse than second in a World Final. What could we lose? But if Barry could upset me then he would win, which he did. Of course I was upset then. But afterwards, no. There was nothing wrong with what he did. How did I feel afterwards? I don't really remember. Probably there were tears. No doubt I was angry with him. But I soon calmed down – maybe not even the same day, but afterwards. And definitely today. He just went for me and I would have done the same thing. I know I would have done exactly the same thing. I probably thought, "Well, bad luck!" or "To hell with that! I'll come and get it next year."

'We were never enemies or unfriendly to each other, but we never became really good friends until after I quit, because he went on for another few years. Now we are very good friends. But of course, on the track, you cannot be friends. It comes to you that he is the one you have to be beating all the time, and he feels the same.'

There was a word and picture analysis in *Speedway Star & News* under the headline 'Was It Dirty?': 'The two people most involved, Briggs and Fundin, made no excuses and they made no accusations.' That is still the case today. 'Fundin gave Briggs the opening,' said the analysis. Briggs took it and 'Fundin still kept making for the line, trying to come across Briggs's course. To put it in plainer words, Ove was crowding Briggs. Then, while Barry maintained his straight course, Ove seemed to lose control. This opinion has been borne out by the majority of riders who took part in the meeting.' Fundin had lost his title with great dignity. The picture showed Ove being assisted by ambulance men, his left hand to his face. The question it asked: 'Was it pain, or anguish that Fundin was trying to hide?' Knowing Ove, it was assuredly anguish. And after all the furore had died down, Craven beat Lawson and Sormander for third place.

For Ove it was destined to be three in a row... World Championship second places, that is. The European winter was spent in South Africa where he continued to make headlines. In January, 'Ove Fundin Breaks Track Record' was one, Dennis Newton reporting that 'Ove Fundin has really settled down and is now showing the fans in South Africa what made him World Champion in 1956 and almost again last year. In a special one-lap record attempt on 27 December he lowered the existing time to 14.6 after Bob Andrews had recorded 15.1 and Roy Bowers and myself had clocked 15.2. In the challenge match between Eagles and Cosmopolitans Ove continued to outride everyone, being hardest pressed when challenged by his countryman, Olle Nygren.' In a league match in Durban, South African champion Henry Long, riding for the Hornets, and Ove, riding for the Rockets, crossed the finishing line to 'tumultuous cheers' following a clash in which they rode the entire four laps side by side with Long just getting the verdict.

The 1958 British season was not very old before Ove and Barry Briggs were lining up against each other again, this time in Austria. In Vienna, before 27,000 people on 12 April Ove's 15-point maximum in a Saturday individual meeting was three better than Barry's 12. The following day a crowd of 22,000 saw the pair of them battling it out at Linz, with Ove once again coming out best with another 15-point maximum. Barry reported: 'I scored 14, dropping the odd point to Ove in my third outing.' The actual racing, he remarked, 'was terrific stuff' and Barry seemed to be more concerned with the fact that his racing leathers went missing on the journey back to Wimbledon to race against Norwich on the Monday than whether Ove had scored any kind of revenge for their Wembley fracas. Perhaps there was some satisfaction in the Monday night Britannia Shield scores: Wimbledon 53 Norwich 43, though Briggs, in borrowed leathers, scored only 9, while Fundin recorded an 18-point maximum. It is interesting to note that in that meeting Ivan Mauger, who went on to be World Champion six times, was unable to get into the Wimbledon team and recorded only a second-half win in the Morden Handicap after riding off five yards.

Ove again got the better of Barry in the Malcolm Flood Memorial meeting at Norwich and in a Southern Riders Championship qualifying round in June at Southampton. There was a free-scoring three-match series of internationals in England with Ove scoring 16, 16 and 15 but with Sweden going down 2-1. In the return series in Sweden his scores were 16, 12 and 11 with Sweden running out 2-1 winners. There was also a 3-0 Swedish whitewash of Australasia and another against Poland. Ove took the Match Race Championship from Craven at the start of the season in May, making history by becoming the first European rider to win the Golden Helmet. He then saw off a challenge by Peter Moore – the man who at that time had beaten him more times than any other rider – and then lost it to Brian Crutcher just before the World Final after being severely unsettled following a warning from an over-officious referee. He also lost his Swedish title to Sormander, and a run-off with Nygren for second place with an uncharacteristic fall.

But where it really mattered, in the World Championship, he came away with a 15-point maximum in the European Final in Warsaw to qualify once again for Wembley. Ove's late sparring partner, Alan Hunt, had let it be known that he considered it far more of an honour and far more important to ride for his country than to ride in a World Final. 'It was the other way round with me,' said Ove. The speedway press noticed that there had been very different attitudes among the two teams of riders in 1956 when Sweden 'murdered' England at Wembley in the first senior international between the nations. In every case, it was reported, the Swedes said what a great honour it was for them to ride for their country and that they would ride all the better for realising it. In the England camp the main topic of conversation had been 'how I beat —— last week' and 'any idea of the score, old boy – we winning or losing?' Hunt was the only one who had said, 'This is the thing, riding for England. Beats all the match races and National Trophy finals – yes, and World Championships too. The greatest honour any man can have in this game is riding for England.'

Ove says: 'I thought it was far more important for me to race for Sweden at Wembley in the individual World Championship than in those Test matches. Far more important. Of course it was a great honour to ride for Sweden, especially when we first used to come to England, because you must remember that England was the home of speedway. So of course it was a great thing. But it was an even bigger honour to do well in the individual championship.'

In the lead-up to the 1958 final he helped Norwich to runners-up spot in the league with an astonishing CMA of 11.66 home and 11.57 away, which included nine maximums, seventy-four first places, six seconds, one third and not one last place, for a race average of 2.9 points a ride in a season when league matches were over sixteen heats and National Trophy matches over twenty heats. So he was all set for Wembley again where he was joined by the four other top scorers from the Warsaw qualifier: Nygren, Sormander and Joel Jansson, all of Sweden, and Hofmeister of Germany. Also in the line-up was Ronnie Moore, who had returned in mid-season after a year flirting with car racing.

The magnificent pot-bellied *Sunday Dispatch* cup had become redundant with the demise of the paper, and the World Championship sponsorship was taken over by the *Sunday Pictorial* – later the *Sunday Mirror* – which put up a unique new trophy, the now famous winged wheel, a tyre carved in wood over a wheel rim from the bike Wimbledon's Cyril Brine had used in his two World Final appearances in 1950 and 1951. This time it was a four-way split on favourites for the title. Reigning champion Briggs, seeded direct to Wembley, and Fundin, plus the strongly fancied Ken McKinlay and Peter Craven who had topped the British-based qualifiers on 27 points each. The track came in for some criticism after it was flooded by a morning rainstorm, which resulted in an unpredictable surface. Fundin became familiar with a bump entering the pit corner, and commented, 'This circuit is definitely not up to championship standard. It's not like any Wembley track I have ever ridden before, very bad.' The referee, Mr E.G. Cope, was also criticised for apparently letting everything go and being too lenient, particularly some 'over robust' riding by Olle Nygren.

The 70,000-plus final crowd was almost 15,000 up on the previous season – it was the first time for years that the final was not televised – and the start was delayed by twenty minutes to allow all the spectators to get into the stadium. The speedway press was speculating on whether Fundin's notoriously 'touchy' temperament might be a disadvantage on the night, but Swindon's George White reported that he seemed more relaxed than in past years because he changed early and spent an hour resting in the Wembley dressing room.

Drawn number thirteen, Fundin established an early claim with wins in heats four and five. Briggs was also unbeaten after two rides, beating Craven and veteran Aub Lawson in the opening heat and Sormander, Geran and Hofmeister in heat eight. Close behind were the usual suspects, Ronnie Moore, Peter Craven and Olle Nygren, on 5 each.

The decider looked like heat twelve, a virtual re-run of the same heat in the previous year's final, with Fundin, Briggs, his New Zealand mate Ron Johnston, and this time the formidable presence of that other New Zealander Ronnie Moore instead of Hofmeister. Moore, who appeared to be on a sluggish motor all night, was left at the start, and though Ove got one of his usual fliers, it was Johnston who took the early lead with Briggs in third place. But on the second lap, Barry blasted round the outside of both of them and claims he took his left hand off the handlebar and 'gave good old Johnno the thumbs up. That was a great psychological boost.' Ove got into second place on lap three but couldn't catch Barry.

Another win for Ove two heats later, over McKinlay and Lawson, kept the pressure on Briggs, who maintained his unbeaten record in heat sixteen. Motor problems for Craven in heat eleven meant he was virtually out of the running for top spot, but another win in heat fifteen from Nygren, Moore and Sormander put him in sight of a rostrum place. Neither he nor Ove could afford to sacrifice another point when they went to the tapes for their final ride in heat nineteen, with Gerald Hussey and Hofmeister. And it was a classic between the pair of them, with Fundin leading and Craven sticking to the outside, avoiding the pit-turn hazard, which found Ove, and passing the chequered flag first.

Ove had dropped a second point, leaving Briggs needing only a second place from heat twenty for him to match Jack Young's achievement of a second successive World Championship. It was a battle between Briggs and McKinlay – which Briggs won to finish on a 15-point maximum. The run-off for third place between Lawson, McKinlay and Craven ended in chaos, with McKinlay and Craven both falling, putting Lawson, the very last of the surviving pre-war greats, finally on the Wembley rostrum at forty-four years of age and rendering him almost speechless with emotion.

If Barry was champion again, equalling Young's titles in 1951 and 1952, Ove had the dubious honour of finishing second for a second successive year, matching Ronnie Moore who had been second in 1955 and 1956, post-war Wembley captain Bill Kitchen who had had filled the runners-up slot in the 1946 and 1947 Speedway Riders Championships, and the great Australian Vic Huxley, who had the same experience in the Star Championships of 1931 and 1932. Ove, when asked afterwards if he considered being number thirteen had been unlucky, laughed and replied, 'I wore thirteen, scored 13 points and won £277 10s prize money. What's unlucky about that?' It was the cash equivalent of just over £4,000 today. Reserves for the night, Brian Crutcher and Peo Soderman – who did not ride – were guaranteed being paid for five starts at £2 10s a start, giving them a total of £12 10s each. This works out at £181.25 in today's values. After it was all over, Barry says that the *Sunday Dispatch* gave him their old trophy to keep.

'Fundin wins gold helmet' and 'Swedish Star Complains About Track Officials!' were the headlines that greeted the beginning of

Ove's 1959 season. He appeared to be starting the year in his usual temperamental style. He had gone to Australia again and was based at Perth with his friend Aub Lawson. His first appearance at Claremont in January coincided with the very last appearance on a speedway track of Ron Johnson who, after more than thirty years in the game, put on leathers and crash helmet again and did a farewell three laps.

Ove, it was reported, 'showed what a terrific rider he is by quickly adapting to the Perth track. He turned in a class performance,' winning one scratch and two handicap races. In his next meeting, showing little respect for his off-track host, and even less for him on the track, Ove beat Aub in a Golden Helmet Match Race series. 'Highlight of the Claremont speedway programme was the Golden Helmet races between Aub Lawson and Ove Fundin, which the latter won 2-0,' said the meeting report. 'Ove had to ride hard on both occasions and won both races by half a wheel. The Swede really thrilled the crowd, riding the straights on his back wheel, the front being well in the air.' Then, later, Ove caused a sensation by protesting about a track official who he accused of holding him back at the start of a race won by Aub from Chum Taylor. The steward ordered a re-run, which was won by Taylor with Ove second and Lawson pulling out because of a seized motor. It was reported: 'The crowd went wild when Ove protested. They were all on his side, though, and cheered themselves hoarse during the re-run, which was a great race.' Ove went on to retain the Western Australia Golden Helmet in two straight runs from a challenge by Ken McKinlay in early March.

The Fundin attitude ensured he was always his own man, beholden to no one. In another incident, again in Australia during a season when he was under contract to promoter Kym Boynton at Rowley Park, Adelaide, he objected to the state of the track's inner line. 'I always used to ride on the white line, and they had sticks poking up on it,' said Ove. 'They had something to do with the speed cars. I rode the bike near there and hurt my hand on those bloody sticks. And I said, "I'm not riding here any more." I was called up to the referee and I called him an idiot. I was so angry, because it was wrong. I said if he read the speedway regulations he would find that there should be only a white line. A curb was allowed, but not anything sticking up there, so I knew I was in the right and that's when I said he was an idiot. So the day after I was called into the South Australian Speedway Control Board to give an explanation. It might have been Kym, who appointed himself my defence lawyer, who said that I was a foreigner and didn't speak English 100 per cent. He said I probably didn't know what the word idiot meant. I said, "I know very well what the word idiot means because we have exactly the same word in Swedish." So they said I would get a £50 penalty. I said, "OK, you can have the penalty, but I'm off." Kym came to me and said he would pay the £50 penalty but I had to stay. I said that I'd stay for two more meetings, and I did two more meetings. Kym was so sure that I would stay because I'd paid for my own flight over there. I'd done it before, instead of being sent the tickets I'd paid my own air fare because I could book it myself and fly when I wanted, and then I was paid for it later on. He was so sure I wouldn't do what I said because he hadn't paid up. But I just flew home, and he never paid me for my air ticket. But it was worth it. And then again, I think it was at my first meeting there that they took my helmet. They said it was no good, it was too soft or something. I was angry at that as well. I was always angry. I didn't buy another helmet – they lent me one.'

When he returned to Europe for the new season he could not have endeared himself to his winter hosts by giving an interview in which he said about speedway in Australia: 'It isn't speedway. It is speed racing. The tracks are too big for speedway. It is the man with the fastest motor who wins, not necessarily the man with the most skill.' He also complained about the rules: 'Every track seemed to have different rules,' he said. 'And I seemed to break all of them. I was in trouble with rules from the moment I got to Australia until the moment I left.'

If Ove's 1959 league average was slightly down – to 11.00 from 11.60 – his form remained phenomenal. He took nine of the minor individual meetings and won back the Golden Helmet from Brian Crutcher, defending it against Peter Craven and Ken McKinlay before surrendering it by default to Craven in September. The Swedish authorities banned him from taking part in the decider at Oxford because they ruled he could not race for three days before their domestic national championship. Ove said, 'I have no option. I have telephoned to Sweden and pleaded with them, but they will not allow me to ride at Oxford.' Craven was equally upset at SVEMO's attitude. He said, 'I don't like winning anything this way. I reckoned I'd have beaten Ove at Oxford anyway. He didn't agree, but we'd have settled it racing. What I find disappointing is that the spectators, through no fault of their own, have lost the chance to see the decider.'

The incident once more called into question the matter of whether foreign riders should be allowed to compete for the British Match Race Championship. As it was, they were, but Ove also lost the Swedish national title, by one point to Rune Sormander. Yet, even though he went on to win it nine times, he says, 'I didn't rate the Swedish Championship very high. If I had I would have asked Norwich to lend me the track spare number two. As far as I remember, I just used the bike I had in Sweden, which was not all that good. The only title I thought special was Wembley, for the World Championship. And also the qualifying rounds, of course.'

In June he set a four-lap world record for a quarter-mile speedway at Jonkoping with a speed of 82kph, and in the same month his racing schedule read: Wednesday 17 June Munich, Thursday Ipswich, the next day Poole with Norwich, back to Norwich for the normal Saturday night meeting, Sunday in Denmark, Monday he was back in England for a meeting at Wimbledon to guest for Coventry, Southampton on the Tuesday, Norwich again Wednesday, Thursday Ipswich, Friday Poole, Norwich Saturday. On Sunday he was racing in France – twelve meetings in twelve days. Later he notched up sixteen meetings in sixteen days.

He was most people's early fancy for the World Championship once again. Barry Briggs was out of the equation for most of the season because he had a row with his Wimbledon promoter, Ronnie Greene, over his return fare from New Zealand. But Ronnie Moore was back in top form. So was Little Pete, and the last of the Big Five had arrived – Ove had recommended Bjorn Knutsson, who was being hailed as 'the latest Swedish sensation', to Southampton as a temporary replacement for

Geoff Mardon, who was out injured with a broken jaw. At Southampton Ove's confidence was so high that when promoter Charlie Knott offered £25 for the first rider to get the track record down from 60.8 seconds to a straight 60 seconds, Fundin, who had set the record earlier with Rune Sormander, jokingly told Charlie, 'If you make the track like it was on the day we did it I will give you £25 if I don't do 60 seconds.'

It took more than a year, but eventually Ove reduced the Southampton track record to under 60 seconds – 59.8 – and reminded Charlie of the offer. Ever the showman, Charlie counted out five fivers on the spot, much to the delight of the crowd and Ove, of course, who has always confessed to being prudent with his financial assets.

A mid-season bout of concussion after a crash in Denmark stopped Fundin from appearing for Norwich at Poole. It was the first time in Ove's five-year association with Norwich that an injury had prevented him from turning out for the Stars. He also missed a home fixture and an away meeting at Wimbledon, then scorched back to score 11 from five rides at Southampton and reached his sixth successive World Final by winning the European Final in Gothenburg with a score of 14.

British speedway literally had a whip round to pay for reigning World Champion Barry Briggs to return in time to defend his title at Wembley, the Speedway Control Board chipping in half his fare and various tracks contributing the rest of the cash. Speculation was that Briggs was wanted back because it was felt he was the only man who could stop Fundin. It was feared that, if Ove won, the Swedes would have a legitimate claim to take the 1960 World Final away from England. Briggs, apart from not wanting to pass up the opportunity to be the first to win the World title three times in a row, was convinced that 'people in high places wanted me back – and badly'. The Wembley showcase and other shared events in a season could often mean a payout of as much as £5,000 per track – a tidy sum that, today, would be the equivalent of something slightly in excess of £72,000.

Top qualifier in the British rounds was Peter Moore with 27 points, followed by Craven and Crutcher on 26 then Ronnie Moore on 25. But instead of Briggs scoring a hat-trick of wins, it was Ove, the odds-on favourite, who scored a hat-trick... of second places. He was denied another World Championship for two reasons – Ronnie Moore, who rode to a virtually untroubled maximum in spite of a slight foot injury and then confessed to using nitro-methane fuel, and the on-track behaviour of the man Fundin looked upon as his greatest friend, Aub Lawson. A single headline told the story: 'Ron Moore's Secret Fuel Won the Title.' Ronnie claimed that nitro-methane was 'becoming the fashion', and his main concern was getting enough of it. 'If I was to stand a chance of winning I would have to use this [nitro] mixed with my fuel. Everybody else was going to be tanked up on it. There was really no alternative.' In the days and hours before the final, Ronnie had toured the model aeroplane shops of London to locate a supply of the magic fuel additive used to power model aeroplane engines. The main advantage of using it was to give better drive from the tapes, something that on World Final night could be decisive. Briggs was also on nitro and, between them, by helping each other out and transferring some of the precious mixture from one bike to another, they both had just enough to complete their rides.

'Everybody else' was not 'tanked up' on nitro. Ove Fundin wasn't for one, and says now that he was shocked when he learned that Ronnie and Barry had used the fuel supplement, though it was widely reported at the time. Then its use was perfectly legitimate but it was later to be banned from the sport. 'There were too many risks in it for me,' says Ove. 'I would have been too afraid it would burn a hole in the piston. And if you stop in a World Final you have not much of a chance of winning the title.' A mere two years later, Ronnie was indignantly denying he was using nitro under the headline in his weekly column: 'I Do Not Use Secret Fuel.' He was responding to a diatribe by Johnnie Hoskins, who had implied that Ronnie and the Wimbledon team were all on nitro. Though previously extolling its virtues in his 1959 World Championship success, he now said, 'The last time I used nitro-methane was well over eighteen months ago.' He told his readers that from 'first-hand experience' nitro was 'pretty dangerous stuff'.

Ove and Ronnie met in their first outing, heat four, and Ronnie says that he made one of the most 'nearly perfect starts' of his career.

The nitro was obviously working. Ove dived under Cyril Roger into second place on the first bend and was followed through by Olle Nygren, but Ronnie won by ten lengths easing up. Ronnie's riding number, thirteen, meant he was out again straight away in heat five, but he coasted past the chequered flag untroubled from Poland's Mieczyslaw Polukard – the first Eastern European to appear in a World Final – Rune Sormander and Joseph Hofmeister.

Ove's second ride, heat six, was crucial. He lined up with Briggs and Lawson, both of whom had won their opening rides. George White made up the foursome. Moore was undefeated, but the other danger man, Peter Craven, was really out of the running having finished last first time out. Eric Linden described the race as one of two 'blood-curdling' rides by Lawson. 'Wily old Lawson again,' he wrote. 'He's into the bend before Briggs and White. Fundin's stone last – but not for long. He belts past White and Briggs with one burst on the pits bend first time round. Briggs chases him while Fundin is after Lawson. They pass the yellow flag near enough to be covered by a blanket. Fundin, flat out round the outside, levels with Lawson, but Aub moves out. Fundin must smash into the fence as Aub gives him no room. But he doesn't – and neither does he win. Very, very, very dicey moment.' Ove had dropped another vital point to his 'teacher' Aub, and really it meant his title chase was virtually over, unless Ronnie made a slip. Briggs had dropped two and could kiss his hoped-for hat-trick of World Championships goodbye. But Ronnie made no mistakes at all, outclassing everyone and riding to a stylish maximum.

Back in the pits after heat six Ove, in a rage, confronted Lawson. As Ove was about to go past, Aub had not only denied him room but had kicked out at him. Strong words were exchanged. Ove says: 'Coming down the straight, going into the corner when I tried to pass him, he looked at me and with his right foot he kicked at me, as if to say, "Don't come near me!" And it wasn't just me knowing it. Quite a few people have told me they saw it. Olle Nygren was one. It was very seldom that I passed people on the outside. It was fear. I never wanted to risk anything. But he was riding so slowly I thought I could pass him by going round him. I can't remember now exactly what I said to Aub, but I know that I was just as sad as I was angry. After all, it was Aub, my best friend in speedway, I could not understand why he did such a thing to me. He ruined that World Final for me. But today I think: never mind, he was a good friend. I don't hold it against him. No way.'

The 70,000 people in Wembley Stadium that night saw it too and didn't like what they had witnessed. They let Lawson know they disapproved of his tactics in very clear terms. If Wembley had possessed a roof then, they would have booed it off. Maybe Aub felt it was his swansong and had ambitions to go two better than the previous year when he had finished third, because he was at it again three races later in heat nine. He took on Nygren and his fellow Swede Arne Carlsson – and came off worst this time. It was another bruising bloodcurdler with the three of them pushing and shoving in a physically bad-tempered encounter. The crowd didn't care for this demonstration either and again booed Lawson, who was given a warning by the referee. His 11 points put him in a triple tie for third place, but it was Briggs who ended up on the rostrum after a spirited tussle with Nygren with Lawson tailed off nowhere.

Ove's comments afterwards were: 'It's a mighty tough sport. But some of this was murderous. I think I am lucky to be second again. Nicer to have won, but Ronnie was terrific. He is a great World Champion.' Ove could afford to be magnanimous in defeat. The speedway pundits voted him top of the world ratings for the third time in four years, above Ronnie, Craven and Briggs. And the word was that, once again, Sweden did not intend to claim the following year's World Final. But it was only a matter of time.

## TWELVE

# THE GOVERNOR

*'I cannot run this business at a profit without Ove Fundin being here. When Fundin is not here we don't make money. The only way this stadium can make money is when Ove Fundin is here.'* – Norwich chairman Harry Wharton.

The voice of speedway throughout the mid-1960s until the mid 1980s, when Independent Television's *World of Sport* programme put the stars of the track into the nation's living rooms on Saturday afternoons, was Dave Lanning. His idiosyncratic TV commentaries were as much of a dynamic contribution to the resurgence of speedway racing as were the new wave of Americans who injected into the sport the magic ingredient of glamour it had been sadly lacking for years. Speedway and Lanning were made for each other. But when *World of Sport* ended in 1988 and the mantle of bringing speedway to the masses was later taken up by Sky, Dave Lanning was allowed to fade into the ranks of forgotten men in favour of an inferior product. This was a great pity – for the sport and for television – because he had a unique talent. He once sat on the sodden terraces of a deserted Belle Vue stadium at Hyde Road, Manchester and linked, live and entirely alone, a hastily cobbled-together show of the season's TV highlights because the showpiece British League Riders Championship Final had been rained off.

Big Dave was not everyone's tank of methanol. He was brash, in-your-face, slick, loud and bristling with ideas. Nor did he suffer fools gladly or delicately. He was one of the great speedway publicists of our or any other time, ranking alongside the gentleman-showman professional promoters who rode the pioneer and boom years – such as Johnnie Hoskins at West Ham, Fred Mockford at New Cross, Tom Bradbury-Pratt at Harringay and the two Charlies, Knott at Poole and Southampton, and Ochiltree at Coventry. Lanning, though, was much more versatile. He did practically the lot in the world of speedway except put on leathers and ride a bike. In his time he was team manager, reporter, commentator, author, gossip columnist extraordinaire – with a lovely line in alliteration – track announcer, disk jockey, centre green presenter and promoter. He was what could be safely described as a smooth operator. As a skilful journalist himself, he knew how to treat the press.

When he was Reading's publicity guru/chief executive – today he would have been described as a spin doctor – you could bet that the crowd knew the name of every visiting journalist in the stadium. Dave would always give them – and their publication – a 'mensh' over the track mike before the meeting started. It was while he was at the Smallmead promotion that he pulled off the biggest cash gamble speedway has ever known. Reading paid out a premium of £1,000 to insure the club AGAINST winning the 1980 British League championship. 'Like every insurance policy, in reality it was a bet,' says Lanning, 'but absolutely, copper-bottomed legal and above board.' When the Racers duly clinched the title there was a £50,000 share-out between riders and management. It was a super-incentive deal – the biggest in the sport's history.

Among Lanning's other claims to fame was that he was Ove Fundin's ghost. In the 1960s a monthly magazine was published called *Speedway Post*. It was a features-led glossy using a bold illustration technique with a column bearing the name of the reigning World Champion who, at that particular time, happened to be Ove Fundin. Except that not a word was written by Ove. It was all ghost-written by Dave Lanning.

Lanning says: 'It was a *Speedway Star* publication and very successful for quite a long time. I don't recall being commissioned to do Ove's column, but in those days I was just out to earn a quid and I'd try to generate any ideas to make a bob or two. I'd known Ove through the 1950s, from when he first arrived in the country. But as far as the ghosting went, he was always very amenable to it. To be honest, I didn't actually speak to him that much, I just used to write the stuff and he'd say, "I think it will be a very good and worthy piece." It certainly wasn't a regular deal for me to call him. I just tried to read his mind and write the sort of things I thought he would say. I don't recall even having to check with him before publication. In those days it would have been difficult for me to afford a phone call to Sweden, or wherever he was, to speak to him. He was always very agreeable, and never disagreed with anything I did. I tried to write in his kind of language. He was always very grateful.

'He could be so prickly and distant, and then on other occasions he would come round and say, "I've brought you some cigars", or "some chocolates for your wife"; or "I've brought something through customs." And he'd present you with something you weren't expecting. Ove could be difficult. He was moody in his prime. He still is – you have to pick your moments with him. I never saw him violent or anything of that nature. He had this habit of cocking his head on one side if something had upset him, and he was sometimes difficult to approach. I've seen him in other circumstances in which he could be quite a handful, though he never was with me. He put Les Mullins through the mangle. Ove never tolerated fools, but he tolerated a lot of hangers-on. He had a lot of people around him who in this day and age you and I would say were peripheral people.

'A man named Eddie Kovacs was a great chum of Ove's for years and years. He purported to be an American. He walked around with a crew cut and a Detroit Tigers outfit. He was always hanging around Ove. He used to meet him at the airport and take him up to Norwich. I don't know what the hell happened to him, but he was a boy from the Old Kent Road or somewhere like that. In those days it was terribly fashionable to be American, or to purport to be American, and he looked like an American. He was an associate of Ove's for a long time, and it was always a bit of a surprise to me that he tolerated Kovacs for so long. Ove always seemed to be commuting, and Eddie always seemed prepared to go to Heathrow Airport and pick him up and take him to Norwich, which in those days was no mean journey.'

Ove says: 'Eddie was a private driver for a Mr Marks of the Marks & Spencer company. He lived just off Queensway in London. He was mad about speedway and somehow he picked me as his favourite. A couple of times he had the use of one of Mr Marks's Rolls-Royces and he took me and also my children for rides around London. He often drove me to and from airports. He had a Morris Minor car painted in the colours of Norwich speedway, yellow and green, and it was full of pictures of me and the Norwich team. Eddie had been born in London but had lived for many years in America and wanted to be thought of as American. He had been a New York policeman. He also had a Harley-Davidson motorcycle he used to like to ride as a cop.'

Lanning recalled: 'I used to write the stuff for Ove's column and send it off to him. He never complained. I remember after one World Final I went to speak to him and he said, "I'm sure you'll write a perfectly good piece." Years later he told one of my sons that I always wrote good stuff about him. Maybe I kind of got under his skin a bit. I always tried to write it in the way I thought he would see it, which is what a ghost writer is supposed to do. The last few times I have seen him he has been effusive in his greeting, and he has always been very, very warm towards me. No way did I ever write anything about him that I didn't mean. I never tried to curry favour in any way.'

Lanning was one of the few journalists allowed in the Wembley pits on World Final nights, so he was able to experience Fundin's behaviour during the really big occasions. 'He was a loner,' says Lanning. 'In the pits at Wembey, if you are looking back down the tunnel, there were some stone steps leading to what used to be the old St John Ambulance balcony. And Ove was always sitting on those stone steps on the right. He made that his corner. That was his place. He always sat on his own. He had the peculiar habit of undoing his body colour, and when he was standing around wearing his body colour when it was done up, he use to put his hands in it as though it was a waistcoat. I can see him now there with his hands tucked in his body colour and his head cocked on the right-hand side. I have a picture of him sitting on those stone steps at Wembley. You tended not to go near him until afterwards. In fact, I tended not to go near him at all and just wrote what I thought he'd want to say.

'He was difficult, and at times not too popular with his fellow riders, and certainly he was not very popular with some of the other Swedes.' Gote Nordin remembers experiencing one example of the Fundin temperament: 'Yes. I remember when we were riding in Gothenburg and he didn't win one heat. He came in and was very upset. He took a brand new magneto and threw it at the wall. He smashed the magneto. It cost him a few quid. The money wasn't that important, but it showed that he was very upset. But I rode with him in England for Sweden against England and we had such a good time then. I didn't have a problem with him when we were riding the Test matches in England. I think he appreciated that as well because after one meeting he said to me, "We had a nice time riding together, would you like to follow me into town for a dinner?" So it couldn't have been so bad then. He took me out to dinner – and he paid!'

Fundin and Bjorn Knutsson were very suspicious of each other throughout their whole time together. Lanning said: 'I remember when we opened up West Ham in 1964, Knutty came there from Southampton and was an absolute sensation. We were getting 15,000 people at a time in there regularly when everybody else was lucky to get 1,500. Bjorn was a smashing rider, I think the first month he was there he didn't drop a point. Those were the days when riders like him were handicapped. I remember him saying to me that it suited him fine, because he started way back on the outside and by the time he got to the first corner at West Ham he was going about 20mph quicker than everybody else. He could just pick his line. Everybody thought Bjorn was invincible, until Ove came down in the Golden Helmet Match Race Championship. The Golden Helmet was a big deal in those days. It was a money-spinner. Ove came and ran Bjorn ragged. That was the night he knocked the best part of two seconds off the track record. But he came into the pits afterwards, chucked the bike at Les Mullins and said it had on "the wrong bloody gear".'

It was Ove's first visit to West Ham for eleven years. The Hammers were enjoying that gate of 15,000 spectators for the third week in succession. Knutsson had been the winner of his twelve rides in the previous two meetings. The match report read: 'So it ended. Bjorn Knutsson was beaten fair and square in his challenge for the British Match Race Championship. Holder Ove Fundin made the gate in both races and left Knutsson trailing.' Ove's times for the two races, at 75.4 and 75.0 were up to five seconds quicker than those recorded in the match that followed – an Easter Challenge Cup fixture, which Norwich won 44-40. Lanning said: 'Quite honestly, the next week we got only about 8,000 because everybody had thought that Bjorn was invincible, and Ove came and put him in his place. The other Swedes had a terrific respect for Ove, and fear of him. Knutsson feared him.'

Their relationship was less than congenial, to say the least. Bjorn recalled: 'We were not very close and not very friendly at the time. We are today, but we were not at that time. Some people you get on with very good and very easy, and some you don't. He was difficult to get on with, and temperamental. I don't really know how to explain it, but he was very, very selfish, you know, in my opinion. I just don't want to speak about it. I'm friends with him today. We are talking about a forgotten time.' Told that the intention had always been to record the truth about Ove as he really is and that he would not mind if he opened up a bit more, Bjorn said, 'Well, you ask someone else.'

Lanning was in the Wembley pits for the run-off between Ove and Bengt Jansson for the World Championship in 1967. Lanning says: 'Banger was going very quickly that year – he had a very fast bike and a new fuel injection system that Wal Phillips and Don Smith had developed. He was going like a rocket. The pair of them had to walk out from the pits up to the start line for the run-off, and Ove completely psyched Banger out. I was standing with Don Smith in the pits and Don was saying, "Come on Banger!" But all the way from the pits to the start line Ove was talking at him, and I thought that there is no way Banger is going to win this run-off because he was in fear of the man and the legend.' As a result, what should have been a climactic end to a World Final was something of an anticlimax, Ove winning comfortably by fifty yards to take his fifth world title. It was a record for that time that was not to be challenged for another ten years.

There were suggestions that Jansson was under orders from the Swedish speedway authorities that night not to beat Ove in the run-off for the title. Bengt vehemently refuted the idea when it was put to him, and Ove is equally insistent. 'Absolutely not,' he said. 'Why should it be? There was no reason. I would not have given it away and he wouldn't have given it away. Who would not jump at the chance to be World Champion? It meant a hell of a lot more to him than it did to me, so don't you worry, he tried his best. Because winning your first World Championship means a hell of a lot. After that it doesn't mean all that much.'

Lanning also recalled another incident, this time at Norwich, when Ove was trying out the new Czechoslovakian speedway machine: 'He was the first to bring in the JAWA, then known as an EsO. They were blue and regarded as something from the dark side of the moon. Nobody had ever seen anything like it. Ove was playing around with the bike and it wasn't really functioning too well. He went into a scratch race final, and the bike was banging and crashing and missing and farting and he missed the start completely. He kicked it and banged it. He had been left at least twenty-five yards behind and he was in against world-class riders. The pits were on the first corner at The Firs and I was standing there and I saw him get the bike going and I swear he went past the three of them on the inside as though they were standing still at quarter throttle. How he did it I do not know. He went inside three absolutely top-class riders who were going flat out and he somehow got the revs up and went past all of them on one corner – I have never seen a manoeuvre like it.

'I remember going into The Firs just before they sold the place. The people who ran Norwich were all hard-nosed businessmen, and the chairman – it wasn't Gordon Parkins, Gordon was just "The Boy" – Harry Wharton said, "I just can't understand this. I cannot run this business at a profit without Ove Fundin being here. When Fundin is not here we don't make money. The only way this stadium can make money is when Ove Fundin is here." I first remember seeing his name when he came to Britain with the Swedish team Filbyterna and they toured the old Third Division tracks. Everybody thought, "Christ, they've got someone here." He didn't look at all like a conventional idea of a speedway rider. He was tall and lanky and thin. He was a beanpole kind of a bloke. People were saying: "There's this bloody bloke with this Swedish team – he ain't half going quick." I seem to remember he was their top scorer.

'I would rate him the best. I have seen all the post-war greats – I didn't see Bluey Wilkinson and the pre-war stars – and I think that in his prime Ove would have beaten Ivan Mauger seven or eight times out of ten. I would place him above Craven, who I think would be next, and then Ronnie Moore. I think Jack Parker would be in there even though he never won a World title, and Briggo and Bruce Penhall and Jack Young – Youngie in his prime was terrific. You can go on through the list. I'd put Crutcher in the top ten I've seen, and Hans Nielsen. You've got to go a long way down before you get to Tony Rickardsson. Ove was "The Governor", he really was. He rode his first World Final in 1954 in which he did nothing. I was at the 1955 World Final, which was the first one I covered. He scored 10 points. That was Peter Craven's final. And the following year he won it. The year after that he should have won it but Barry Briggs stuck him straight into the fence in the run-off.

'When I was ghosting for him, I remember calling his home and being told he was running an oil company and had gone off driving a tanker to Baghdad, or Basra, or somewhere round there. They said, "We don't know where he is but he'll be away for a fortnight." He'd done it because he was bored.

'In my opinion, he is the best all-round rider I have seen in his prime. I will go to my grave saying that. I was fortunate enough to see him when he was in his prime, and I saw him very early in his British career back in 1954 and 1955 when he first rode for Norwich. In my opinion, prime time, he would have beaten anybody else in their prime time. Fundin. I love him dearly. Every time I see him now it's a delight. For my money, he was the greatest of all time.'

It was another phenomenal year for the man they were calling 'Fantastic Fundin'. Ove's lowest score in the 1960 Britannia Shield tournament was 15, his lowest league score was 13, his lowest in the National Trophy was 16. Over twenty-eight official matches he averaged 16 points a match. Having lost the Golden Helmet by default the previous season, he took it back with 'immaculate ease' from

Ronnie Moore in what was described as 'a thrill-packed decider', 2-0 at Ipswich. World Champion Moore had appeared to be completely cool in the pits before the start, in contrast to Fundin, who was inevitably strung up with nerves. But once on the track Ove made no mistake, smashing the track record by two-tenths of a second in the first race – then complaining that his engine was 'missing'. But in the next race he took almost another second off the new record. 'What a performance,' said the match report.

Ove held the Match Race title for the rest of the season, beating Barry Briggs and Ronnie Moore again. His temperament had shown when, after rain forced the postponement of Ron How's first-leg challenge at the beginning of September, How broke a wrist in the World Final and Ove refused to accept a last-minute substitute challenger, claiming the title by default. His reasoning was that he had lost by default the previous year and if the rule was good enough to apply against him, it should also apply in his favour. He was also involved in that other incident with How, when hotheads in the Wimbledon crowd had gone after his blood following their controversial decider in the Gold Cup, resulting in him handing back the trophy. In The Laurels, again at Wimbledon – that far-from-happy hunting ground – Ove was vastly superior to anyone else, winning his five rides for a 15-point maximum. The meeting had been run on the twenty-heat classic championship formula with a 'forced climax' of two semi-finals and a final – the method now used to decide the modern World Championship Grand Prix – with a high-class field of virtual World Final standard that had included Ronnie Moore, Craven, McKinlay, Young, Knutsson, Briggs, Peter Moore and Nigel Boocock. It gave a second chance to riders Ove had already beaten, and he came third in the first semi-final to Craven and Ronnie Moore. Then Ronnie went on to win the final. For once the Wimbledon fans appeared to sympathise with Ove. It was reported that 'this method of running championships is not generally popular'. Many fans were of the opinion that 'Ove wuz robbed' and were at a loss to understand why, if a man had raced against all his opponents and won the meeting with an unbeaten score, he had to go out and win the meeting all over again.

Norwich could also claim to have been robbed of the National Trophy after running into a controversy with referee Arthur Humphrey and going 'on strike' in the second leg of the final at Wimbledon. The Stars took a 16-point first-leg lead over the Dons to Plough Lane, but in heat nine there was 'trouble – as usual – for Norwich at Wimbledon'. Ronnie Moore spun into the fence and damaged a hand. His partner, Jim Tebby, fell at the first turn and was still on the track when Fundin and partner Johnny Chamberlain were completing the lap and were almost upon him. Only then did the referee put on the stop lights, ordering a re-run with all four riders due to an 'unsatisfactory start'. Norwich were outraged. Ronnie Moore withdrew from the race, and the meeting, with a badly bruised hand and was replaced by reserve Gil Goldfinch. On the last bend, Tebby and Chamberlain crashed. Chamberlain was excluded and Tebby, whose machine was picked up by track officials, pushed home for third place and then collapsed. The fact that he was not excluded for 'receiving outside assistance' was the final insult for Norwich who went on strike and refused to continue. It was fully ten minutes before the Stars were persuaded to change their minds, and the incident must have unsettled them because the Dons finally ran up a score of 69-39 and an aggregate win of 115-101. Norwich's crumb of comfort was that Ove scored an 18-point maximum. But Wimbledon were league champions for the third of a four-year winning run, and the Stars slipped one place in the league to fifth, compared with the previous year. But there was some consolation for Ove in winning the Swedish Championship for the third time and leading Sweden to victory with a 12-point maximum in the newly introduced World Team Cup. What a performance indeed.

But the best performance was at Wembley on Saturday 8 September. Ove became World Champion for the second time in another dramatic finale, a three-man decider – the first since 1951 – determining the title-winner after Ove finished the evening on 14 points with Peter Craven and Ronnie Moore – and this time it was Ronnie who could become the first to win the World Championship three times. Briggs, who had made the break from Wimbledon and spent the season at Johnnie Hoskins's New Cross, could too, but he had an off night and was down in sixth place on 9 points. His night was made no better by him being served with a driving summons in the pits as he was about to go out for his last ride.

Craven, who had not dropped a point in the qualifying rounds, equalling Australia's Vic Duggan in the 1947 Speedway Riders' Championship qualifiers, was well on the way to setting a unique record by going through the entire competition unbeaten until he finished second to Ove in heat eighteen. Little Pete had electrified the 70,100 crowd, and the entire pits, by winning heat two by twenty lengths from Briggs and posting a new Wembley track record of 68.8 seconds. It was Ronnie who had beaten Ove after an incredible duel between the pair of them in heat ten, with Briggs well back in third place. Moore was unbeaten after three rides but Craven was faced with two races in succession in heats twelve and thirteen. After winning heat twelve from Ron Johnston, Jack Young and Poland's Henryk Zyto, he had to take on Moore straight away in the following race, and the Empire Stadium erupted when he passed the chequered flag one length ahead of Ronnie. It looked as though popular Peter had the title within his grasp. But everyone had reckoned without Fundin.

They lined up alongside McKinlay and Sormander in heat eighteen, but it was Ove who emerged from the first turn in the lead. Craven chased him for the entire four laps and then on the last bend hit a hole and was thrown forward onto his handlebars, somehow managing to stay on the bike, though obviously in pain. Back in the pits he all but collapsed and had to be helped from his machine. With Moore winning heat nineteen, one of the best World Finals for years ended with a sensational climax – a three-man run-off for the crown.

In the draw for starting positions, Craven was on the inside, Moore on the outside with Ove sandwiched between the two of them in the middle. Ronnie confessed to 'quivering like a jelly'. He had hoped that after five hard rides the meeting would be over, but instead he was facing the toughest race of the night.

Ove says: 'I can't remember the way they chose the gate positions, but I got the middle one – which was the worst one. It was my bad luck to draw the worst gate, but someone had to have it. When I came up to the gate I concentrated harder than ever to make sure that I was first out, because I knew that if I didn't make it my only chance would be to shut off and try to come back. It's easy with not the very best riders, but with riders like Peter Craven and Ronnie Moore you couldn't afford that. There wasn't much of a chance. Therefore I was really concentrating. I just shut off at the gate – that's one of the instances I do remember. And then they never came near me as far as I remember. I didn't even have to look for them.'

The concentration paid off. Ove made a marvellous start with Ronnie close up and Craven marginally behind them. The crowd went delirious as, down the back straight, Ove moved out into the path of Ronnie who attempted to go past him and ended by scraping the skin off his knuckles on the fence. It made him lose his cool and, in the same place next time round, he tried to force a way past Ove on the inside. Fundin was ready for him and closed the gap. Ronnie ran into him and says he thought he had broken his wrist. The ground it caused him to lose allowed Ove to put enough distance between them to give Ronnie no chance of catching him. Craven made a last-lap challenge on Ronnie, but had to settle for third place.

Ove denies he ever employed gamesmanship in situations of such vital importance as that. 'What could I have done?' he says. 'Do the Ivan Mauger thing and come the very last to the tapes? No, I don't think I ever did. If I was ever last up to the gate it would be because they were changing the gear on the bike, or something. I always liked to be first at the gate. If you look back to whenever I raced, you will see that I was nearly always first. Because if you come up first it gives you time to settle down and go through in your head what you are going to do. If you come up there last you come in a rush, and nothing is good in a rush. If you do something in a rush you always forget something. Aub Lawson taught me that. To always arrive at least one hour before a meeting. You can look at the gate, look at the track everywhere, walk the track. Instead, most people just come, get dressed, warm up the bike and then they are out. That's no good.'

When Ivan Mauger and Bernt Persson were in a run-off for the title at Wembley in the 1972 final Ivan confessed that he deliberately rode a slow circuit of the track before coming to the tapes because, he said, Swedes don't like to be kept waiting like that. It was done as an unsettling tactic.

Ove says: 'Nobody likes to be kept waiting like that. I think everyone was angry with Ivan – of course I didn't race that many times against Ivan but he always came up last and then stopped far away from the gate. Your front wheel is supposed to almost touch the tapes and the starter is supposed to make sure you are there. But he did it and did it and did it until the referees probably got so tired of it they let him get away with it. And then it is so easy, you only need that much to roll on and you've got a rolling start. Every race like that should be stopped. But there again, I think the referees knew it and they couldn't have cared less anymore. We have to get this meeting over, we can't stay here all night – that sort of thing. But this is only what goes through my mind.'

What was going through his mind after that momentous decider at Wembley was, like Ronnie, terror. 'I honestly thought I'd had it when Ronnie Moore beat me in heat ten,' he said. 'I never expected Peter to beat him later. When he did, and I knew I had another chance for the title after all, I worked it out that if I could beat Peter we would all likely be in a run-off. The thought terrified me.' He added that he had no idea what he was going to do with the £500 top prize but, he said, 'I've never heard of it being hard to spend.'

The season earned him top place in the world rankings once again. Publishers *Speedway Star & News* remarked that it was 'an unprecedented run of successes that lends weight to the opinion of many speedway experts that Fundin is the greatest rider the sport has ever known'. It was an accolade that none of the pre-war speedway giants had achieved. But behind the scenes, in British speedway's corridors of power, the name of Ove Fundin was not top of the popularity poll. Before the year was out it was confirmed that the 1961 World Final would take place in Sweden, at Malmo. And there was revolutionary talk not only of breaking away from the FIM, but of a blanket ban on foreigners and 'finding our own riders to replace them'.

'It was my doing,' says Ove. 'Of course I was kind of proud. I had already won twice, so of course they screamed for it and they got the

backing of all the other Continentals in the FIM. Britain had only one
vote, but Sweden had all the Continentals with them: Poles, Czechs,
Austrians, Germans, Finns, Danes, Norwegians. We wanted the World
Final to rotate from then on. They just used me to get it. It wasn't
my home track. We used to ride there once a year. It was very much
like the one in Gothenburg, designed by the same man, and it even
looks like the same track. But being in your home country makes a
big difference. Makes you a little bit more cocky, I suppose, and you
know that the others are coming from so much further away than
you, and you feel at home.'

In the run-up to the 1961 World Final Ove reckoned he had clocked
up one million miles in his racing career since he first joined Norwich
in 1955. Rumours persisted that the club was under the threat of closure
and the site being developed for housing, but as in previous years the
rumours were denied. There was no Aub, who stayed at home because
his wife was facing a serious operation, so the Stars relied on Ove more
than ever. He didn't let them down. In the league he turned in an average
of 12.2 points a match and 2.9 points a race, though the Stars slipped
down to seventh place. He also fended off challenges for his Golden
Helmet from Peter Craven, Peter Moore and Ron How. But the threat
of Bjorn Knutsson was growing, and Ove eventually lost the Match
Race Championship to him – the first time two Swedish riders had
met in the competition, the first leg of which at Southampton ended
with Ove and Les Mullins having to plunder in the dead of night a
Rotrax frame from Alec Jackson's shop in the Harrow Road. That did
have a happy ending, Ove winning the European title in Vienna with
Bjorn in second place. There was also the initial Internationale success
won amid a storm of hostility at Harringay.

There were two series of Test matches – Sweden v. Great Britain in
England, and Sweden v. the British Commonwealth in Sweden. The
Swedes lost 5-0 in England and took their revenge with a 5-0 win in
Sweden, where a remarkable performance by Ove saw him drop only
two points in the entire series, scoring 16 in the first Test at Vaxjo and
then sweeping to four successive 18-point maximums at Gothenburg,
Norrkoping, Stockholm and Malmo – a confidence booster for the

forthcoming World Final. An illuminating little paragraph on Ove's abilities emerged from the second Test in Sweden at Gothenburg, which recorded, 'Ove Fundin again proved that he can team ride, nursing Soren Sjosten to 5 points and a total of 17 points in their four rides together, the maximum being 20.' But Ove did not like having to race what he called the 'bloody British Empire'.

He says: 'I remember being very, very angry about the fact that in the so-called English team – or British team – there were Australians and New Zealanders in it. If you look at those teams, there was Ronnie Moore, Barry Briggs, Peter Craven, Ron How, Peter Moore and all those people. It seemed we rode against the rest of the speedway world, because the Germans, the Finns and the Poles and the Russians weren't there at that time. I thought it was very unfair. And even later on, in the World Team Cup, they turned up with the whole empire, didn't they? We were all of us very, very upset about that. But we managed to beat them anyway. Maybe that was one of the reasons why we beat them because we were so angry. It wasn't fair, was it? Poor little Sweden.'

Poor little Sweden? At the time Sweden was considered the leading speedway nation, even though they had lost that year's World Team Cup by a single point to the emerging Poland. But even SVEMO boss Carl 'Pom Pom' Ringblom went on public record to claim that the Test series was a mistake because the Great Britain team was too strong.

This time the reigning World Champion did not have a 'free pass' to the final. The rules were changed and instead of being seeded direct to Malmo, Ove had to take part in the qualifying rounds like everyone else, which he did, only dropping a single point – scoring 15-point maximums in his rounds at Vetlanda, Visby and Oslo, 14 at Gislaved and topping it off in Vienna to lead the eight-strong Continental contingent to Malmo ahead of Knutsson, Sormander, Gote Nordin and Leif Larsson of Sweden, Florian Kapala and Stanislaw Tkocz of Poland and, the first Russian to reach a World Final, Igor Plechanov, of whom Ove was destined to see a great deal.

At Malmo on 15 September Ove Fundin became the first to win the World Championship three times. 'Fundin is the Greatest Champ Ever,' screamed the headlines. But the crowd gave their most

tumultuous applause to second-placed Knutsson. He was pulled out of
the presentation parade Mercedes by jubilant fans and thrown in the air
– the traditional winner's 'bumps'. 'Surely the unluckiest runner-up of
all time?' said the meeting report – though perhaps correspondent Jack
Rollin had not been around when Australia's Jack Biggs missed the 1951
title by one point at Wembley, and then lost a three-man run-off for the
championship behind Jack Young and Split Waterman. Yet it was, without
doubt, Sweden's night, with Ove taking the title, Knutsson second and
Gote Nordin third. Things seemed to be going in threes, as it was the
third time one country had provided the top three – America in 1937,
England in 1949 and now the Swedes. Barry Briggs, Ronnie Moore and
Bob Andrews were the only British-based qualifiers to make any kind
of impression on the dominant Swedes, coping with a slick track in a
meeting that opened in steady drizzle. Even Peter Craven, who crashed
spectacularly in his first ride in heat two, was way down on 6 points.

Knutsson recorded the four fastest times in the four races he won, in
several instances having to fight his way through from the back. But in
the race that mattered, heat sixteen against Fundin, disaster struck. He
tried to ride round Ove on the first turn and fell, striding away from
his crashed bike in disgust and disappointment. Olle Nygren was in
Knutsson's pit crew at Malmo. He says: 'Bjorn was faster than Fundin
all night. Much faster, because he had a good special cam in. In heat
sixteen he had fourth gate and Fundin was third, I think. But I said
to him, "For Christ's sake don't go round Fundin." But he tried to go
round Fundin and that was the end of Knutsson. Ove shovelled him
out. He was tough. You have to be.'

The meeting was full of drama, both on and off the track. The starting
gate threw a fit of mechanical temperament and the tapes were broken
several times, by Knutsson in the very first race, Ron How in heat three
and in heat fourteen Nordin got tied up with the tapes and Tkocz ended
with them draped around his neck. Yet no rider was excluded for tape
breaking. In the end the Swedish officials had to resort to starting races
with a hand-held piece of elastic. The decider looked to be that heat
sixteen when Fundin and Knutsson met, both unbeaten, with Briggs
and How also in the line-up. But Bjorn's fall gifted Briggs two points

and Barry won his final ride in heat seventeen to finish on 12. Ove's last ride was heat nineteen and a maximum appeared a mere formality. But Gote Nordin was also in the race. He was on 9 points and a win would put him level with Briggs. With Knutsson in devastating form, it was practically guaranteed that he would win his last ride in heat twenty, which he duly did easily, by half a lap. The opportunity was there for a three-man run-off for the minor positions with Sweden in with more than a chance of making a clean sweep by taking the first three places. In the pits Sweden's top administrator, Arne Bergstrom, took Ove on one side and ordered him to let Nordin win heat nineteen.

Ove says: 'I wasn't sure I was going to win the meeting, but I think I was more sure than in England that I could do well. There was a lot of pressure, and Bergstrom always wanted to arrange everything. Which he did here. He actually forbade me to win the race. I could have won it on 15 points, but I did it on 14 points because I had to give away one point to Gote Nordin. If I helped him, team rode with him and let him win, then he would have a run-off with Barry and Bjorn Knutsson. So I did it. In the run-off Bjorn won and Gote was second, so the three of us were first, second and third. That Bergstrom... everyone was afraid of him. He was more or less a dictator, which was a good thing for Swedish speedway, as he pretty much introduced it. But if I hadn't listened to Bergstrom that night he would have banned me from riding in England the next season. It was good for Swedish speedway. Of course, it didn't matter to me whether I won it on 14 points or 15 points, as long as I won it.'

Knutsson says he did not know that anything was being arranged for Ove to help Gote win heat nineteen: 'I didn't know that until afterwards. I never thought very much about it, I was riding very well in 1961 and I beat Ove just about every time. I think I should have won the World title in 1961 to be honest, but I didn't have enough experience. I was very unhappy that I happened to have Ove on my inside when we met in heat sixteen. He went wide and I fell on my bum, as you probably know. I don't know about Bergstrom telling Ove to let Gote win but I presume, or think, it would be like that. I was not aware that anything was going on at the time.'

When Ove and Gote left the start in heat nineteen, with Florian Kapala and England's Cyril Maidment, it must have been quite obvious what was going on. One report said: 'The champion safely negotiates his fellow countryman into first place.' Barry Briggs observed: 'The only point he [Ove] dropped was a gift to fellow countryman Gote Nordin in his last ride. Ove throttled back to allow Nordin to collect a win, which gave him 12 points.' Gote, asked if he remembered anything about the incident, said: 'I do about this occasion. Early in the meeting Ove and I made an arrangement to give him points in heat nineteen if he needed them. But later on, when I had ridden my fourth race and we were ready for heat nineteen, we realised that it was me who needed the points. If I had three points I should be in the run-off for the second, third and fourth. Bergstrom came up and said to Ove, "You have to give Gote three points in this heat." And Ove said, "Yes, all right." Ove was acting under orders from Bergstrom.'

Olle Nygren was in on the whole thing. He confirmed: 'Of course Gote Nordin was aware of what was going on. He was told by Bergstrom: "You have to try and stay with Ove and Ove will help you and nurse you, and then he will let you win." That's what he was told.' Bob Andrews was a fascinated witness to the incident. He says: 'I was kneeling down making out I was busy doing my bike and got the gist of it. Not word for word because my Swedish is not too good. Bergstrom was laying down the law, and the body language told me enough, with English coming from Ove. Ove wasn't a happy chappie. I was annoyed with myself because in my race before I was in front of Nordin and Craven and Tkocz. I nearly spun around on myself and was hit by Nordin, which straightened me up. I went from last to third and missed second by a small margin. Had I won that race, I would have been in the run-off for second place.'

When it came to it, there was Gote, Bjorn and Barry Briggs. So was there also an arrangement between the two Swedes? 'No. We didn't say anything about the heat or the run-off,' says Gote. 'Bjorn took it as a normal heat. So either of us was out to win that one. There was no arrangement to block Briggs. He tried to get his points, but he didn't get more than one. After it was all over we didn't do anything special, but the newspapers did. They were taking a lot of pictures of Ove, Bjorn and myself with our wives. There was a lot of press interest because it had happened only twice before – the Americans in 1937 and the English in 1949.' Barry claimed that in the run-off, started by the elastic band released by a Swedish official, he was not even near the gate when it was released, but it had been 'poetic justice for the best rider of the night – Knutsson – to get second place'.

Ove denied that anyone had ever offered to sell him points or asked to buy any from him. 'I was never in need of doing it. The only time I could have sold a point would have been that incident but there was no mention of paying me for what I did, not even for the money I lost on the point. They didn't even make that up for me. As far as I remember I didn't even get a thank you for it. Though Bergstrom did. He came up to me and said something like: "That's exactly the way I wanted it. Thanks. Now we can only hope that Gote will win the run-off and then we will have the three of you."'

The question of 'buying and selling' World Final points has always been vexed. But there is no doubt that it went on, no matter how much we would all like to believe that the supreme prize in speedway racing is and always has been decided on pure sporting endeavour. To pretend that point trading never did take place displays extreme naivety and a disinclination to live in the real world. Ove is quite unequivocal on the subject. He says: 'No. I have not bought or sold World Final points either way. But I'm quite sure it has happened. If you look through all my finals there wouldn't have been any need for me to do it. I don't think I was ever in a position to buy a point. Of course earlier on in a meeting, like in that 1956 final when I scored only one point in the first race, should I have gone up to someone in that first race and paid for that? That would be stupid because you would have to buy the whole bloody meeting.

'Aub always used to go on to me about Jack Biggs in his last race in the 1951 final when he needed only one point to win the World Championship. Aub told me that they approached him and asked him, "Are you willing to pay something for a point?" This is what Aub said – I never heard it from Jack Biggs. Aub said there were people in that race who had no need of the points because they couldn't win anyway. One was Aub himself with only 5 points. Look here, that point didn't mean a thing to him. He could have given that point. It doesn't matter where you are – fifth or sixth. Fred Williams was another one. He had scored only 6 points. Aub specially said that an offer was made, but Jack said, "No thank you." Because he was so sure of himself. Aub said that he was quite mean and he was so confident. That's why they all went out and beat the hell out of him, that's what Aub said.'

Only Split Waterman, the other rider in the race, was in with any chance of getting on the rostrum. He had 9 points. That year's title holder, Fred Williams, described how Lawson came up to him and said, 'Has Jack said anything to you?' Fred told him, 'No.' And Fred said, 'So we just went out and fixed him – we all moved out on the first turn. It's terrible really, but that's what we did, because he had said nothing.' Waterman won the race, putting him, Jack Young and Biggs all on 12 points and in a three-man run-off for the title. So Biggs had a second chance, but even then he failed, finishing last. Young won and Waterman was second.

There was a phrase for trading points. It was: 'Can you cover for me?' Olle Nygren explained that 'can you cover for me?' meant: 'Will you talk to the other riders and more or less ask them to stay out of my way?' Money wouldn't change hands on the night, says Olle, but of course it would have done at another time. 'Everybody did it,' says Olle. 'We learned it from our Mr Bergstrom. I was in the Swedish Championship qualifying rounds once, and I was winning, winning, winning. Then Bergstrom said one of the riders in my own team needs to win this race and you are in it, so you have to be second. I said to him, "I don't want anybody to tell me such things. If I am beaten I might be second but if I try I might win it." So he said, "No, that's an order." Everybody did it. It was all in the game – the name of the trade. If you didn't do what they wanted, Bergstrom and SVEMO could make it difficult for you.

'All of us hated SVEMO because they always worked against us. They never helped us. Fundin hated them because he could have ridden more in England and got even better. But he had to ride poxy open meetings and league matches. So they stopped our permits to prevent us going to England. They actually tried to stop us going. I could have earned a fortune, but they banned me and stopped me. That's why I started road racing – to get away from them. But when Fundin won that 1956 final – it was like Ingemar Johansson beating Floyd Patterson for boxing's World Heavyweight Championship in 1959. You would never have thought a Swedish boxer could win a world crown, but everyone remembers that. Fundin had the same effect. Not with the journalists because they didn't like anyone riding a bike. They said that it was not a sport because you had an engine helping you.'

Malmo was described as 'one of the best organised finals'. That, and the success of their riders, emboldened the Swedes to consider applying for the 1962 final as well, at Stockholm. Writer Jack Brodie, reviewing the situation, concluded that 'most observers agree Malmo outshone anything that has gone on at the Empire Stadium – and few will deny the lavishness of these presentations.' Brodie went on: 'Sweden will point out that England staged fifteen finals on the trot, and that their request to stage the meeting for a second time under these conditions is reasonable.' He reported that Russia too wanted the 1963 final, and Poland and Austria were other candidates waiting in line for later on.

Perhaps Brodie was not at Malmo at all because plenty of people should have been questioning 'the lavishness' of the presentations. Maybe he was at another final, otherwise he would have been among the observers who witnessed the debacle of the malfunctioning starting gate, and the pathetically amateurish introduction of a piece of elastic to start races in the most important meeting of the speedway year on the world stage involving the sport's finest riders; and that the crowd had been a mere 25,000 in a stadium with a 31,000 capacity, even though the cost to British fans of flying 'with the riders' to Malmo was only £20 return, in-flight refreshments and stadium tickets included. Wembley had been pulling in almost three times as many spectators as that, even in the darkest days. The Swedish ambitions were dashed when the World Final returned to the Empire Stadium in 1962, though the inevitability of the finals being shared around had to be faced if the sport's major competition was to be a genuine World Championship.

In January 1962 Ove was voted, if not top of the speedway pops, top of the world rankings once again, for the fifth time in six years. During that winter he went ice racing, signing for two meetings in Moscow and then another four in Siberia, because he wanted to see what the Soviet Union was like and because travel had always been one of his 'vices'. The Russian conditions followed him back to England where Norwich's opening meeting of the new season was snowed off.

Individually the season began well. Ove took back the Match Race Championship from Bjorn Knutsson. As World Champion, Ove was the first challenger on 8 May, springing a surprise by winning the first leg 2-0 at Knutsson's home track, Southampton. Fundin won the toss for the first race and from the inside put in a faultless ride. In the second, though Bjorn was first away, Ove closed the gap brilliantly to ride inside Bjorn on the first corner of the third lap and win unchallenged. Bjorn was described as being 'off colour'. He had fallen while sleepwalking and injured a leg that required thirty stitches in the wound. Southampton promoter Charlie Knott wanted to call off the Match Race, but Bjorn insisted on riding. Three days later in the second leg at Norwich Ove again won 2-0 to become champion once more. The first race was a steady win but in the second Bjorn borrowed Barry Briggs's bike and almost caught Ove on the last lap. Fundin went on to win the final of the Malcolm Flood Memorial Trophy from Briggs, Ronnie Moore and Eric Williams. Knutsson, obviously still suffering the effects of his sleepwalking mishap, scored only 4 points and did not make the semi-finals. Ove kept the Golden Helmet for the season by beating Briggs and Peter Craven later on.

It was in May that Ove, to his acute annoyance, learned that even though he was World Champion he was going to have to ride in all the qualifying rounds of the competition to get to Wembley – there would be no seeding of the title holder direct to the final this time. His reported annoyance was, apparently, putting it mildly. When he was told, he was said to have given 'a snort of supreme disgust'. But on his way to the final he helped Sweden win a two-match Test series against Russia and also won the Swedish Championship for the fourth time and the Internationale for the second time.

46. *Right:* Fundin with his hero, Ronnie Moore. 'Ronnie could have gone much further if he had been more selfish,' said Ove.

47. *Below:* Champion again: screen star Norman Wisdom about to make the presentation to Ove on his second title success at Wembley in 1960. Runner-up Ronnie Moore is on the right and third-placed Peter Craven on the left.

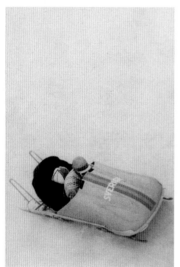

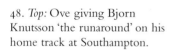

48. *Top:* Ove giving Bjorn Knutsson 'the runaround' on his home track at Southampton.

49. *Above:* Bobsleighing.

50. *Above right:* Long-tracking.

51. *Right:* Ice racing.

**GEAR RATIOS FOR 42 TOOTH CLUTCH**

| E. | C/Shft. | Rear Wheel | | | | | |
|----|---------|------|------|------|------|------|------|
|    |         | 55   | 56   | 57   | 58   | 59   | 60   |
| 17 | 14 | 9.7  | 9.88 | 10.05 | 10.23 | 10.41 | 10.58 |
| 18 | 14 | 9.17 | 9.33 | 9.5  | 9.66 | 9.83 | 10.0 |
| 19 | 14 | 8.68 | 8.84 | 9.0  | 9.15 | 9.31 | 9.47 |
| 20 | 14 | 8.25 | 8.4  | 8.55 | 8.7  | 8.85 | 9.0 |
| 21 | 14 | 7.85 | 8.0  | 8.14 | 8.28 | 8.42 | 8.56 |
| 17 | 15 | 9.05 | 9.22 | 9.38 | 9.53 | 9.71 | 9.88 |
| 18 | 15 | 8.55 | 8.71 | 8.86 | 9.02 | 9.17 | 9.33 |
| 19 | 15 | 8.1  | 8.25 | 8.40 | 8.54 | 8.69 | 8.84 |
| 20 | 15 | 7.7  | 7.88 | 7.98 | 8.12 | 8.26 | 8.40 |
| 21 | 15 | 7.33 | 7.46 | 7.60 | 7.73 | 7.86 | 8.0 |
| 17 | 16 | 8.49 | 8.64 | 8.81 | 8.95 | 9.11 | 9.26 |
| 18 | 16 | 8.02 | 8 16 | 8.31 | 8.45 | 8.60 | 8.75 |
| 19 | 16 | 7.59 | 7.73 | 7.87 | 8.01 | 8.13 | 8.28 |
| 20 | 16 | 7.21 | 7.35 | 7.48 | 7.61 | 7.74 | 7.87 |
| 21 | 16 | 6.87 | 7.0  | 7.12 | 7.25 | 7.37 | 7.50 |
| 17 | 17 | 7.99 | 8.13 | 8.28 | 8.42 | 8.57 | 8.72 |
| 18 | 17 | 7.54 | 7.68 | 7.82 | 7.96 | 8.09 | 8.23 |
| 19 | 17 | 7.16 | 7.28 | 7.41 | 7.54 | 7.67 | 7.80 |
| 20 | 17 | 6.79 | 6.91 | 7.04 | 7.16 | 7.28 | 7.41 |
| 21 | 17 | 6.47 | 6.58 | 6.70 | 6.82 | 6.94 | 7.05 |

52. Ove's gear chart.

53. Lining up to pounce: Barry Briggs about to exploit a rare gap that has appeared between Ove and the white line. (Alf Weedon)

54. The Terrible Twins – the bikes, that is. Norwich's two track spares receive the expert attention of Les Mullins and Olle Nygren.

55. The man who had a big-meeting habit of putting one over on Ove, Russia's Igor Plechanov, squeezes in close at Mallila in 1967.

56. *Opposite above:* Going for gold – the Golden Helmet: Ove about to race Ronnie Moore for the British Match Race Championship in June 1960. Ove had lost the title by default the previous September, but took it back from Ronnie after winning this match at Norwich and a decider at Ipswich. Don Clarke, speedway correspondent of sponsors the *Sunday Mirror*, is with Ronnie and his sports editor George Casey is with Ove.

57. *Opposite below:* Saying it with flowers. This time it's the CTS Trophy, and Aub also has something to smile about – a new tyre. The gentleman on the right is Norwich director Jack Thompson, and that's his wife Phyllis on the left.

58. Introducing son Eric to 'Old Faithful', Norwich Track Spare No. 2.

59. *Above left:* Teacher and pupil: Aub Lawson congratulates Ove in front of the main grandstand at The Firs in 1960 on being World Champion and British Match Race Champion.

60. *Above right:* Another World Final – but this time Olle Nygren is in Ove's section of the pits to offer help and advice.

61. *Right:*
Psyching people out, Briggs style: Barry 'Mr Cool' Briggs takes a laid-back look at a Wembley World Final practice session, while the Swedish camp – Arne Bergstrom and Ove – look on all smiles to show they are not convinced.

62. *Below:*
Smuggling the spoils: Ove transferring Czechoslovakian liquor from the Russians' tour bus after avoiding customs checks.

63. A tough cookie: Jimmy Gooch, the man who 'sorted out' Fundin and was sacked for it.

64. With a wire brush you don't have to have too much mechanical knowledge to go to work on a tyre.

65. *Above:* Celebrity golf pairs on the course at Malmo in the 1974 Scandinavian Enterprise Open. From left: Kjell Johansson, boxer Ingemar Johansson, Tony Jacklin and Ove.

66. *Below:* World Pairs Champions 1968: Ove with Torbjorn Harrysson. (Trevor Meeks)

67. Ove watches from the Wembley terraces as his bikes are tested for the 1963 World Final, crude bandages round his injury.

68. *Above left:* Some famous last words: 'I'll have a ride.' Unable to resist the temptation, Ove thought he'd 'just try it' and crashed. Wimbledon boss Ronnie Greene is holding his foot with *Sunday Mirror* speedway columnist Don Clarke looking on. Nigel Boocock is cradling Ove's head.

69. *Above right:* You won't be needing this then! Comedian Charlie Drake takes away Ove's support during the 1963 pre-meeting parade. But it was Ove's night for the fourth time, confirmation of an unprecedented sporting achievement.

70. *Right:* The picture of a pensive Ove that appeared in *Speedway Post* following his ban in 1966.

# THE MAN WHO WON'T BE THERE

HE sits at the back of the pits in Vaxjo, Sweden, patiently cleaning his goggles.

He awaits the call of action to compete in the Swedish Championship round.

He answers it by getting a 15-point maximum to qualify for the Swedish Final for at least victory there would be some consolation.

He can remember, of course.

He can remember 1954 when he scored two points in his first World Championship Final.

He can remember 1956, 1960, 1961 or 1963 as the years he won the World title for a record four occasions.

He can remember every World Final since that 1954 debut. After all he has ridden in them all.

He will watch the 1966 World Final with spectators.

He was suspended at the time of the Swedish Qualifying Rounds.

He is said, by some, to be the greatest of them all.

He will be missed on the track at Ullevi even if he is watching in the stands.

He is OVE FUNDIN.

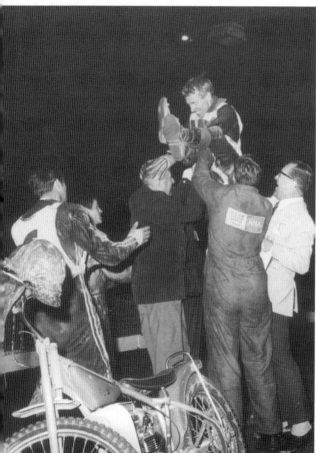

71. *Above:* Swansong for the master: Ove leads fellow Swede Bengt Jansson at Wembley in the vital run-off for the 1967 World title. (Trevor Meeks)

72. *Left:* Crowning glory: Ove being given the traditional bumps after his record fifth triumph in the 1967 World Championship at Wembley, with fellow finalists Barry Briggs, left, and Rick France joining in. The hybrid EsO/JAP machine that carried him to victory is in the foreground. (Trevor Meeks)

73. *Opposite below:* Doing a favour for a friend: Trevor Redmond persuaded Ove to join Wembley in 1970 and here he is at the Empire Stadium wearing the famous Wembley Lions race jacket. (Trevor Meeks)

74. *Above:* The boss. Businessman Ove at the wheel of one of his trucks at the start of another personal delivery.

75. *Above:* Soccer star: Ove playing in a charity football match in Tranas.

76. *Left:* The author with Ove outside the Fundin home in France. (Picture: Ioanna Fundin)

77. *Below:* This is how Ove likes to do his motorcycling these days. (Picture: Annika Fundin)

78. *Above:* Driving his computer: Ove in his office at home.

79. *Right:* Mr President: Ove being inducted with the presidential chain of office by his old friend Reg Fearman on his election as president of the Veteran Speedway Riders' Association in 1993.

80. *Below:* The picture gallery: Ove in front of his favourite action study.

81. The winning combination – Mullins and Fundin. Les and Ove together again at a recent Norwich reunion.

82. An awards ceremony for being Swedish speedway's Man of the Millennium.

83. Still winning: Ove accepting the Rider Cup, the Veteran Speedway Riders' Association golf trophy, from modern Poole promoter Matt Ford.

It was the first year of handicapping the Big Five and, as a consequence, Ove's National League performance was poor by his standards – even worse than his first season in Britain – with an overall average of 9.49 points a match, and Norwich slumped to fifth place in a league of only seven teams. Then, on 25 August, only fifteen days before the World Final, Ove crashed with Wimbledon's Ron How at Norwich and ended up in hospital with a nasty leg injury. Norwich supporter Keith Farman was at the meeting. He says: 'We had season tickets for the grandstand. It was in heat two. Fundin and How were racing neck and neck and, as they came past us How, on the inside, moved out and took Ove hard into the pits bend fence. I was up out of my seat and got to the safety fence together with a lot of the other Norwich fans. We all believed that How had deliberately fenced Ove. This was the only time that I ever got really mad with a rider and, like all the Norwich fans, booed How. It got a bit heated with all the stadium booing, and later when How was back in the pits someone threw a brick at him. They were racing so close, and Fundin could not avoid a collision. Both riders were thrown into the fence. How, fortunately, was uninjured, although he did not ride again. Fundin was taken to hospital. We were told that How's engine had seized. But did How have engine trouble? At the time it certainly did not look as though he did, and that night there were not many Stars supporters who believed that he had.'

Ove insists that it was an accident. He says: 'Ron How seized an engine in front of me and I ran into the back of his bike – not him, but his bike. It was a handicap year. Ron How would have been on the gate before me.' Les Mullins remembered the accident well: 'When Ove got injured that night at Norwich, when he and Ron How crashed and he injured his leg quite badly, that was a fortnight before the World Final and he was favourite to be the first to win the World Championship three times in a row. Nobody else had done it. I was in the workshop and I didn't know how badly he had been hurt. The doctor came in to me and said, "Come and have a word with your man, I can't do anything with him. He won't go to hospital." In the ambulance room Ove had his leg covered with a big lump of cotton wool. I said, "What's the problem, Ove?" He said, "They want to send me to hospital." So I said, "Well, there must be a reason otherwise they wouldn't want to send you to hospital." I asked the doctor if I could have a look at his injury. He pulled away the cotton wool and there was a big gash on his leg. They were worrying about damage to the main tendon. They wanted to get him to hospital to get it together. I just put it back and said, "There isn't an argument, is there? He'll have to go to hospital." I won't say exactly what he said. He just blew his top and said, "I thought you were my friend. I thought I could rely on you." And I thought, "Oh, here we go again." They put him in the ambulance and away he went. We were going up north I think for a meeting and on Sunday we thought we'd better just pop into the hospital to see how he is before we went. At Norwich Hospital we walked in the ward. Well, as soon as he spotted me, me being the one who had sent him off to hospital, it was: "You're no friend of mine anymore. You've had it, mate!" The nurse said, "He's a pain."'

Ove says: 'I was in hospital overnight, and the next day I refused to stay. I probably wasn't too nice to them. Someone came to get me out because I didn't have my car or anything. They put me in plaster. I remember I had to have it redone it a couple of times, because I rode one meeting in Gothenburg and I had to go and see this doctor in Vienna. He took me to the hospital and they put another plaster on it. The doctor more or less refused because he said, "If you go out there again it's very likely that in ten years time we will have to operate on it and you will finish up with a stiff leg."

'It was quite a bad one. You can still see the scar even now. I still have trouble with it if I go running. Two things that stiffen it up for me are when I go running or sit in the car for a long time. I have to exercise. Even after I finished speedway I used to go to the doctor quite often to build up the muscles again. But it doesn't bother me when I cycle, strangely enough. You know when you run – I've forgotten exactly what it is – but when you run you come down with maybe 1,000 kilos of weight on your foot. With cycling it's only movement, and on the contrary that does it good. I suppose I have been lucky with injuries. As I said, if you don't start off a bit wild you won't get anywhere. And if you do start off wild, there's quite a chance that you'll hurt yourself – and you'll never get anywhere either. I suppose I was lucky that I have nothing permanent.'

The day before the accident, Ove had gone to Belle Vue and beaten
Peter Craven in the first leg of the August Match Race Championship.
After both had machine problems, Ove won 2-1. Four days after the
crash they were due to meet in the second leg at Norwich, which
Ove had to forfeit because of his injuries. The World Final was a mere
seven days away.

Les Mullins says: 'When he got out of hospital and they had strapped
him up, I talked to him about it and he said, "Well, we'll go to Wembley.
We'll try." At the meeting he was in a lot of pain, and the funny part
about it was the gateman came up to me and said, "I've got someone
who says he's Ove Fundin's doctor down at the gate – Konrad. He wants
to come in." I said, "Yes, that's okay. He's got to come in to give Ove an
injection, so I understand."' According to Ronnie Moore, Konrad was
the most colourful character in the pits. He was wearing the national
costume of Lapland – all oranges and blacks and browns – and he had
brought reindeer skins and antlers as gifts for the top three riders.

Les recalled: 'He came up and oh my God. He was dressed all in
this Laplander gear. He had brought ice to pack round Ove's leg. And
that's how he got through the meeting. He finished third. I think that
was one of the most fabulous nights. To think that he could even get a
third under those conditions, because there were no punches pulled in
those days. They would knock him off as soon as look at him to win
the World Championship, whether he had an injury or not. Afterwards,
when we went up for the meal in the Wembley restaurant that night,
they all stood up and applauded.'

Ove says: 'My friend, Dr Konrad Basler, he was Yugoslavian, he gave
me an injection in the foot. He came over to stay with me a couple of
days beforehand. He wanted to see a World Final. Being a doctor he
said, "I'll fix you all right, don't worry." I was prepared to ride without
any painkillers. Dr Carlo Biagi, the Southampton doctor and a friend
to all injured speedway riders, designed a special boot for me to wear.
You know when people have flat feet, they give you a lifting insert
into your shoe. He fitted one of them into my boot so that I could
stand on the footrest. It was the right foot, which you put all your
weight on. But even with the insert it was too painful so Konrad gave

me an injection. It was the painkiller they give you at the dentist's. I couldn't have injected myself because I'm too scared.'

On the pre-meeting parade, Ove limped out with the aid of a pair of crutches and a wire cage supporting his injured knee. Though he won his first ride in heat three, the title really slipped away with a second-ride last place in his toughest race, against Barry Briggs, Peter Craven and Bjorn Knutsson, and then a third in his next. But two wins in his final rides, amazingly, put him in a run-off with Bjorn Knutsson for the last place on the rostrum. Ove led all the way with Bjorn falling in a desperate last-bend effort. It was Craven's night, a second title for him, and a second place for Briggs. It was also the final when people began to take note of the EsO machines ridden by Russia's Igor Plechanov. Though his score was a modest 7 points and tenth place overall, the age of the EsO, latterly the JAWA, was on the horizon.

Two days after the final Ove met the man who had taken his World Championship title from him in the Match Race decider at Wimbledon and, shrugging off the injuries that had made it such a difficult night for him at Wembley, 'in a brilliant exhibition of riding', beat Craven 2-0 to retain the Golden Helmet until the following season.

At the beginning of the 1963 season, the Speedway Riders' Association and the Speedway Control Board decreed that teams would be allowed only one foreigner each. So Norwich threatened to pull out of the league unless they were allowed to include both Fundin and Nygren in the Stars side. They got their way, and Norwich had one of their most successful seasons. They were runners-up to Belle Vue in the league and went on to become National Trophy winners for the second time, beating Belle Vue in the final. This may have been something of a hollow victory, coming as it did just after the tragic death of Peter Craven. The Wizard of Balance had top scored on 14 points for the Aces in the first leg at Manchester on 7 September – only one week before the World Final – when, ironically, Norwich were without Fundin who had crashed and was out of action with foot and shoulder injuries. Belle Vue took an 18-point lead to The Firs on 28 September, four days after Craven's death, but the Aces were also without their other top scorer, Dick Fisher, and the remnants of the once fine team that had seen them top the league had no answer to

Fundin, who was back and in devastating form. Newly crowned World Champion for a record fourth time, Ove led the Stars to a 30-point win with a 15-point maximum. Ove's encounters with Craven during the year had included first losing – and then winning back – the Golden Helmet, which he successfully defended against Bjorn Knutsson in September.

For Fundin 1963 was another tremendous year. After struggling somewhat the previous season, the first year of handicapping, he appeared to have adapted totally to the mammoth task of coming from the back in every race through having to start twenty yards behind. He scored more points than anyone else in league and National Trophy matches, 349, for an average of 12.03, despite the irritating injuries. The Big Five had become the Big Four early in the year, when Ronnie Moore crashed and broke a leg, and later decided to retire from speedway completely. The 'Big Three' behind Ove were Bjorn Knutsson on 311, Barry Briggs on 298 and Peter Craven on 279 – although Nigel Boocock popped into the big time with a total of 311 as well.

There was no let-up in the anti-Fundin feeling. Controversy and animosity continued to centre on Ove. The worst, and most unsettling example, was the public bribery allegations at the Wimbledon Inernationale where he made it three wins in a row. 'I have seen some most unpleasant scenes at different tracks,' said Ove. 'People who don't like to see me winning, people who don't seem to like seeing any successful Continental winning.' He could not understand the hostile attitudes on the terraces. He was always sociable, always willing to sign autographs. 'What do the British fans want?' he asked in desperation.

About this time, Sheila Blakeman-Shead was a massive Ove Fundin fan. Then a schoolgirl and now a deputy head teacher living in Linconshire, she recalls: 'I remember that speedway fans just wanted anyone to win except Fundin. I had been to speedway matches at Wolverhampton, which is where I lived, for as long as I can remember and have fond memories of falling asleep on my father's shoulder on the way home. But the hero of my life was Ove Fundin. We used to travel to Coventry's home matches and any international event staged there just to see him. I was sixteen years old and quite a good artist, I subsequently did a degree in Fine Art. I had drawn a portrait of Ove that my father insisted

I give to him, which I did at Coventry, a very embarrassing moment for a sixteen year old. He seemed genuinely pleased, and after that he recognised me at any track I went to and would come over and chat. I did a small oil painting of him and made dolls in leathers with helmets and full Norwich gear for Eric, his son, which I also gave to him.

'I saw all his World Championship wins, even travelling with my parents to Gothenburg and to Germany for the World Team Cup. I spent holidays in various parts of the country with my parents, as long as it meant that I could go and see a meeting when Norwich were the visitors. Ove had so much time for his fans. Even with his leg in plaster at Wembley, arriving at the arena for the World Championship he still had time to recognise me, come over and say hello and introduce me to other riders. He gave me a lift home once from Cradley Heath. He was on his way to Manchester and realised that Wolverhampton was on the way. It was exciting to be steered by Ove through crowds of autograph-hunting fans to his car, if only for a lift to the nearest roundabout to my home. He played on his fame, of course. I know this is not a big deal, but something must be included about how approachable he was and how much time he had for his fans.'

For the second year in succession, Ove was not fully fit when it came to the World Final but, compared with 1962, his shoulder and foot injuries were not quite so serious. No crutches this time, but a walking stick accompanied him on the parade and presentation at the beginning of the meeting. Though Olle Nygren says, 'That was probably a bit of phsychological warfare,' Ove insists it was not. Les Mullins said Ove told him, 'We'll go down to Wembley for practice, and we'll get Olle Nygren to try the bikes.' Nygren says: 'I was not his adviser – I couldn't tell him what was happening on the track, that was up to him. I tested his bikes that year, 1963, when he got injured and he had a stick and limped at Wembley. He had five bikes – two or three JAPs and two EsOs. He couldn't test them. I took his practice rides on the track. He said you have to sort out which is the best one from the gate, and I did. I picked the right bike. It was a JAP. But he rode JAP engines in EsO/JAWA frames – they were good frames.'

Les remembers: 'Ove said to me, "All I want you to do is give me a bike that will start well. If it starts well, I'll do the rest." Those were his exact words. Olle was carrying a little bit of weight in those days. We tried the bikes out and he came back and said, "They are good. Yes, they'll do." Then suddenly Ove said, "I'll have a ride." So what he did was go down the home straight and into the bottom bend and fall off. I said to him, "Why didn't you keep off it?" He said, "I thought I'd just try it."'

Ove ended up with a big crowd round him – riders, reporters and photographers – being cradled in Nigel Boocock's lap, his injured leg bound up with scarves and his head in his hands. He says: 'I'd tried to take part in the practice and I just couldn't stand on my foot. It was too painful, that's why I fell off.' Barry Briggs claims that Ove was blaming it all on him. According to Barry they had been practising together with Bjorn Knutsson and a 'desperate' Ove had tried to pass him on the inside. 'Unfortunately there wasn't enough room and Ove went thumping to earth. When we came round and stopped, there was Ove lying flat out with Nigel Boocock holding his head and laughing. Ove was trying to win another Oscar. I offered him a ride back to the pits and on the way he asked, "What were you doing, Barry? You were going so slow, and you made me crash."' Barry confessed to thinking: after that Ove is going to be no good at all on final night.

Ove's injuries had restricted his scoring in the World Team Cup in Vienna – a mere 7 points – again won by Sweden and led by Knutsson on 11 and Soderman on 10. Knutsson had taken the Swedish title, topped the Continental qualifiers in the European Final of the World Championship in Gothenburg with a 15-point maximum to Ove's 13, and was strongly fancied for Wembley – provided he could overcome his well-known big-night nerves. Craven had led the British rounds by a single point, 42, from Briggs on 41, and both were obvious danger men. But the handsome Norwegian newcomer Sverre Harrfeldt, who was with Wimbledon, was tipped as a likely shock contender. At 62,000, the crowd was not sensational, but the meeting certainly was.

The Barry Briggs assessment of Ove's ability to perform well on final night took only as long as heat three to end up – with Barry – in the Wembley shale. Harrfeldt and Knutsson both dropped points – the Norwegian to Boocock in the opening heat, and Bjorn to Craven in heat two. Fundin went to the gate with Briggs, Ron How and Russia's

Boris Samorodov in the next. Ove's front wheel came up as they left
the tapes with Briggs disputing the lead with him round the first bend.
They got only as far as the fourth turn when Samorodov rode into Ron
How and the race was stopped. How was carried off and Boris excluded,
but the furious Russian, in his first World Final, refused to leave the
track. There was almost fifteen minutes of chaos while, to a chorus of
booing, officials tried to persuade Boris to go quietly so that the race
could be re-run. As the others got ready again, Samorodov appeared on
the track once more before finally bowing to the inevitable and retiring
to the pits to more derision and scornful boos from the terraces. In the
re-run Fundin was first again, with Briggs impatiently challenging. On
the last bend of lap three, Barry's patience ran out and, roaring round
the outside of Fundin, he hit a slick patch and came crashing down. All
he could do was remount for the odd point while Fundin, in spite of
his painful foot and shoulder, skated past the chequered flag to record
the fastest time of the night. Neither the commotion with Samorodov
nor his nagging hurts was able to weaken Fundin's resolve. He lived for
nights such as these and absolutely nothing was allowed to interfere with
his concentration. He didn't even want to know who was in his races
or who his next opponents were.

He says: 'I think I wanted to know if there was anyone I needed to be
– I wouldn't say scared of – taking extra notice of. And of course I wanted
to know which gate I was on, which is quite important. I always picked
my spot out of the way at Wembley. Arne Bergstrom used to come to
me at Wembley and try to tell me what to do. He couldn't ride himself.
He had been a manager and I think he wanted to offer good advice. But
I didn't need good advice – it's too bloody late anyway on the night. I
didn't want him to tell me what to do. I knew what to do, he didn't. But
I didn't even want to look at the others. I didn't want to know what was
going on. I wanted to be out of the way of the other riders. I wanted to
concentrate on my racing and not care about the others.'

Ove clocked up another win two heats later, but disaster struck Craven
in heat six. Badly away, the Wizard of Balance fought his way to the
front and then his wonderful balancing skill deserted him for once and
he came down in front of How and Jim Lightfoot, remounting like

Briggs for the odd point after Per Tage Svenson of Sweden dropped it as well. Briggs went on to win his next three rides, one of which was at the expense of Knutsson. Craven crashed again in heat nine and was stretchered off with a knee injury. The 1962 champion's title was gone – and within a few days he would be dead. Samorodov won the race and, to make up for his first-ride wrecking excursion, was quietly picking up the points. He ended the night on 11 points in fourth place. It was his first World Final and, but for his heat three disaster, he could have been Russia's first World Champion. Knutsson overcame his nerves after two rides and took a win at Fundin's expense in heat eleven. But after the fourth round Fundin was leading by one point, needing a win from his last ride in heat eighteen to clinch the title. Against Peter Moore, Lightfoot and Leo McAuliffe, he made one of his trademark lightning starts, but decided to ride an ultra-cautious race and won – in the slowest time of the night. The headlines proclaimed: 'It's Ove's Title for the Fourth Time' – this was a record. His one fear, as he cruised back to the pits towards the inevitable reception committee of fellow riders waiting to throw him in the air in celebration, was that they might be rough with him. He was scared of landing on his injured shoulder or leg – 'and that might cripple me'.

'The guy with the gammy leg and the battered shoulder made it,' reported Eric Linden. 'Ove Fundin, winner of the Speedway Championship of the World for the fourth time. And now, who can possibly argue that this Swedish firebrand is not the greatest rider who has ever sat on a saddle? At Wembley he overcame the handicap of three broken bones in his right foot and strained ligaments in his right shoulder, in a fantastic display on a fantastic night.' Ove admitted that the night had been his greatest thrill. 'Never before am I so happy about winning a title,' he said, 'because this was the title I was sure I wasn't going to win.' There was the missing Ronnie Moore, a situation he thought would inspire his old rival Barry Briggs to be even more determined, and there was the hostility at some tracks. 'I have never had such unpleasant scenes before,' he said. Then there were the injuries and the fall in practice. 'I take a great risk riding patched up. Walking across for the parade before the final started was agony. I am thinking that if the leg goes after, say, one race, I am finished. So I think I must be careful. I concentrate on gating and don't try anything ambitious on the turns.' But in the end, it was, one reporter commented 'as near a perfect exhibition as one could wish to see.'

While Ove was winning that record fourth World title on 14 September, Mona was giving birth to their fourth child. They said they had provisionally called the child Charlie. But Ove says: 'It was Paul. Everybody kept asking us what we were going to call him and we said we only had a working name for him and that is Charlie.'

During the season Ove was at last voted his country's Sportsman of the Year, receiving his award proudly from Prince Bertil, the brother of Sweden's monarch King Gustaf VI. It was against all the bureaucratic odds because, even in Sweden, speedway racing was not considered comparable with other sports. Ove says: 'I could have became Sportsman of the Year much earlier, but they didn't recognise professional sport. Even Ingemar Johansson, the world heavyweight boxing champion, he was never Sportsman of the Year because he was a professional. I was the first one that they accepted and that was only after some people brought it up and said that I had been outstanding a couple of years before and they said it was time. We did give it to tennis players, who were not professional in those days, but they earned lots and lots of money. Of course, when I rode I was considered a professional. Tennis and ice hockey are the highest-paid sports around these days in Sweden, but they weren't professional. We did have a handful of professional footballers, but that was all.'

Perhaps it was not altogether surprising that when the year's official world rankings were published in February Ove was voted number one for the seventh time in eight years. That fourth title confirmed it and set the seal on a career of unprecedented sporting achievement.

Teams in British speedway's National League, the sport's premier division and the equivalent of today's Elite League, where riders were – and needed to be – world class to compete, had by 1962 been reduced to their lowest number since the great revival of 1946 and the mid-1950s slump. A mere eight sides began the season in the top flight: Ove Fundin's Norwich, near neightbours Ipswich, Southampton, Wimbledon, Coventry, Belle Vue, Swindon and Oxford. But in July Ipswich closed and the results of the fifteen matches they had ridden were deleted from the records. So the league was down to seven, and its fortunes were destined to remain at that level for two more seasons until the cessation of hostilities between the Speedway Control Board and the 'black' Provincial League promoters following the RAC Shawcross Inquiry, which smoothed the way for everyone to kiss and make up, and bring about yet another major speedway renaissance with the forming of the one big British League in 1965. The Provincial League came into being in 1960, and the prime mover behind it was a north of England slum landlord-cum-entrepreneur, the late Mike Parker, a former midget car driver who operated out of a hardware store in the notorious Moss Side district of Manchester. Parker was a man of such ruthless and questionable ethics that his former business associate in Northern Speedways Limited, Reg Fearman, was finally moved to describe him as 'a pirate, a bandit and a bastard if ever there was one. It came to the point where if he'd been lying in the gutter on fire I wouldn't have pissed on him.'

Parker began running meetings in 1959 at stadiums such as Bradford, Liverpool and Cradley Heath, where speedway racing had been staged previously. The meetings were unlicensed because they were over only fifteen heats when the statutory requirement was a minimum of eighteen heats. There was no shortage of talent prepared to turn out for Parker. He was able to recruit riders put out of work by the shrinking National League. Foreigners were banned and the original idea was to encourage young newcomers, with teams having no more than three 'experienced' riders. But the very maverick nature of the new set-up produced some bizarre situations. Fearman, a former West Ham star, promoted at Stoke, another of his former clubs, and also rode, as did veteran Pete Lansdale at Exeter. When Rayleigh, promoted by Wally Mawdsley, visited Stoke and one of his riders failed to arrive, he borrowed a bike and leathers and not only rode but scored 2 points that helped win the match.

To add to the general feeling of speedway anarchy, some of the highly experienced but faded stars soon began to appear in Provincial League teams: Wal Morton at Liverpool, Geoff Pymar at Yarmouth, Trevor Redmond and Johnny Hole at Bristol, Harry Bastable at Cradley, Ken Middleditch at Poole, Len Williams at Sheffield, Ray Harris and Les Jenkins at Stoke, Graham Warren at Wolverhampton and even the great

Australian pioneer international and former Crystal Palace and New Cross idol Ron Johnson at Edinburgh. In spite of all this, the Provincials prospered and, reported Peter Morrish, the 'legitimate' National League promotions 'found little cause for joy.' Some degree of panic appears to have set in. Yet another attempt by the major league to exclude foreigners proved abortive, but a method of handicapping riders was introduced based on reviewable graded ability. Though the idea was a bit of a shambles – speedway tracks ended up with three sets of starting tapes – it was 'rescued', if that is the word, by Coventry promoter Charles Ochiltree. Journalist Howard Jacobi reported that Ochiltree was able to end the assessment system, which was unpopular with the riders, whereby they were regraded every month according to performance and replace it with a permanent arrangement that had 'star' riders starting twenty yards back, reserves (numbers six and seven in the teams) starting off scratch and all other riders starting ten yards back. 'Promoters have sanctioned pay increases of more than twenty per cent,' wrote Jacobi, 'which they feel sure will be available from the increase in attendances that a firm system of handicapping will bring in its wake.'

Writer John Hyam extolled it as 'the scheme that could prove the ultimate saviour of speedway racing in this country'. One official was said to have remarked, 'The time is ripe for a real speedway revival.' The reality was that speedway, once again, had lined up its drinks in the Last Chance Saloon. The crowds did not improve noticably even with the handicapping system, which was supposed to produce better-quality racing. The designated 'star' back markers, Barry Briggs and Bjorn Knutsson, both then with Southampton, Wimbledon's Ronnie Moore, Belle Vue's Peter Craven and Ove Fundin at Norwich, became known as the Big Five.

Fundin recalled: 'There was Ronnie, Barry, Peter, Bjorn and myself on the third gate. On the second gate there were quite a lot of people, but most were on the first gate. A lot of the time you were sitting back on your own – except when you met Belle Vue when Peter would be there, and if you met Wimbledon Ronnie would be there. I didn't like it. It was a bit unfair. Do you know what they did? They gave us half a crown extra a point. Half a crown [the equivalent of marginally more than £1.32 in today's money], for starting back there. I didn't mind too much when it was dry. But when it was a rainy meeting, or when the tracks were over-watered to start with – and they very often were – you got filled in with all that shit. Yet when you look at the results, the five of us were still the best scorers. The way I looked at it was that the good riders were the good gaters. Peter Craven was not a bad gater at all. When we went off the third gate, he would often beat me out of the start – and I was considered good. But it was true that he could also come from the back. My advantage was being on the inside. You couldn't choose which gate position you started from, but it didn't matter because I always went for the inside anyway. I was very often first out of the first corner even after being handicapped twenty yards.'

Barry Briggs remembered: 'They were lucky to get us to agree to being handicapped, I think. The first year of handicapping it was all right because blokes raced you. Most of them would hear you coming up behind them and leave you some room. The second year they f——ed you. If you were on the outside there was no room. I was forever scraping the fence or taking short cuts over the grass because there was nowhere else to go.' He didn't blame his opponents, he said. He would have done the same to them on the basis that 'if these bloody blokes are so good, let them earn their money'!

'We went to Coventry one night,' said Briggs. 'The track there was easy to ride, but for the back markers it was hard to pass. So we reckoned we had better get half the bike off the track – use the verge and the bit of dirt that most of the normal riders couldn't use. So what they did was they put the track rakes on the inside so you couldn't go near it. Handicapping possibly did a job for speedway, but you can imagine, especially for me who did my own work, you'd go into the first corner and you'd be covered in shit, and hours of work had gone just like that. I know I got more money, but the chances of getting hurt... well, Ronnie broke a leg, Craven was killed, Bjorn was going like a train and he was going to seriously hurt himself because he was taking monster chances. Ove and I were riding like crap. There was only just so much you could do.'

Even though Barry insisted that he and Ove were both 'riding like crap', Craven had a different view of the system. In the first year of handicapping, the Wizard of Balance considered that, far from taking the edge off his racing, he said he had never ridden better in his life than he had that season. 'The handicap has added to my racing. I now feel a much better rider than I did in 1955.' That was the year he won his first World title.

In the second season, 1963, Briggs said that standards had improved so that there were a lot of good riders around to whom he, Ove and the others could not really afford to give a twenty-yard start. But the fact is that the handicap system made little difference to the Big Five's club records. They still topped their team's averages and the league scoresheets. Remarkably, in 1962 Briggs and Knutsson were within a point of each other at Southampton – Briggs on 230 and Knutsson on 229. The following year there was a four-point difference – Knutsson on 239 and Briggs on 235. Craven was on 221. Fundin outscored them all on 263. The unfortunate Ronnie Moore in May broke a leg in a crash trying to make up his twenty-yard handicap on two riders who had collided ahead of him. In his book, *The Ronnie Moore Story*, Moore told reporter Rod Dew: 'Because of the dirt being flung up by the front markers, I had my head down, and when I did spot the fallen riders I stood no chance. I went sprawling. My bike shot up in the air... it thudded down on my left leg. It didn't need a doctor to tell me that the leg was badly broken just above the ankle.' The break was so bad that Ronnie decided to call quits on his track career and retired.

Craven's death, following a racing accident in an inter-league challenge match at Edinburgh, devastated everyone connected with speedway. The shock and distress it caused throughout the entire sport at the time is still felt even today. There are those who insist that on the night of the fatal accident, 20 September 1963, Peter, who had, according to local reporter John Gibson, put on a dazzling display 'to take full points from his first three races', went out for his final ride in heat twelve having agreed to start off twenty yards to demonstrate the handicapping system to the crowd because Edinburgh was in the Provincial League where there was no handicapping.

My considerable researches into the incident indicate that the crowd did not like the idea of Peter being handicapped, because they wanted their local hero, George Hunter, who had already been beaten once by the double World Champion two races previously, to have another chance of defeating the illustrious visitor 'fair and square', with both riders starting off scratch. In the fatal race it was Hunter who took an early lead. He was about to be passed by Craven on the first bend of lap two when he fell. In avoiding him Peter was hurled into the fence, dying four days later from his injuries.

Knutsson's attitude to the handicap system was: 'It was very, very hard, and when you knew you were twenty yards behind it didn't make you very happy. Of course people saw more passing, the best blokes were behind and they had to pass the others to win. But that's the way it was. It was to try and make speedway come back. Because speedway was very, very down in the early 1960s they tried to make it better, but I wouldn't think it did so really. One good thing was that you earned more money. I didn't ever have any problems with passing from behind. But I was pleased when they stopped it, because that is how it should be, everybody starting from the same position and the best man winning.' Barry Briggs observed that Knutsson's way of dealing with the handicap system was to shove opponents out of the way, and he was convinced that 'Knutty's' ability to come to terms with handicap racing probably speeded up his development and made him the world's number one at that time.' Indeed, Bjorn Knutsson joined the elite World Champions club at Wembley in 1965, the year after handicapping was abolished. The year before handicapping was introduced, 1961, Fundin had the incredible average of 11.73 points a match. There was a dip to 9.49 in 1962 – which could be put down to a year of adjustment – but it was the only season in his entire ten-year career with Norwich that his average dropped below double figures. By 1963 it was back up to 11.44, and the following year, his final year at The Firs when handicapping was dropped, it was 10.71.

The system had begun to get Briggs down long before then. He was punishing his machinery, it was costing him a fortune in blown motors, he was 'taking a lot of dirt' and his confidence – a vital ingredient for speedway success – was also a casualty. He said: 'The problem was that when someone finished ahead of you off the handicap, they figured they had beaten you. They hadn't really beaten you, but the thing about any individual sport is that you wear blokes down. It was all right saying you were the best, but you had to give everybody a start, and then you got covered in shit. The blokes at the front in the end thought they had beaten you, and that was bad for you because when you met them in a "proper" meeting [when there was no handicapping and all riders started level on scratch] they thought they could beat you and you didn't want them to figure that. Ivan Mauger was worse than me on that. When we did the World Champions' Troupe tours in Australia and New Zealand in the 1970s, we were living with the other blokes and they all thought we were the same.' It was obviously a big psychological advantage for Briggs and Mauger to stay, preferably, separate and a little aloof from other competitors so that the carefully nurtured mystique that they were invincible – or at least that they were better – could be maintained.

In his book *Briggo* Barry wrote that the extra money and effort involved in the handicap system was a poor reward for riders like the Big Five who, in effect, were being penalised for dedicating themselve to reaching the top of their profession. He wrote: 'Eventually, Ove, Bjorn and myself decided to draft a joint letter to the Speedway Control Board. We asked for the whole handicapping system to be abolished. The scheme had outlived its usefulness.' Their action is verified in *Speedway Star & News* dated 10 July 1964. But in an interview for this book Briggs said that others were involved in the campaign as well: the two Boococks (Nigel, who was with Coventry, and his brother Eric, at that time with Middlesbrough) and Ivan Mauger (who was really beginning to become prominent at Newcastle). But speedway riders do not stick together, said Briggs. 'I know that when Ivan makes a decision he stands by it. Cynthia [Nigel Boocock's wife] said, "Your promoter is going to be up your arse on Monday." And somebody else said, "Oh well, I'll open a fish and chip shop." Oh, yeah? By the Monday morning it had all fallen to pieces...'

In the end, Briggs decided to go it alone and issued an ultimatum to the speedway authorities: 'Drop handicapping or I quit the sport!' He was that passionate about the situation, and he may have felt that his threat carried some weight because, following his second World title win in 1958, he refused to return to race in Britain for the 1959 season after his promoter at Wimbledon, Ronnie Greene, would not stump up an extra £30 for his return fare from New Zealand. Eventually it was paid by contributions from the Speedway Control Board and numerous tracks because, he claimed, as reigning World Champion 'people in high places' wanted him back to defend his title and forestall the season's biggest money-spinner from being taken away from Wembley – possibly by Sweden because of Fundin's success. Finally, it worked. The Control Board 'decided to have done with the whole business and wiped out the twenty-yard mark there and then.'

Ove said: 'I wasn't aware that Barry minded so much. I never said anything. I was never involved in anything like that. I rode my races and I didn't really have much to do with my own team, never mind having anything to do with speedway politics.'

In the meantime, more accolades had come Ove's way. In 1961 he was awarded a speedway 'Oscar'. And in 1963, the year of his fourth World Championship win – then a record – came Sportsman of the Year in Sweden. The first – and only – Speedway Oscars ceremony took place at the sumptuous Waldorf Astoria hotel in London. 'We were all there,' recalled Ove. 'There should be a picture of myself somewhere together with Ronnie Moore, Peter Craven and Stan Stevens.' The 'Oscar' was an engraved silver cigarette box, which he still has at home – but Ove did not, and never has, smoked. 'It happened only one year,' he said. 'They meant to do it every year, but it was probably too expensive for them, because to invite a lot of people to the Waldorf Astoria doesn't come cheap. Reg Fearman and Vic Gooden were promoters at the time, and driving Rolls-Royces. I still remember those two Rollses sitting outside the Waldorf Astoria when the rest of us had to go and find somewhere to park wherever we could. I remember asking one of them – I think it must have been Reg, but it doesn't matter – and I said, "It has its advantages to drive a Rolls." Then he said to me, "But it has its disadvantages too because you can't stop outside a hotel without some flunky rushing out all dressed up, opening the door for you and expecting a tip of at least a tenner."'

'What were the Oscars for? Don't ask me. What do they give Oscars for? It must have been for the best speedway rider. What else could it have been? It couldn't have been for the best-looking speedway rider, or the nicest. When I say it was the Oscars, I think someone must have called it the Oscars. It was only a publicity stunt by the Control Board to invite the media. You have to attract their interest with something. They probably minuted it at the Control Board.' They didn't, but Ove merited his as World and Match Race Champion, Peter Craven for being the outstanding British rider, Ronnie Moore for being the outstanding Commonwealth rider and Stan Stevens, then of Rayleigh, for being the outstanding novice.

This was a period of highs and lows, for Norwich and for Fundin. In the first year of handicapping Ove had to watch his big rivals, Briggs and Knutsson, spearhead Southampton to the 1962 National League title, while Norwich finished fifth – two places from the bottom. The era of the great Aub Lawson was finally over and Ove had been joined at The Firs by his Swedish nemesis Olle Nygren. But it took the threat by manager Gordon Parkins to pull Norwich out of the league in 1963 before the authorities gave special dispensation for the one foreigner per track rule to be waived and Nygren be allowed to stay. Nygren's arrival propelled the club to its most successful season in the top flight, finishing runners-up to Belle Vue in the league and, for the second time in its history, snatching the National Trophy from the famous Manchester side in a memorable and emotional final following the death of Peter Craven. At The Firs the Norwich team and supporters paid their respects to Craven and a collection was made for his dependants.

Fundin, having become, in the words of one pundit, 'the greatest racing machine that speedway has ever known,' by winning the World Championship for that record fourth time, should have been on top of the world. After all, he confessed, 'It's funny. I win the World title three times, I come second three times and third once. All big moments, exciting occasions. I win match races, Internationales and Swedish Championships, but never, never before am I so happy about winning a title than my fourth World Championship.'

But, at the close of the 1963 season, he wasn't happy at all. There had been hostile scenes at some tracks. 'People who don't like to see me winning,' said Ove. 'People who don't seem to like to see any Continental winning. It is not my fault that I am born in Tranas instead of Birmingham or Bow, so why do they boo? This time I feel perhaps it is an unlucky year for me. I have never had such unpleasant scenes before.'

## THIRTEEN

# THE MAN THEY LOVED
# TO HATE

*'Fundin has been booed, bashed, threatened, barracked, stoned, pelted with rubbish, accorded police protection and sundry other delights, more times than he cares to recall. Ove takes it all terribly personally.'* – Angus Kix

The Internationale was a major annual FIM-inscribed event involving the world's best riders, a World Final in everything but name. It was given to Britain in 1961 as a sop for being deprived of its status as the only country to stage the sport's premier meeting when, that year, the World Final went for the first time to another federation, Sweden. British promoters had enjoyed a gigantic shareout from their Wembley monopoly for a quarter of a century since the first final in 1936, a bonanza only temporarily interrupted by the Second World War. Being deprived of the lucrative proceeds from the Wembley finals every year was a huge financial catastrophe.

Anne Gillespie, secretary to the Speedway Control Board for many years, recalled: 'The money from the World Final was split between the British promoters. We always used to say the Control Board was non-profit making and the money we made was ploughed back into the sport. When I was with the Control Board I remember that after each World Final at Wembley we got together with the officials and riders and paid them their start and points money and travel expenses before they left to go home.'

Former BSPA chairman Reg Fearman said: 'Never did I see any split of income with the other federations. The Control Board, via the Auto-Cycle Union, paid a staging/licence fee to the FIM, and expenses were very considerable. The rent for Wembley and making the track were the highest costs, plus of course travel expenses for so many people, including numerous FIM officials and members, their hotels and entertaining etc. After all of the expenses were paid, the Control Board would top up its reserves – but the sum escapes me. After 1965 the surplus would be paid to the Promoters' Association, which would then top up its reserves and then divide the balance between the British League tracks. When the Second Division was formed in 1968, the Division Two promoters were soon clamouring for a share of World Final revenue. They were given one share between them, which equalled a British League track's share. I'm sure that as far as the Wembley World Final is concerned, the other national federations had no share. Russia's Igor Plechanov told me that he had to collect the Russians' money from Wembley World Finals and Test matches in cash and take it in a suitcase to the Russian Federation in Moscow. And they gave him peanuts.'

The first Internationale was staged at Harringay. One of London's most sumptuous stadiums, the Green Lanes complex, now long since 'redeveloped' into a supermarket, had been among the originals to pioneer the new sport of dirt-track racing in 1928. But, following the early post-war boom, crowds had plummeted and the management pulled the plug on speedway before the end of the 1954 season. So effectively the opening Internationale took place on a genuinely neutral track. The line-up that first year included not only the Big Five (Fundin, Moore, Craven, Briggs and Knutsson – they finished in that order) but also a formidable array of other star names of the calibre of Jack Young, Ron How, Doug Davies, Split Waterman, Peter Moore, Arne Pander and Bob Andrews. The opening of Eric Linden's meeting report was: 'Ove Fundin is the greatest rider I have seen. Despite the boos and hisses and catcalls of the crowd, there is no doubt that he won the Speedway Internationale title on brilliant merit.'

Out front the paying customers were taking it out on Ove. He had been booed the moment he set foot on the track at the pre-meeting parade. He was World Champion at the time, the man the crowds loved to hate and behind the scenes he was, once again, involved in a furious row, this time of such magnitude that it threatened to set off the biggest international storm in years. It was not only in danger of jeopardising the forthcoming Swedish Test series, but the return of the 1962 World Final to Wembley could yet, according to Linden, 'blow up in our faces'.

Ove won a run-off with Ronnie Moore after both scored 14 points. But he had ridden under protest because the Speedway Control Board had banned the use of the Czechoslovakian Barum tyre, even though FIM regulations permitted it. Fundin was told: 'Ride a British Dunlop tyre or you'll be thrown out of the meeting.' The ban was because the Speedway Control Board was under the mistaken impression that the Barum was not available to all competitors. But, reported Linden, Fundin had eighteen Barums and was 'willing to let all the boys have them'. The SCB wouldn't budge so Fundin protested, put in a complaint to the FIM and also the Swedish authorities who were demanding action be taken against Britain. Ove recalled: 'In that very first Internationale I was at I can remember that cut tyres were not allowed. I was the only one to turn up with an uncut tire. Guess if I was angry! Well, the meeting went on and I won it, maybe because I was so mad.'

Linden, in spite of waxing lyrical at Ove Fundin's performance, described the meeting as 'three-quarters of the time, the worst "show-piece" I have ever seen. Riders were complaining about the state of the track from the start. And it certainly seemed in poor shape.' Maybe it had been a mistake to stage such an important event in a stadium, no matter how prestigious, that did not have a permanent speedway cir-cuit – a criticism now being levelled at some of the present day Grand Prix tracks. Apart from Peter Craven and Ronnie Moore putting on a neck-and-neck show in heat thirteen that yanked the crowd to life, and ended in Moore's first defeat, there had been little excitement. So maybe the spectators decided to add a little atmosphere by showing their displeasure and putting Fundin – again – in the firing line.

Fundin-baiting had gone on for years. It is not unknown for the speedway public to take a dislike to a particular personality. England's first World Champion, Wembley's Tommy Price, had endured the sometimes violent hostility of rival supporters, particularly at Wimbledon where he had even been threatened with an iron bar. The hugely successful career of six-times World Champion Ivan Mauger was later to be punctuated by demonstrations of extreme unpopularity. The boos and catcalls merely bounced off Price and Mauger, and inspired them to ride even harder. They bounced off Fundin too, but he was of a much more sensitive nature, and he took it personally.

It seems to be a peculiar trait in the psyche of British sporting fans. The paying customers don't care for someone winning too much, as Rick Eldon observed in *Speedway Star & News*: 'When Fundin was an unknown, and mowing down the giants, they loved him for it and they cheered him for it. Now they have switched their allegiance and cheer the men who can beat him. That is sport. It happens all along the line. Everybody loves a game little 'un and most people don't care for the champ.' Mauger became far too successful for the fans' liking. Fundin was also guilty of that, coupled with the fact that he had what was described as a 'robust' style, and his situation was made worse by him being a foreigner, though when it comes to their sporting heroes and villains, the British can never be accused of being a nation of xenophobes. The truth is that they adore building up their own national icons, and display an equally poweful demonic delight in tearing them down, as has been the case with soccer star David Beckham.

Mauger recalled an occasion when Swindon fans had thrown stones at him. 'And everyone hated me at Coventry. It was the same at most places, except my home track,' he said. He confessed that the universal dislike was one of the spurs that made him try all the harder 'to prove everyone wrong'. He didn't, he said, intentionally set out to be unpopular: 'I set out to win. If I upset a few people along the way, tough luck!'

By 1959 the anti-Fundin brigade had pushed Ove to the point where he was considering quitting Britain. And the boo-boys were to blame. In an interview with Linden, Ove said, 'I am sick of it all. Even at Norwich I have been booed, by my own crowd. Don't ask me why. I don't know what makes them do these things.' At Swindon Ove said that fans 'threw stones at me while I was on the track. Not enough, they even throw stones at my car.' Maybe they were practising for a future visit by Mauger. Ove said he would have been far better off riding on the Continent. 'I could have been getting a lot more money in Europe these last two or three years, but I was happy with Norwich and I love England. Now these things are happening, can you wonder I am thinking of quitting British speedway?' He was to endure far worse in the future.

Typical were these headlines: 'Fundin Barracked by Southampton Crowd. Uncalled for Treatment After his Great Riding', 'Is Fundin Getting a Raw Deal?', 'Fundin Trouble... Another Furore' and, 'Fundin Booed Again!' Don Watts reported from Wimbledon on 26 June 1961: 'The unsporting section of the Wimbledon crowd gave Ove Fundin a good booing when he put in an appearance at Plough Lane for his Match Race clash with Ron How. This bad behaviour... reflects badly on the sport, and it is time for them to acknowledge the fact that as a rider, tactician and sportsman, the Swede is a credit to speedway.' No doubt the Dons' fans went away happy because Ron How beat Ove 2-1 in the first leg of his Golden Helmet challenge, though Fundin went on to win the second leg at Norwich and the decider at New Cross.

Perhaps the fans were recalling the incident the previous season when there had been another almighty rumpus at Wimbledon in the Gold Cup Final when How and Fundin were in a run-off after tying on 14 points. Under the headline, 'Ove Gives Cup Back' Watts again reported: 'The race proved to be the most controversial seen for many seasons, and tempers flared among hotheads in the Plough Lane crowd after Fundin appeared to bump local man How off course. How was trying to ride outside Fundin on the pits turn when the riders closed together and How lifted out of his saddle... but managed to regain control of his machine to set off in a vain attempt to overtake his rival. As Fundin came back to the pits, a section of the crowd swarmed through the pits gate after the Swede. His fellow countrymen Birger Forsberg, Bjorn Knutsson and Alf Johnsson helped track officials and police hold back the menacing fans. Despite handshakes between Fundin and How, the crowd refused to be pacified and Fundin handed back the trophy at the presentation. After the meeting police had to clear a way for Fundin to leave the stadium.' In an ironic payoff, Watts commented: 'Racing generally lacked spice – but the aftermath of the run-off satisfied the excitement seekers.' No wonder Fundin was being described as 'speedway's most controversial figure'!

It was not only the fans on the terraces who supposedly 'had it in' for Fundin. There was an alarming incident in 1958, again at Wimbledon and again involving a British Match Race Championship challenge, this time a decider against Southampton's Brian Crutcher. The referee, a Mr G.F. Little, took it upon himself to take Ove aside before the first heat of the Match Race to issue a warning about his starting technique. It just so happened that Mr Little had been chosen to referee, within the month, the World Final at Wembley for which Ove had once again qualified. Fundin had been standing in the pits when Mr Little had approached him. 'I think he is a supporter, so I talk,' said Ove. 'Then I find it is the referee and he is warning me about my starting. He tells me I will be disqualified and fined £5 unless I start properly and fairly. I do not know what he means so I ask him to explain. He says that when I come to the first white line in front of the tapes I must stop. When I see the green light I must move up right to the tapes in two seconds. He says I am always slow in moving up. So what if I am a little slow? He can hold the tapes until I get there. I am not starting any different now to ever before. So before the Match Race I am worrying. And then the referee tells me that he will be in charge at Wembley too this year, so I had better watch out there. And already now I am worried about the World Final.'

That night Crutcher took the Golden Helmet from Fundin, who didn't even look like he was trying. Unusually, Ove was beaten off the start in both races and Crutcher equalled the track record in the first. According to the match report, 'Fundin never looked at all happy in either heat and seemed to have difficulty in controlling his machine. Nevertheless, he was a gallant loser and was the first man to congratulate Crutcher upon his victory.' If Ove was a gallant and gracious loser on that occasion, it was the first time in his racing career. He was always furious – with himself – whenever he lost a race. But the crowd – and presumably the reporter – were unaware that he had been so unsettled by the pre-race confrontation with Mr Little.

Writer Rick Eldon found out about it and went into battle for Ove with all guns blazing. Confronted, Little admitted warning Fundin. 'But I also had to warn him here last week about the same thing,' said Little. 'I received complaints and explained to Fundin exactly what he was doing wrong.'

'What about the Wembley warning?' demanded Eldon.

Little replied, 'All I said was: "It's better to be told now than to be pulled up at Wembley." And it is, isn't it?'

'You weren't inferring that you would be in charge of the Wembley final this year and that you'd have an especially keen eye on Fundin?' Eldon challenged him.

'As a matter of fact,' said Little – and, reported Eldon, 'a grin spreads across his features... the kind of grin of a man who has reason to be satisfied with an honour to come' – 'I will be in charge of the World Final.'

Norwich put in an official protest over the incident. They asked for a re-run of the Match Race on the grounds that the referee's warning had placed Fundin at an unfair disadvantage. The Control Board upheld the protest and sacked Little from the World Final. It was announced separately that the referee for Wembley would not be Mr Little after all, but Mr E.G. Cope. The Control Board didn't agree to a re-run of the Match Race decider, but Ove reclaimed the Golden Helmet from Crutcher at the beginning of the 1959 season.

When Fundin was reminded of the incident, he said: 'There were one or two referees who weren't too keen on me. They showed it by trying to stop me somehow. I do remember being warned by some bastard. A referee has the right to say, like they do in boxing, "make it a good clean fight," and all that, but then they should talk to both riders, shouldn't they?'

After Ove's initial 1961 Internationale success, he went on to win it three times in succession. The top prize was always a nice, shiny, brand new speedway machine. Yet in all my years of watching speedway I had never seen one of those beautiful bikes – all chrome and glistening

– being ridden in anger on the track. 'I never rode them,' said Ove. 'I always used to sell them. The first one that I won I sold to Norwich – and they put the engine in my bike. I remember whenever I won an engine, Norwich speedway paid me for it. Same with the bikes. They bought them off me. If I had sold one to someone else, that I would remember – but I don't. I just took the bikes back to Norwich and they gave me some money for them.'

Probably the worst and most unsavoury row involving Ove happened at his third Internationale win in 1963. It plunged the sport into a huge bribery scandal and speedway became the object of the most damaging kind of publicity in the national press. Following a dramatic heat nineteen in which the Wimbledon idol, Norwegian Sverre Harrfeldt, crashed out when needing two points from a second place to win the meeting, and before the biggest Plough Lane crowd for a decade – well over 14,000, said the reports – promoter Ronnie Greene went on the microphone and announced publicly: 'Evidence has been handed to me that two riders were paid not to win.'

By implication, Greene's accusing finger was pointed at Ove Fundin.

Ove had won his first ride, dropped points to Leo McAuliffe in heat seven and old rival Bjorn Knutsson in heat eleven, but pulled himself up by his bootstraps by winning his fourth in heat fifteen from Barry Briggs. In his final ride, heat nineteen, he had to face Harrfeldt, Peter Moore and Peter Craven. As a climax to such a big meeting it couldn't have been scripted better. A win would have put Harrfeldt on maximum points. If he finished second the trophy was still his. Fundin had to win, but if Harrfeldt was third there would be a run-off between the pair of them. Craven, though well down on points, could spoil the party for everyone.

In the event Fundin won it. Craven was second, Moore was third, and Harrfeldt crashed in what was described as 'a dusty mix-up.' The meeting report recorded that 'the crowd booed their hearts out, for a second place would have meant the Norwegian winning. And suddenly the ousted favourite, Ove Fundin, was not only back in the running but he'd won the darned thing for the third time.' And the downed and disappointed Harrfeldt was back in the pits vainly protesting.

Fundin, sitting on his machine on the track awaiting the prize presentation in full view of what was always a hostile crowd, was understandably furious at Greene's comment and took to the public address system to defend himself. He said, 'Mr Greene might just as well have accused me and Peter Craven and Peter Moore. But I tell you that race was not fixed.' Then he offered to donate the new machine he had won to any Wimbledon rider if Ronnie Greene could prove the charge.

Eric Linden reported the whole embarrassingly unpleasant goings-on. Though in his match report he had written that 'from well over sixty meetings I have seen this year this was far and away the best of them all', his commentary referred to the sensational incident as 'the most serious charge I can remember being made. The timing of it. The place. It could not have had a greater explosive effect if Ronnie Greene had owned every newspaper in the land.' And in they came, said Linden. Scandal and sensation. It meant speedway getting a mention in papers that normally treated the sport with contemptuous indifference – though the *Daily Sketch* laughably reported erroneously that it had all taken place at Wembley.

Fundin was – naturally – among those who called for a full-scale Control Board inquiry. *Speedway Star & News* editor Paul Parrish revealed that since the storm had broken, 'reports have appeared in some circles that spectators at the Internationale are prepared to back Mr Greene's allegation. The date of the inquiry will be determined after the Control Board have spoken to their lawyers.' To this day Fundin proclaims his innocence: 'Nobody asked me if I would buy any points. I wouldn't have done anyway. I've never been questioned by the Control Board, but I have had two letters – one about one time at Southampton congratulating me for throwing my bike down to save a rider, and one when the Control Board gave me an award in 1961 that they called the Oscars of Speedway.'

Later, in a formal statement, the Speedway Control Board said that 'exhaustive inquiries had been made, statements had been taken from the track official who had reported his suspicions and the four riders who it was thought were concerned. As a result it was decided there was no evidence at all that could be placed before a court indicating that any improper arrangement was made.' The incredible thing is that Ronnie Greene escaped scot-free. His public comments over the stadium microphone were considered by many observers to be extremely inflammatory and probably slanderous – though this was never tested – and did the sport enormous damage. However, with the dispute between the National League and the Provincial League about to reach civil war proportions the Control Board did not want to rock its own boat, which it was about to steer through some extremely perilous and equally stormy waters.

Before the rumblings of the bribery rumpus had died down Fundin and the Norwich team, who were both having one of their most successful seasons – visited Wimbledon and had the affrontery to beat the Dons on their own track 40-38. The victory was achieved, said the reports, 'with only half of Ove Fundin'. Certainly, as Parrish observed, the Dons 'starved Ove Fundin of a win in the match... they had Sverre Harrfeldt chalking up his first maximum, including a double over Fundin.' But, wrote Parrish, 'The threats to Fundin possibly had something to do with his off-colour performance.'

Ove had been warned by a policeman before the meeting not to venture into the pits without an escort. 'The policeman said he had been tipped off that a gang was out to get me,' said Ove. 'How can I concentrate on racing with that happening here? I am almost afraid to go near anyone on the track out there. Anyone falls off and I am in more trouble.' He appeared to have recovered his composure later in the meeting because, though he failed to win a race in the league match, he cleaned up the second half, winning the All-Star Scratch Race from team mate Olle Nygren, Wimbledon's maximum man Harrfeldt and Ron How, and also the five-man Mitcham Handicap from Gerald Jackson, Bob Andrews, Roy Trigg and Colin Cotterell, who had let Wimbledon down by failing to arrive in time to ride for them as reserve in the match.

The perceived threat to Ove did not materialise, though there were elaborate precautions enabling him to leave the stadium safely. The police, if not actively guarding him, were certainly very much in evidence and Ove's car was taken from the main car park by the pits. He was spirited from the pits in a decoy car and his trailer of bikes taken to the front where Ove did a quick switch from where he was able to make a safe getaway.

He didn't always escape from Wimbledon so easily. Ove says now: 'When they used to boo me at Wimbledon I rode so much better. They used to boo me there quite a bit. Once they got onto my car – I had a Mercedes and they went all around it with a penny or something and scratched it. On the sides, on the bonnet, everywhere. I was so angry. They had to protect me when I went out to my car. What had I done? I had only won races. I was there to win races. But it only happened at Wimbledon, I remember. There are always some individuals who don't like you – but on the track you can't hear them anyway. It made me more angry, made me ride better. Sort of, "I'll show you bastards!"'

A regular and frequent observer of the mayhem was Ernie Hancock, a frequent contributor to speedway journals and producer of a booklet paying tribute to the late Peter Craven, which has become a rare collectors' item. At the time Hancock was recording audio commentaries of meetings for a company named Track Tapes and, after Ove had been reduced to tears in the Wimbledon pits by another particular example of cruel crowd behaviour, Ernie went to him and asked him what was wrong. Ove said, 'The people out there do not like me. They call me names.'

So Hancock suggested starting a fan club and he called it the Friends of Fundin League – FOFL for short. He said: 'There were about 200 members. Each had a membership card and a biography of Ove. I had a rubber stamp made of Ove's signature so – now it can be told – I'm afraid they didn't get an authentic Ove Fundin autograph. But FOFL lasted until Norwich shut down in 1964. It was non-profit making. All the money went on badges and the other items of membership. Neither Ove nor I made a penny out of it.'

If Ove was not exactly the darling of the crowds, neither was he always 100 per cent popular with his fellow riders. Bjorn Knutsson may have helped hold back the baying pack of enraged supporters that night at Wimbledon in 1960, but all was not sweetness and light between the two Swedes, even though there had been a recommendation from

Ove to Southampton manager Bert Croucher that Bjorn would be a worthwhile replacement for his star Kiwi Geoff Mardon, who was suffering from a fractured jaw.

A golden haired upstart of eighteen named Terry Betts began to learn his speedway trade at Norwich in the early 1960s. He was to go on to achieve international stardom, but at the time they partnered him with Fundin so he was able to observe closely the character of the man. They probably made him Fundin's partner because no one else wanted to ride with Ove then – perhaps understandably – because not only was Fundin a prolific points-scoring machine, but if you rode with him you were also up against other riders of his calibre. It was a prospect that could be heartbreaking for a young and ambitious lad with designs on becoming a speedway star.

Trevor Hedge, now a skilful and hugely respected engine tuner, but then another aspiring youngster just beginning what would be a distinguished career, remembered: 'When they had handicap racing years ago at Norwich, I tell you people didn't want to ride with Ove. We used to put all the names in the hat the previous week – I'm sure without his knowledge – and the one who was drawn out had to ride with him the next week. It used to be known as the short straw. People just didn't want to ride with him. Jimmy Gooch had the problem with Ove. I didn't because I probably wasn't fast enough. Except once, that I remember, I'd kept in front of him, and we came into the pits and he swore at me because I'd filled him up. "Look at me," he said. "My leathers!"'

Jimmy Gooch, a tough cookie ex-paratrooper, after Army service, began his speedway career with Wembley in 1950 and put his name to an entertaining weekly column in *Speedway Echo* magazine entitled 'Diary of a Novice'. He was highly experienced when he joined Norwich from New Cross in 1962. At the beginning of the 1964 season, Gooch 'had the problem with Ove'.

Terry Betts witnessed the Fundin-Gooch problem. He said: 'There used to be a lot of aggro with Fundin because he was so good. Jimmy Gooch partnered him once and every time Ove used to pass Goochie he'd run his front wheel up his leg. Goochie told him, "If you do that anymore I'm going to sort you out." In the next race Fundin did his usual and Goochie had a go at him in the pits and laid him clean out. There was all hell to pay over that and Goochie said he wasn't going to ride with Fundin any more. In the end they had to put Reg Trott with him, and then it was me.'

Phil Clarke, who had retired from racing by then, says the incident was hushed up to a certain extent: 'From what I understand, Jimmy said to Ove when he came in the pits that he didn't think much of what had happened and suggested he didn't do it again. They went out in their next race and the same thing occurred, and when they came into the pits Jimmy socked him – rather severely. Ove went down, and that was the end of Jimmy at Norwich. He never rode for Norwich again. The directors didn't like an incident like that.

'All tracks to a certain extent would have puddles on the white line, and Norwich was particularly prone. The first time I went out with Ove I think I took the outside position, but not being able to communicate with him very well because he knew little English at the time, I didn't explain to him what I was going to do, perhaps. I left a space on the inside for him that, if you're team riding, the man in front has got to do – be out a little bit – to give his teammate the room to manoeuvre on the line. But Ove was keen to win and he went over the white line with both wheels. He should have been excluded, really. And I was actually covered in white slime and shale – a real mess. I think I told him I didn't think much of it, but you couldn't really get through to Ove very easily in those days, he was very determined. It didn't happen a second time because I was aware of the possibility and kept out of the way. But it wasn't a very good introduction. I was his team partner until he became a heat leader in his own right, and the Jimmy Gooch incident was not a complete surprise.'

Jimmy Gooch described Ove as 'the grieving Swede' but when asked what he meant he said, 'Never mind. It's something between me and him. But that incident is a long time ago – forty years. He went over my foot. And with his skill there was no necessity to do that. He did it a couple of times. He was a bit bolshy on the track at times, because he was a World Champion, you know what I mean? You get this in every sport, and it was just one of those things, I suppose.

I don't know why, I would say myself that I reacted out of character, I'm not usually a fisticuffs man, I never hit anybody in my life, but that particular day was probably the trigger, I don't know. I just went off my head and went back to the pits and just clouted him. He fell down. They carried him out on a stretcher. Well, Norwich sacked me on the spot. Then the team went on strike until they straightened it out and I was transferred to Oxford. It ended okay. And that's about it.

'But if there is any slant on it at all, I'd like you to put it as defamatory on my side because I was really out of order from the point of view that, legally, he wasn't penalised by the steward at the meeting, so technically he was totally within his rights to do what he did, despite the fact that I felt otherwise. This happens a lot in all sports, especially today in football. A lot of the fouls we see are probably not seen by the referee. The thing is, he was not penalised on that day so really I hadn't any right to go near him or accost him in any way, so I was out of order. But if you do leave a slant on it, leave it in his favour.'

Another witness to the incident was a very young teenager, Bruce Blanchflower, now a millionaire builder whose fortune was founded on handouts from the speedway stars who came to Norwich. They paid him – varying amounts – to clean their leathers, and Bruce remembered: 'I saw Ove get a poke in the mouth one night from Jimmy Gooch. Jimmy said Ove filled him in twice. Jimmy got the sack for that. If Ove got beaten by one of his own team, we used to stand and watch and he'd throw everything on the floor and rant and rave, and throw things about the workshop.'

Jimmy Gooch was transferred to Oxford and helped them win the 1964 league title. Ove says that he remembers nothing of the incident.

Terry Betts said: 'Ove didn't ever knock you off, he'd just give your leg a bit of a burn. He had to win, that's what made him so good. It didn't matter whether it was a Norwich rider or an away rider, as long as you were second and he was first. Nothing else mattered. That was the difference between Ove and other riders, and that is why he won the World Final five times. You have got to be that type of aggressive rider, you don't get to be World Champion five times by being a nice bloke in speedway. The only really nice guy who ever became World Champion was Peter Collins. All the others have had a mean streak on the track. Ove was quite happy to get a 5-1 with you, as long as he was the one who won it. That's why he was so good, the fact that he had to win everything. He had to win. Give the bloke his due, you could tell by his record that was the streak you had to have. Being friendly didn't come to much if you had a run-off in a World Final.

'You can't be friends with opponents and then have that killer instinct on the track. You have either got that in your make-up or you haven't. Fundin had it and the only rider in my day who didn't have it but still won a World Championship was PC. Mauger, Olsen, they all had that aloof type of superiority over anyone else.'

# FOURTEEN

# OVE AND THE EsO

*'A two-valve JAWA was just about as good as you could choose… It actually did everybody a favour. The cheapest speedway I ever had was the first five years of the JAWA two valve. Ove had it but he wasn't the type to develop it, or put up with the shit that went with it.'* – Barry Briggs

According to the late speedway writer Cyril May, the first EsO speedway machine to be seen in Britain appeared in the possession of Ove Fundin in early 1961. The Czech company gave him one, but he rode his JAP-engined bikes in all the important events. Alec Jackson Exports Ltd in north London became the original UK distributor for EsO motors in 1965, but the following year Barry Briggs became the sole UK concessionaire for the complete EsO at his Southampton premises.

Apart from this brief acknowledgment, tidied up a little by me, and a few passing references in the World Championship section, Ove merits, amazingly, a mere four-line paragraph in May's book *Ride It: The Complete Book of Speedway*, which, dismissing as it does with such brevity the Fundin global contribution to the sport, would not seem to be as 'complete' as it perhaps ought to be. The JAP engine had dominated the sport for thirty-five years from 1930. The EsO – or JAWA, as it subsequently became – has been around for forty and is still going strong, though it was challenged by the British Weslake for a while and its present main competition is the Italian GM engine. By 1965 Ove had been testing the EsO for four years and was under contract to the EsO/JAWA organisation:

*Contract between Mr Owe Fundin, Jawa Works and Motokov, Praha*

*1 /   The Jawa works agrees to lend to Mr Owe Fundin for 1965 season only two EsO 500 D.T. motorcycles, one EsO 500 D.T. engine and the set of spare parts.*

*2 /   During the season the Jawa Works guarantee an immediate delivery of spare and component parts, not included in the aforementioned set of spare parts.*

*3 /   Mr Owe Fundin agrees to absolve the maximum number of races on the Jawa EsO motorcycles as far as conditions of the racing circuits allow. He is not in a position to sign any liability to take part in the finals of the World Championship on the EsO machine, as for the time being he is not used to it to such an extent to guarantee expected results. He will do his best, however, to take part in final race on EsO motorcycle if the condition of racing track and the motorcycle allows.*

*4 /   If Mr Owe Fundin gains the title of the World Champion on the EsO motorcycle he will receive a special reward (the conditions will be stipulated later on, on the basis on number of races absolved and achieved results).*

*5 /   If he is forced to use the JAP motorcycle in the final the agreement on the special award is void, however, for the publicity reasons, he will keep both machines and the spare engine as a present.*

*Praha 13.4.1965*

And it was signed by Ove and representatives of the Jawa-Works Motokov Praha.

When the trials began in that first year, 1961, Ronnie Moore commented on the latent competitor for the ubiquitous JAP in his weekly magazine column under the headline: 'EsO can rival JAP. Czech speedway engine could be a winner.' Ronnie wrote: 'After years and years of unchallenged supremacy... the JAP engine is likely to get its greatest rival ever. I have ridden this new bike, the Czech EsO, and believe me it could well be a winner. The machine I rode belonged to Ove Fundin. It's got a few bugs in it at the moment, but it doesn't take a mechanical expert to work them out.'

Ronnie said that the new engine 'means that a man can experiment with some very odd gearing ratios – some of which will guarantee to get a novice out of the gate faster than the slickest starter.' 'How come I rode the EsO?' said Ronnie. 'Ove wanted to learn something. Riding the machine himself he never knew what it behaved like at the starting gate. So I did a few practice starts – and he watched for pointers. When you are a champ, you're never too proud to learn.'

Well, Ove was a self-confessed non-expert when it came to the mechanics of the game, but when you get right down to it he couldn't be bothered, did not have the desire or the patience to work out the bugs. As Ove was renowned as one of the sport's slickest starters, perhaps he was none too anxious either that novices should be able to get away from the tapes as fast as, or faster than, him.

Ove says: 'They asked me if I would like the dealership for England, Sweden and wherever I wanted it. First of all I said no because I was a speedway rider, I didn't want to be a sort of businessman. I was only interested in riding. I had no time for it. But afterwards I did feel a little bit betrayed when Barry got the dealership for it. I thought it was unfair when he started importing them and selling them in Britain. Suddenly everybody had to buy them and the JAP was history.'

Briggs's version is that Ove didn't use the EsO extensively 'because he didn't get the thing working properly. Because he wasn't mechanical and he was lazy. I introduced it by hard work and suffered by it. The thing stopped on me. So I'd try changing things. Luckily in the end I got repaid for it because I became the agent for it. Ove had it but he wasn't the type to develop it or put up with the shit that went with it. And it's not that he wasn't a businessman. His trucking business was highly successful. He is very smart. Maybe the business part of speedway didn't bother him, but it wasn't the lack of business sense. I just couldn't imagine him importing the bloody thing because it's not him. It was offered to me and I thought: "I'll give it a go."

'It actually did everybody a favour. The cheapest speedway I ever had was the first five years of the JAWA two-valve, because the second-hand bikes had a tremendous value. The good blokes could offer their old ones when they'd done a season, and someone could pick up a really good bike and the whole thing just revolved round that. Today it's impossible. The riders today, with all the money they are spending... it's ridiculous. It's money going out of the sport and it doesn't come back because it doesn't give anything to it. A bloke who can spend the money today can probably win.'

A year after the first experiments, in May 1962, Ove's old journalist friend Angus Kix wrote: 'Fundin has told me he is sending his EsO back home to Sweden. Quite a few bods in this country will say good riddance. That is because they fear this bike. They fear it because it just might prove a cracker, better than the present machine. And that is going to cause a lot of expense. Riders who wanted to compete with anyone on an EsO would have to buy themselves one. And few of the boys are in a position to start shelling out a couple of hundred smackers for a second machine these days. So they heave a sigh and mentally give Fundin a pat on the back for getting rid of the monster. Not, I think, that he wanted to. I doubt whether the boys would have let him ride the machine in their company. With one look you would say that speedway riders are killing progress in the sport. Maybe they are, but a speedier bike is not going to mean better racing. I'm not against progress. But I am against it if it means that in order to get it we have to dump dozens of riders overboard because they can't pay their way.'

Trevor Hedge remembers vividly the impact of the new piece of engineering. He was a young man with obvious talent, but in 1962 had struggled with First Division Norwich in the National League. So, in 1963, he was loaned to the new promotion at Provincial League Hackney. He said: 'I blew up an engine at Long Eaton and I had no money or anything. I went into the Norwich pits the next morning and Ove saw the bike. He said, "What have you done to that?" I said,

"I blew it up." "So what are you going to do now?" he said. "I don't know, really," I told him.

"'I'll lend you my bike," he said. The EsO. A brand new EsO he had, and he lent me that bike. I don't know if he ever did anything like that for anybody else. We know what he was like and how he used to carry on, for him to come to me and say "You take the EsO" was wonderful. The first meeting I rode on it was at Rayleigh. And he said to me, "What's the track like there?" And I said, "I don't know. I've never been there."

'He went into the office and telephoned and asked how big the track was. He came back and he had about two sprockets hanging up in the workshop and he said, "We'll put this one on the back and that will be good."

'I used the thing and I couldn't go wrong. It was like driving an automatic. You let the clutch go and turned the throttle on and it just took off. It was absolutely marvellous after riding a JAP. I had a two-gallon drum of methanol and I know I used the lot – that's how much fuel it used. It was super of him to do that.'

Trevor was somewhat in awe of Fundin. Just how much was demonstrated on a trip to Leicester by the pair of them. Trevor says: 'I was only a kid when I first went there. One night he wanted me to take him to Leicester for an open meeting. I don't think Les Mullins could go with him. He said to me, "You know the way to Leicester, Trevor, you take me."

'I drove him all the way there in his Mercedes 190 diesel, and he slept in the back. I pulled up in the pits when I got there and parked the car. He was such a nasty tempered bugger really that I daren't wake him up. But I didn't know how to switch the motor off. I didn't know how to stop the car, so I left the engine running and left him there and I cleared off somewhere else for about half an hour. I was too scared to wake him up. Well he would fly up in the air. That's how he was before a meeting. But he won the meeting – and that night all the top notchers were there, Briggo, Knutsson...'

In April 1963 Fundin's first challenger for his Golden Helmet was Peter Craven. The first leg was at Norwich and Ove won the first race by some fifty yards. In the second, Fundin's engine failed on the third lap. In the decider, 'taking no chances', according to reporter Derek Hunt, Fundin came out on his EsO machine and won comfortably from the start. By May, the whispers among the riders about banning the EsO had begun to grow. It was reported: 'Ove Fundin has one, and used it against Peter Craven in the first leg of their Match Race at Norwich recently. But only, note, after his number one machine had given out. Now I'm told that Chum Taylor [riding for Oxford at the time] is using an EsO engine in his frame. So far the boys are just watching. But if those EsOs start moving real fast, expect a clamour to get them banned. The riders said they were not against progress, but, as one said: "We wouldn't care what we rode. We'd all change to the EsO tomorrow if it was going to improve the racing... and if somebody would buy them for us. The plain truth is, we can't afford to lash out another £300 or so on a new bike [around £3,900 in today's money]. And so far from giving the JAP a little competition, it might well have them pulling right out of the market."'

Ove says: 'When I first brought the EsO over here, I remember Peter Craven was chairman of the Speedway Riders' Association, which was very strong. One thing they controlled was the foreigners who could ride in Britain and those who couldn't – so it was very strict. We had to get a labour permit. The labour permits were controlled by the riders, the SRA. I brought that EsO, and I even used it in one of the match races against Craven. I beat him on it and he wasn't too pleased. He and one or two of the other riders took me aside and Craven said, "Look, Ove, that thing that you are riding, it's too good. You know that times are bad. We aren't getting much money. A few of us could easily afford to buy this other bike, but that would only make us even more outstanding (he was talking about the Big Five, Ronnie, Barry, Bjorn, me and himself), so if we used the EsO it would be unfair. If we allow you to use it everyone is going to have to buy one of those things. And it is all right for the handful of us, we can afford it, but all the others they can't afford it. So please don't use it. Or, if you do, we will have to think again. We might ban it. And it would be much better if you don't use it."

'It was not threatening. No way. Absolutely not. It was very friendly. And I very much agreed with him. Because I always thought that one of the good things about speedway then was that anyone – any Smith and Jones – he could buy a bike and start speedway. Of course it cost more than playing football, but it didn't cost all that much. I mean, it's impossible to get into road racing, not to talk about car racing. But speedway, you could buy any old bike and you could win a World Final on it – you didn't have to be factory sponsored or anything. That's why I thought it was good. So I lent the bike to Trevor Hedge and he rode it. And then of course the EsO people were rather cross. They weren't very pleased.'

They were even less pleased when Ove Fundin sped to a record fifth World Championship title at Wembley in 1967, knowingly sacrificing that unspecified award in Section 4 of his EsO contract. He was riding an EsO frame... with a JAP engine.

Speedway in 1964 was in a perilous position, like the heroines of the old silent movies who were tied up and swooning away as a fate worse than death came nearer and nearer. But then, just before disaster struck, the heroine was rescued in the nick of time. And so it was with the sport.

The Provincial League teams were running 'black', outside the diktat of the Speedway Control Board. They were twelve strong and doing very nicely. But the National League was in dire trouble with only six clubs, having lost Southampton. Virtual anarchy broke out when the maverick promoter Mike Parker rejected on cost grounds an ultimatum to take his 1963 table-topping Provincial League Wolverhampton into the premier division to make the numbers workable. When he told the National League promoters what they could do with their major section he was given 'another chance' by being 'invited' to take Wolverhampton into the National League, only to comment: 'When I heard the latest statement, I just can't repeat what I said. How many times have they got to be told? I have said in the press, I have told them to their faces and I'll say it again now. Wolverhampton will not go into the National League.' And, he said, nor would any of the other tracks in which he had an interest, which included Newcastle, Hackney and

Newport. 'We don't want this dispute,' he went on, 'but if they want a fight, they can have a fight, and by the time we have finished with them they will know they have been in a fight.' He added on behalf of the Provincials that they did not want to operate as a pirate league but they were damned well going to do so, and lawyers had been instructed to go right to the FIM if necessary to get an inquiry into the running of the sport.

The Control Board attemped to force an amalgamation of the leagues into one big sixteen-team set-up. At the same time it refused licences to tracks at Sunderland, Glasgow White City and Newport, where the promoters virtually stuck up two fingers to the Control Board and said they would operate anyway. The Speedway Riders' Association said that if the two leagues were compelled to merge they would not support work permits for foreign riders, taking great pains to point out that the ban would include Ove Fundin the World Champion. The speedway press was quick to leap to Ove's defence and ask why the SRA had to pick on him. It was argued that it could be taken 'as a compliment to the greatest rider in the world that he alone should be named'. But it could also be argued that maybe it was time everyone 'stopped picking on Ove just because he is great'. Only the reopening of West Ham – without the sport since 1955 – saved the National League.

At Norwich the spectre of closure began to loom again, this time larger. 'Could it be Last Year at the Firs?' was the alarmist headline over a story in March that predicted that developers would take over the stadium in October, and had Gordon Parkins insisting, 'An offer has been been made and has been turned down.' The continued specula- tion inevitably unsettled the riders. Reg Trott, captain of the Stars in the final year, said, 'It has not been pleasant riding at Norwich with the axe always ready to fall. A thing like that changes the atmosphere of the place.' But throughout the season attendances at The Firs were among the best in the country, and the lively after-match club room's swinging atmosphere was unique in the sport.

Though in only his thirtieth year, there was evidence that Ove was, almost imperceptibly, beginning to lose that super-fine edge of skill,

brilliance and ruthless determination that had placed him top of the
world rankings for seven out of eight years. Norwich won the Easter
Cup, described as 'a minor pot'. The competition was a bit of a mis-
nomer because the trophy did not become the property of the Stars
until high summer. In the league the team – just like Ove – slipped
very slightly, to third place from the previous year's runners-up spot.
The fortunes of Norwich and Fundin were inextricably linked, and if
the sparkle had gone off one then the other did not shine either. Ove's
scoring was down more than 100 points on the previous season, Olle
Nygren heading the Norwich scorers, though from six more matches
than Ove who nevertheless was still on 10 points a match. When the
totals were totted up for the 1964 season five of the first six places
were occupied by Swedes. Soren Sjosten (Belle Vue) was top, followed
by Bjorn Knutsson (West Ham), then Nigel Boocock (Coventry), the
sole Englishman in the top eight. Olle Nygren was fourth, Ove fifth
and Gote Nordin sixth.

It was the year that a Russian Test side, led by Igor Plechanov and
all on EsO machines, visited Britain for the first time, losing the series
against Great Britain 3-0 but winning massive popularity. Ironically
in July a four-man Russian team went to Norwich and won against a
full-strength Stars side. Derek Hunt reported: 'Those fantastic Russians
won the hearts of all East Anglia with an endurance test that can hardly
be equalled in speedway history. Four Russians took on Norwich on
their own. Four men riding nine times each on their first visit to The
Firs stadium, and what is even more fantastic they won.' There was no
explanation as to why the Russians turned up with only half a team,
but they pipped Norwich 55-53, with Russian skipper Plechanov,
whose riding during the tour had made him an outsider to topple
the Swedes in that year's World Final, scoring 19 points. Ove scored
an impeccable 18-point maximum, and the pair had by no means seen
the last of each other.

With the scrapping of the handicap system Barry Briggs's confidence returned with a vengeance and, before a 16,230 crowd, he put
a stop to Ove's run of successes in the Internationale by winning
the August Bank Holiday meeting at Wimbledon. As usual it was a

field of World Final quality and though Briggs ended Ove's reign of three wins on the trot, in the last race of the night Ove issued the strongest possible reminder that he was still lethal, by stopping Barry's hopes of a maximum to take second place overall. As well as the Internationale, Briggs steamrollered to the Gold Cup, the Midland Riders' Championship and, released from the handicap stress, eighteen league maximums, finishing off his run up to the World Final with the British Championship at Wembley. In contrast Ove did not seem to be quite the force he was. He won his fifth Swedish title, beating Rune Sormander in a run-off after both had scored 14 points, and though Sweden won the World Team Cup for the fourth time comfortably from Russia, Great Britain and Poland, Ove's score was only 6. In his Continental qualifying rounds for the World Championship, instead of turning in his usual string of maximum scores, he was slightly off the pace and doing just enough to qualify. When it came to the European Final, the last round before the World Final, a Pole no one had heard of with an almost unpronounceable name, Zbigniev Podlecki, walked off with the title at Wroclaw having scored a 15-point maximum. Bjorn Knutsson, the world title favourite, was second on 13, while Ove's score was 11, level with Russians Boris Samorodov and Plechanov. And though the final was to be staged again in Sweden, and for the first time at the magnificent Ullevi Stadium in Gothenburg, it was a track Ove did not like.

On the eve of the World Final there was open speculation that Ove was about to retire. It was reported that only the Golden Helmet stood between him and any decision to quit because he had a secret ambition to better the legend of the old Match Race maestro Jack Parker, the man who had taken him to Australia a decade before and set him on the road to greatness. Parker's British Match Race Championship record was won 22, lost 3. At the time Ove's was won 19, lost 5. Both had been involved in the competition over eight seasons, Parker variously from 1931 when it was the British Championship and unofficially regarded as a world championship, Ove continually since 1957.

But there were other factors too. Ove says that he does not recall being unsettled by rumours of The Firs being sold to developers: 'I cannot remember any talk about Norwich going to be closed in 1964, but I guess I didn't care too much.' There was his growing family to consider, too. He says: 'I could live on my speedway earnings, but only just. As far as I can remember, we got £1 per start and 25s per point. When you see what they are getting today, it's a joke. But at the time it was okay for me. In any case I raced to win, not to earn money. But I had to think about the future.' He had been considering life after speedway for five years, which is why in 1959 he had begun his trucking business, at first engaged in transporting and selling domestic heating oil and later branching out into general haulage, operating all over Europe and the Near East. 'That,' says Ove, 'had a great effect on my retirement.'

The day of the World Final dawned miserable and, at midday, turned Scandinavian wet. It was the worst weather ever up until then to bedevil a World Final night. At the 7.30 p.m. start time there were ankle-deep puddles and more than half the track was underwater. But the Swedes simply drove truckload after truckload of sawdust into the stadium and spread it around until all the water was soaked up. It took fifty minutes, and the rain was still falling when the first four riders cruised up to the tapes for the opening heat. Reigning champion Fundin was given a huge reception by the 25,700 home crowd when he went to the line in heat two, alongside the in-form Briggs, Polish surprise packet Podlecki and Dick Fisher. Though Ove led into the first corner, Briggs surged round the outside to set up a big lead. It was the first of a five-ride maximum by Barry that took Ove's title away from him and gave Briggs his third World Championship. Ove won his second ride from the more-fancied Knutsson who, apart from havng to cope with his well-known big-occasion nerves, had been badly shaken in a car crash the previous day. Ove dropped another point to Russia's Samorodov in his third ride, but won his fourth and fifth – the last in heat twenty against Plechanov – which put them both on 13 points and in a run-off for second place. Ove made the start with Igor right on his back wheel looking as though he was on tow and the wily Fundin countering his every move to pass until the last bend. A fantastic burst of back-straight speed carried Plechanov past Ove on the outside to take the runners-up place, and the performance was described as 'surely the greatest ride that didn't win a World Championship'. It was the first time a Russian had been in such an exalted position and so close to the title, but though Ove was relegated to third, it was the ninth time in as many years he had stepped onto a World Final rostrum.

So Briggs was the new World Champion. His end-of-season form was little short of sensational, and exactly one month after his Ullevi triumph he also took away Ove's Golden Helmet, winning the first leg 2-0 and also the second at Norwich 2-1. Ove's motor had blown levelling the scores at The Firs, and in the decider he had to go out on Reg Trott's bike. But though he was allegedly able to ride it as well as Norwich Track Spare No. 2, it wasn't enough to prevent Briggs depriving him of the title. There was little satisfaction for Ove either in going on to win the individual meeting that followed – the Kings of Oxford Trophy, which was named after its sponsors, a local motorcycle company. Ove won the trophy on 14 points, beaten ironically in the last race by Briggs, who had four winning rides but pulled out of his third with motor trouble. To cap a fantastic season, Briggs was voted runner-up to athlete Mary Rand in the BBC's Sportsview Personality of the Year award – amid unproven rumours that the result had been diplomatically 'doctored' because the BBC could not contemplate a speedway rider winning their prestigious and top-rated event. In February Barry was voted number one in the world rankings ahead of Fundin.

The loss of the Golden Helmet to Briggs wrecked whatever ambitions Ove had of beating Jack Parker's British Match Race Championship record. Reporter Derek Hunt wrote of the 10 October meeting at which Ove finally lost the Golden Helmet that of course it was a 'very sad one. It was officially the final match at The Firs – ever. Also, Ove Fundin is retiring. On Wednesday 14 October there is a riders' benefit meeting.' Ove was down to ride in that, but it was rained off and the real final meeting at The Firs took place on 31 October without Fundin, who had a prior engagement on the Continent. In an inspired turn of phrase veteran Manchester newsman Frank Maclean was moved to comment: 'Norwich without Fundin is like playing Hamlet without the Prince.'

The local paper reported that 'the final curtain was rung down on thirty years of speedway history at Firs Stadium. It was a night of nostalgia, recalling the "good old days" of cinder tracks and leg-trailers.' Nostalgic names from the past were there: Wilf Jay, Phil Clarke, Len Read and Jack Freeman. But the major disappointment of the night was the fact that the biggest name of them all, Ove Fundin, could not be there. 'He was the man, above everyone else, who had done most to keep the name of Norwich in the forefront of the speedway world.' When it was really all over and the last motor had been silenced, the faithful fans went to their familiar club room to remember the good times over a drink. It was a scene very much like it had always been. The difference was there would be no more Saturday nights spent like that, and for many it did not strike home until they were leaving the darkened, quiet stadium for the last time.

There was a brief – a very brief – last hurrah in November when a massive headline appeared that proclaimed: NORWICH SAVED. The story underneath revealed that The Firs may have closed, but a new site for speedway had been found and 'there will be National League racing there next season'. The names behind the venture were Maury Littlechild, described as a haulage contractor and mushroom grower, and former Norwich Speedway board member Jack Thompson. It didn't happen, though the Littlechild family, with Cyril Crane, did open nearby King's Lynn the following year.

Avarice had finally proved irresistible to the directors of The Firs at the end of that 1964 season and the stadium and its commercially valuable fourteen-acre Holt Road site was sold to a property company for the sum of £75,000. The metaphorical shutters came down not only on thirty-four years of speedway in Norwich, but also on Ove Fundin's life as a speedway star – though the career of the man considered to be the greatest speedway rider the sport had known up to then was not about to be extinguished without one more single flash of defiant brilliance.

Ove says: 'I did decide to quit in 1965 when Norwich closed. I still consider that my retirement. Then I came out of retirement in 1966 because I was talked out of it, first of all by Reg Fearman, who was already a good friend of mine. He said, "Please come over and help me." I said, "I have my business to run." I can't remember how many meetings I did, but it wasn't very many. Maybe a handful. That was for Long Eaton. No doubt I flew into London Airport and he drove me to the track, and probably I was still asleep. He gave me a bike and I rode around and then went back home again.'

Out of the chaos of the bitter dispute between the National and Provincial antagonists, the British League was born in 1965. After the Shawcross Inquiry into the running of the sport, one big league was formed of eighteen teams and once more British speedway tottered back from the brink. The 'helpless heroine' was saved again from a fate worse than death. But the move did herald a much healthier future for the sport, with control passing to the British Speedway Promoters' Association (BSPA) made up of members with a direct financial interest in the game. Even if Norwich had not closed down, it is questionable whether Ove would have raced in Britain anyway because the commuting Swedes were banned. Only foreigners resident in the country were allowed to race for British teams. But even with the inter-league dispute settled, there was a new pre-season crisis. The entire house of cards was threatened with being brought tumbling down when the riders refused to accept the offered 1965 British League pay rates of £1 a start and £1 a point. They wanted £1 5s a start, £1 10s a point and £8 maintenance money. But preserved BSPA Management Committee official records show that what they got was £1 5s a start and £1 5s a point. There was more for open meetings on a sliding scale depending on the number of heat leaders taking part, and if there were imported foreign riders in the meeting. Maximum pay, for thirteen or more heat leaders, or two or more imported foreigners, was £1 15s start and the same per point. Novice riders, non-contract and second halfers got 12s 6d and 12s 6d. Travel expenses were 4d per mile. British Final rates were £2 and £2, Nordic/British Final £2 10s and £3 10s, European Final £5 and £5, Internationale £2 and £2. Agreed Internationale admission prices were: ground 5s adults and 3s child, stands 7s 6d, 10s and 12s 6d adult and child. If you wished to go to the restaurant it would be be £1 10s including dinner. To give a comparison, that £1 10s including dinner at the Internationale would be the equivalent of a little over £18 today.

Ove was in Britain for the Internationale in June, but this time he was well down with a mere 6 points in a meeting won by the enigmatic Australian Charlie Monk. There was trouble right from the first heat. Ove and Cradley's Ivor Brown reached the first corner level and the two of them clashed. Eyewitness reports describe how 'Ivor tried to do to Ove what he did to all other riders: that is lean all over them and intimidate them on the first corner.' But Brown, new in the big time from the Provincial League, was unaware that trying to move Fundin was like trying to move a brick wall. Ove carried on as if Brown wasn't there, and Ivor went into the fence, sustaining severe buttock injuries. Ove was excluded by the referee. In the fierce Black Country rivalry between Cradley and Wolverhampton, Brown was hated like no other rider by Wolves supporters. In the early 1960s, in Dudley Wood Road on a bridge over the 'cut' (canal), a piece of grafitti appeared that said, 'Ivor is a bastard', painted allegedly by some aggrieved Wolverhampton fans. After the Internationale incident another piece appeared that said 'Hurrah! Ivor is knackered!' Both legends were still there after more than forty years of wear and tear. Since Ivor Brown's recent death it has been revealed that he was the un-named rider Ivan Mauger referred to graphically in his autobiography *Triple Crown Plus* in chapter thirteen, entitled 'The Man I Hated'.

Back home, in the Swedish Championship Ove was runner-up with 14 points but the title went to Gote Nordin. In the World Championship he beat Bjorn Knutsson in a run-off in the European Final at Slany, Czechoslovakia after both had scored 14. But Knutsson was not to be denied, becoming World Champion at last at Wembley. Ove dropped points to Nigel Boocock in the opening race and Knutsson in his second ride in heat eight, but went on to win his other three, in his third beating Briggs and in his fourth beating Plechanov. Then, in a repeat of the previous year in Gothenburg, he and Igor lined up for a run-off for second place, both of them on 13 points. And Plechanov won again. But in finishing third, Ove set a unique record of never being out of the first three for ten consecutive years – an achievement that has yet to be equalled.

Ove's 'coming out of retirement' in 1966 in answer to Reg Fearman's Long Eaton SOS was short-lived. He was banned by the strict SVEMO in April after he apparently told them he was taking part in a car race when he was required for a World Championship qualifier. The suspension stopped him adding to his sequence of twelve successive World Final appearances, and almost certainly prevented him winning a record sixth World title before Ivan Mauger managed it in 1979, and of course Tony Rickardsson in 2005. Efforts to find out the exact circumstances of the ban drew a blank at SVEMO, and Ove said he couldn't remember but added, 'I probably went somewhere I shouldn't have done or went somewhere without permission.'

Reg Fearman says: 'Ove had retired and I phoned him in 1966 and said would he come over and ride for Long Eaton. He said, "Yes. Sure." You know what he's like. It was one phone call, and he had his business going then. He just rode for the same arrangement he had at Norwich, which was a machine supplied and maintained. We did that, and Ray Wilson looked after it and transported it to each track. Ove turned up to race just like he always had done. We paid his fare backwards and forwards, whatever we had to do, like with all the Swedes. He rode for start and points money at the going pay rate – although he never did ride purely for money. Ove's reason for racing was to win. Truly. For some reason the money didn't matter. I don't know if he had always been of independant means, but I do know that he, along with my other riders, received their pay cheques in the pits and I had to ask Ove why his cheques had not been cashed. He unzipped a pocket in his leathers and pulled out a fistful of pay sheets and cheques.'

'Reg Fearman asked me to ride for Long Eaton, but I was never happy there,' Ove says, 'I didn't like the track. I didn't like having to go there. I was very busy and I was arriving at the last minute. I did it only because Reg was a good friend of mine. But I didn't do many meetings for them. You can look up the records.' It was only five matches for an average of 9.636.

'He raced for me for about two-and-a-half months,' says Fearman, 'then SVEMO banned him. They banned him because they wanted him to ride in the World Championship and he said no. So they suspended him, which buggered me up. I rang him and said, "What's happening now?" He said, "They've banned me because I wouldn't ride in the World Championship qualifier." It was a total ban, and for the whole of the rest of that year. I don't think he was that bothered anyway. He hadn't ridden in England since Norwich had closed. That's how I got him. He hadn't ridden in England, and when I offered him this, it was like Ronnie Moore coming back, and he said yes.'

Ove says: 'We had to have written permission from the Swedish Motor Federation before we were allowed to go and ride in Austria, Germany or Poland, or wherever. But I didn't do it and they banned me. I think I said to myself, "Why should I ask them if I may go or not? What can they do to me?" Well, they did ban me after that. They stopped me. They banned me a couple of times, and I am still banned I suppose, although I have done a few things since then. Nowadays I am very friendly with Rolf Sunderberg who has just quit, and I always say to him, "You know next week I am going to England to race in one of the Golden Greats meetings, and I'm not going to ask you for permission. What will you do to me if I don't ask your permission?" "You are already banned," he says. It was a bit of a joke.

'I know Barry thought that SVEMO turned themselves inside out to do anything and everything for me. But on the contrary, they banned me and they didn't help me or Nygren. They didn't help anyone. It didn't work that way. It's not Poland. In Poland they did those sort of things. In Poland they rigged races and let them get away with rolling starts. SVEMO is an office. They handle licences and permits for meetings. Those people never went to meetings.

'When Norwich packed up I did a season in Formula Ford car racing and I got backing from BP. They gave me a car and a trailer. I raced maybe twenty meetings all over Scandinavia and won only once, but a couple of times I had the fastest time. I wanted to have a go at it. It's not all that easy. At the end of the season I gave it up. I didn't have time for it and I went back to speedway. I didn't really like it. It is a snobbish sport. For instance, the mechanics did everything. I hated it when they and the helpers had to load the car – the driver wasn't supposed to do that. And they always had a dinner the night before the race – not afterwards, like after big speedway meetings in Sweden and Poland. I did a few meetings in Sweden – not much – and then the following year, halfway through the season Soren Sjosten got hurt and Belle Vue said, "please, please come as his replacement, just for a few meetings." That was another weak moment and I said, "OK, I'll come".'

During 1966, Ove had also acted as general adviser and manager to the Swedes. That year he became a father for the fifth time when Niclas, his youngest son, was born, and he told journalist Dave Lanning that he wanted a fifth World title because he now had five children. So Belle Vue's timing was right. In 1967 the Speedway Riders' Association changed its attitude to foreign riders, and more of them arrived in Britain than ever before. But by mid-season several teams were struggling, among them Belle Vue and King's Lynn. The East Anglian side was desperate to sign Ove because of his Norfolk connections, and it was estimated that he would bring in an extra 2,000 people a week at Saddlebow Road. At Belle Vue Soren Sjosten had broken a leg, and they wanted Ove too.

King's Lynn were bitterly disappointed when the BSPA allocated Cradley Heath's Howard Cole to them and Ove to Belle Vue. The BSPA were very wary of the problems that he had experienced in 1966. They therefore asked him to sign an agreement committing him to all Belle Vue's fixtures until the end of the season. Ove was stopped from riding until he signed it. He was due to appear for the Aces at West Ham on 20 June, and arrived with his equipment ready to race. He told the crowd that he had seen no agreement and knew of none. He was given a sympathetic response but did not ride that evening. On behalf of the BSPA Charles Ochiltree said that the agreement still allowed Ove to ride in World Championship meetings and even Swedish League meetings, but it did not permit him to miss meetings because of Continental engagements or car racing appointments, as had happened in 1966.

Even though the matter of the agreement was eventually resolved – though exactly how appears to be a mystery – Ove still did miss meetings. He failed to appear at Newport for a challenge match in August and was fined £20. Frank Varey was furious when Ove did not turn up for the Northern Riders' Championship Final at Sheffield, especially as he had ridden in the qualifying rounds and had made it through to the final legitimately. Belle Vue had assured Varey that he would ride, but Ove was on his way to a World Championship meeting on the Continent. Even so, he topped the Belle Vue averages on 9.647 after riding in only twelve league matches. In several international series, against Russia, Poland and Great Britain, Ove scored freely but not sensationally, apart from an 18-point maximum in one against England at Exeter. The Swedish Championship and the Czech Golden Helmet were the major successes, and on his way to that year's Wembley World Final there was a 15-point maximum in the Nordic Final, but he scored only 8 in the European Final, which was dominated by Poles Andrzej Wyglenda, Andrzej Pogorzelski and Antoni Woryna, and – that man again – Russia's Igor Plechanov, the top ten going through to Wembley.

Controversy continued to follow Ove around. On 15 September, the night before the World Final, he was due to ride for Belle Vue at King's Lynn but failed to arrive. A message reached the stadium to say that his car windscreen had been smashed near Newmarket, so King's Lynn sent someone to pick him up, but he couldn't be found. To this day, King's Lynn fans are miffed about his non-appearance, and what has always seemed to them to be a questionable explanation. But Ove says of the incident: 'SVEMO did not allow Swedish riders to race three or more days – I can't remember exactly – before the World Final or any other big meeting. I never liked all the rules SVEMO had, but if I had raced that night I would for sure have been banned again, and for a long time. But Dent Oliver, the manager of Belle Vue, knew that I could not be with the team that night.'

It was a clue to how seriously he was taking the World Championship again. He had been out of the mainstream of British speedway for three years and the speculation was that his heart was no longer in the sport. The commentators were calling his performances 'lack-lustre' and his connection with Long Eaton 'ignominious'. It seemed at first that he had retreated into the speedway shadows at the start of that season, but his quest for yet another World Championship changed all that. The results of his progression along the road to Wembley had made it clear that here was the Fundin – The Fox – of old, full of the familiar fire, driving dedication and the menacing will to win. Wembley was where he felt at home – much more than in Gothenburg in his native land – so much so that there had been an incident at the 1964 World Final when Fundin had rounded on Swedish journalists for daring to compare Ullevi with Wembley.

Two weeks before the final he had won an EsO machine in the Czech Golden Helmet meeting at Pardubice. But he was unhappy with it and experimented continually with it right up to the official practice day at Wembley. He was so concerned about the motor that he arranged to borrow a stand-by engine from Sverre Harfeldt, who was not in that year's final. But Sverre blew it up just before the practice. Eventually Ove decided to ride the machine that had been prepared for him by Dent Oliver, Harold Gardner and Guy Allott at Belle Vue; an EsO frame with a JAP engine. Throughout the meeting he shouted at his mechanics because he said it wasn't fast enough. The previous year, Barry Briggs had ridden unbeaten to his fourth World Championship, and there was a double irony in that he had done it in Sweden at Ullevi and on an EsO, the first rider to win a World title on the Czech bike. Ever the businessman, Briggs had issued an ultimatum to the manufacturers: if they wanted him to ride their machine in the World Final, they had to guarantee to make him the United Kingdom concessionaire. It was the real start of the EsO/JAWA revolution in British and world speedway.

Harold Gardner, now nearing ninety, had begun his career at Belle Vue in the early 1930s during the club's great pre-war era. He was team mechanic and later machine examiner at The Zoo. He said: 'I met them all at Belle Vue. I even had a few rides myself. But I looked after Max Grosskreutz for a long, long time. Dent Oliver set it all off with Fundin, who wasn't very happy with the EsO as it was. He liked the JAP engine. So it was suggested that we popped a JAP engine into his EsO frame. Dent asked me if I could make him a bike that would get to the first bend before anyone else. I thought I could as well, and I did. At first Ove thought that we wouldn't be able to do it, but we said, "Bet you we can." And that was more or less how it ended up. I set about it, weighed it all up and made one or two adjustments before we got it right. It was fine. He got on it and said, "This is for me." It would certainly get to the first bend very, very quickly. The main thing was getting the gear ratio right. It was done more or less in my spare time.

'My contact with Fundin was mainly on race nights. But occasionally he would pop down during the week just to see how things were getting on. He didn't know a lot. He wasn't very well versed mechanically. But you could talk to him and I think he understood eventually. He wasn't very good on clutches. We had to put a decent clutch together for him. As far as his so-called ego went, he didn't lose his temper at all with me. He was a gentleman to us, actually.

'He wasn't very hard on motors. He rode them hard but he was cautious. He wouldn't over-rev them, and he was very fastidious about the correct gearing. That was the main thing. I did nothing particularly special for that year's World Final, apart from build the bike and put the engine in the right position so that there wouldn't be too much wheelspin. It just had a very nice engine prepared by Guy Allott. I made sure nothing was going to fall off it, and that it had the right tyres and the right tyre pressures. I was at Wembley, but just as a spectator. It was as simple as that. Everything I've told you is actually as it happened.'

On the day of the final, Ove drove down from Manchester with Wilf Lucy, Belle Vue's chief mechanic. There was no time for a nerve-calming afternoon visit to the cinema on that day. The night's line-up was bristling with some of the brightest up-and-coming talents desperate to take over his mantle: Ray Wilson and Eric Boocock of England, Bernt Persson, Bengt Jansson and Anders Michanek of Sweden and the young pretender Ivan Mauger of New Zealand, as well as the old guard of Briggs, liberally tipped to take a fifth title, and Plechanov.

Ove led a phalanx of Swedes in his first ride, which had him lining up with Jansson, Michanek and danger man Briggs, who had experienced motor problems on the pre-meeting parade. Briggs had observed the way Ove was behaving in the pits before their first ride and was convinced that the hybrid JAP/EsO machine meant he was taking the meeting very seriously, plus he had 'two of his mates to help him in the first race'. Mates or not, Jansson and Michanek saw only Ove's back wheel, and so did Briggs, who finished third. Heats seven and twelve went the same way for Ove, and after three rides it was obvious that Mauger was becoming the real threat. Both of them led with three wins each. But Ove, with the number seven on his race jacket, was programmed for his fourth ride in the very next race, heat thirteen, and dropped his first point to Plechanov who gated like a dream and led Fundin past the chequered flag in the fastest time of the night. In heat fifteen, Jansson broke Mauger's unbeaten run, which left the pair of them with Plechanov and Ove all on 11 points.

The decisive race looked like heat eighteen when Ove was due to meet Mauger in their final ride. It was Ivan's second final and he was in with a real chance of realising the ambition he had planned and strived to achieve for a decade, that of taking speed-way's supreme prize for the first time. They went to the tapes with Persson and Pogorzelski, with Ove off the inside gate and Ivan off the outside. The two of them left the tapes at the same time and went into the first turn level. Then, according to Mauger, Persson came off gate three and rode into him. Ivan went down and referee Arthur Humphrey immediately excluded Persson for foul riding. He angrily refused to leave the track and a fierce argument followed between Persson and the referee while Mauger tried to straighten out his badly bent machine. There was consternation and chaos in the Swedish section of the pits, where everyone seemed to be arguing. Humphrey refused to change his decision and Persson – later to be described as 'the complete destroyer' by Briggs, following a crash in the 1972 World Final, which resulted in the loss of one of his fingers – was eventually led away after being threatened with suspension from future World Championships. Another row erupted when the Swedish reserve, Leif Enecrona, tried to take Persson's place in the re-run but was unceremoniously ordered back to the pits. When the race finally began again Ove's experience told over the shaken Mauger and he led from start to finish.

The last race, heat twenty, brought Jansson and Plechanov together, and both could end the night on 14 points. There was a false start when Plechanov tried to duck under the tapes and Jansson won the re-run. It meant a two man run-off between Ove and Jansson for the title. For Jansson there was the pressure of becoming World Champion for the first time. For Ove there was the pressure of becoming World Champion for a record fifth time.

Experienced observer Dave Lanning is of the opinion that Ove talked Bengt Jansson out of winning when they walked side by side to the starting tapes to toss for positions in the run-off. Barry Briggs, down the list on the night in fifth place, was equally sure that 'the Swedes conned Jansson' out of the title. 'Ove and Bergstrom convinced him he had no right to win,' said Barry. 'He was the better rider on the night, but by the time the race started Banger was psyched out.'

In contrast, Ove was described as 'ice cool' and made one of his characterisitic jet-like starts to ride an almost perfect race, apart from offering a slight chance to Jansson on lap three. Ove, by no means as race fit as he would have been if he had taken part in a full British season, having to all intents and purposes been retired from full-tme competitive speedway for two years, and riding a hybrid machine, neither JAP nor EsO – or perhaps both – had risen to a height no one had a right to expect of him, except perhaps himself. He had set new standards that were to remain the stuff of legend. An attempt had been made to diminish his third victory in 1961 at Malmo when Bjorn Knutsson had been described as 'the best rider of the night', and here it was, with his unprecedented fifth win at Wembley, happening again. But on both occasions, Fundin's fierce tenacity, determination, temperament, talent and desire to win had enabled him to triumph. It was both the beginning and the end of a speedway epoch.

The day after the final a picture appeared in a Swedish newspaper of Ove leaping over a bench in London's Hyde Park. The headline read: 'My wife is worth a medal too – I'd never have done it without her.' And the caption read: 'How glad he is... Ove Fundin goes to town the day after winning the 1967 World Championship – he leaps a bench in Hyde Park happily and easily.'

'I won that fifth title without taking it all that seriously,' he says. 'I mean, I did take it seriously when I was racing, but before I used to take it seriously all the time, twenty-four hours a day, 365 days a year. But in 1967 I took it seriously only when I was at the racetrack. I would fly in for a meeting and then fly home again. I took my work with my business more seriously. And then they were on to me in Sweden all the time: "Oh, you've got to ride. Now you are World Champion again, you've got to race." So I did a few meetings up until 1970, and then no more. When the season finished in 1970 I finished.'

'A few meetings until 1970' included two more World Championship Finals, in 1968 at Ullevi again where Ove scored only 7 points and in 1969 back at Wembley where he scored 9. The pretender to Fundin's throne, Ivan Mauger, finally ascended and Ove could only watch as in those meetings Ivan won the first two of his record three consecutive World Championships, another accomplishment still to be equalled. But even then Ove wasn't really finished. He was to be caught out in another 'moment of weakness' by another old friend. And it was, once again, Wembley calling.

Trevor Redmond, who had ridden for the Lions in the 1950s, had teamed up with wealthy businessman Bernard Cottrell to reopen Wembley after taking over the Coatbridge licence. The relaunch of the famous Wembley Lions was done on a grand scale, as befitted millionaire Cottrell and the exuberant and extrovert showman Redmond. Top radio disc jockey Ed Stewart provided the between-races entertainment and the announcer was Bob Danvers Walker, whose voice was well known on the nation's cinema newsreels. Redmond contacted Ove and told him, 'You will love Wembley. Come and do a few meetings.' Ove says, 'He was another of my good friends. I can't tell you how many meetings I did for Wembley, but it was not very many. I never took it seriously any more. Well, I took it seriously when I was there, but I forgot about as soon as I left.'

The Lions, in their distinctive red and white, were reborn at the Empire Stadium on Saturday 30 May in a local derby against London neighbours Hackney. On a track where he had experienced so many nights of glory, Ove didn't disappoint the crowd, reported to be 20,000, or his good friend Redmond, top scoring on 9 points and leading the side to a 41-37 home win. But he was to ride only fourteen matches for Wembley – eight away and six at home – for an average of 7.932, much reduced from the years when he was at his best.

'When Trevor opened Wembley,' says Ove, 'I had even less time. I was working very hard at my business, but I couldn't resist going to Wembley. Freddie Williams was the team manager. Bernard Cottrell used to pick me up at Heathrow in his Rolls-Royce. I had a few hours before the meeting and I spent some time in his penthouse near the stadium and I was very impressed. But of course he and Trevor fell out – they ended up deadly enemies, but I don't know why.'

Wembley lasted another season before speedway was evicted, because of planned extensions to the soccer season, by the ungrateful stadium authorities – had it not been for weekly speedway since 1929, the original Empire Stadium may well have ceased to exist before it did. Ove made his farewell racing appearance on the Wembley stage he had graced with such historic tenacity, such brilliance and such formidable mastery, when he led Sweden to another World Team Cup win in 1970 against Great Britain, Poland and Czechoslovakia. There were also his eighth and ninth Swedish individual championships in 1969 and 1970. And though he'd had to wait a long time for league championship medals, there was a second Swedish league title with his team Kaparna to go with their first in 1968.

The highest league position Norwich had reached during Ove's career with the Stars had been runners-up in 1958 and 1963, and yet throughout all those years of fabulous achievement in Britain, he was never approached by another – perhaps a more glamorous, more wealthy, more ambitious, more successful – club to switch allegiances. 'Not once. Not once. Never, ever,' he said. 'People ask me that today. I had an e-mail the other day – maybe Oxford – from someone who said I always enjoyed it when you came to our track and only wish you had ridden for our team. Did they never ask you? I wrote back and told him there was not anyone asking – until after Norwich closed. Then several came in.

'I know Ronnie Moore turned down chances to leave Wimbledon
with offers of more money, but no one offered me anything. When
you are young you want to make money, but no one came to me and
said we'll give you more money to ride for us. I wish they had done,
especially one of those London teams. But even if they had I don't
think I would have left Norwich. I liked Norwich and the people of
Norwich liked me. I was happy there. Maybe when Norwich closed
down I would have gone to another team, or if I'd been approached by
someone else before Norwich, because I would have much preferred
to have been with one of those London teams, even though I don't
like big cities. But it would have been so much more convenient for
me to be right next to the airport.

'I never rode for the money. I was happy with what I did receive,
it was more than I used anyway. And when you are young you don't
think of saving or investing. I wish I had done now – now that I'm
older and wiser. Even the bit I made – because I didn't need it – I
could have invested it. If I had invested in property in England, look
where I would have been today. I could have bought terraced houses
for a hundred quid each – a whole string of them.

'Mind you, when I rode on the Continent in open meetings that was
a different story. They would say I could have so much. I could ask for
so much. When I rode in Austria I said I wanted 10,000 schillings, but
that included my travel. I had to pay everything out there. I wanted to
make my own arrangements because I would have someone to bring
down a bike. For sure I could not take the track spare from Norwich
and put it on a plane.'

Ove says he never had a final race and, indeed, this is true, because
he still gets astride a speedway bike. One of his most recent escapades
was to open, with former English international Malcolm Simmons,
the speedway section of the midsummer Motorcyle World event at
the National Motor Museum, Beaulieu in Hampshire, but his last
really competitive race on a speedway track was in October 1970. It
was, by all accounts, a spectacular exit. Ove says: 'I got knocked over
by bloody Ray Wilson in a Test match at Stockholm. He put me in
hospital for two days.' There had been a six-match international series

between Great Britain and Sweden in England in July that Sweden had lost 5-1. Ove had ridden in only the first match at Glasgow when Great Britain had won 66-42. Ove, as captain, had failed to score and the leadership of the Swedish side was then taken over for the rest of the series by Anders Michanek. A return three-match series in Sweden took place in October with Ove restored to the captaincy. He scored only 1 in a 45-63 defeat at Gothenburg, but his form picked up in the second Test at Malilla with a useful 15 points in Sweden's 73-34 victory. The crunch came in the third and final match at Stockholm on 6 October.

Ove won his first two rides and Sweden held a slight lead. But in his third outing, against the Great Britain pairing of Ray Wilson and Eric Boocock, Ove missed the gate and is then reported to have made a 'wild attempt' to make up lost ground on the first bend. What happened next, according to an on-the-spot report by Neil Wahlgren, 'changed the course of the match'. Ove caught up with the Great Britain pairing and cannoned into Wilson, but lost control and crashed into the fence. He was then hit by his partner Tommy Johansson, who flew over the fence and landed on the terracing. Fortunately neither he nor any of the spectators was hurt, but Ove was taken to hospital with concussion. Wilson was excluded, and a furious row developed, with the Great Britain team protesting so vigorously that, after some time the referee relented and allowed Wilson back in for the re-run. It proved to be the turning point of the meeting and Great Britain won 61-47 and the series 2-1.

The Swedish press carried a picture of the crash and of Ove being carried away on a stretcher under the headline 'Varldsmastarens sista tavling? Har slas han medvetslos' – Is This the World Champion's Last Meeting? Ove's version is this: 'He knocked me off against the fence. And that is when I quit after this. The newspaper was asking, "Is this the World Champion's last meeting? Here he is knocked unconscious." I was in hospital for two days, the only time I was with concussion. I think it was the last competitive race I had. I had already more or less stopped racing anyway, so it didn't really matter. He was a bastard, that Wilson. He was ruthless. He ran into anyone. I wasn't the only one.'

Earlier, Ove had been in pursuit of yet another World Championship and had reached the British-Nordic Final at Coventry. But his score of 7 points meant he qualified only as a reserve for the next round, the European Final in Leningrad. It really looked as though, instead of having the opportunity to set one unique record and thwart another – win a sixth World title himself and spoil Ivan Mauger's run of three in succession – it really was the end of the Fundin World Championship line. But Bengt Jansson broke a wrist and Ove took his place, putting him back in the running. He reached Leningrad, but never arrived at the meeting. The reason was a final show of temperament.

He says: 'I flew in there with the chairman of the Swedish Motor Federation. At the time he was secretary to the Defence Minister in Sweden, later he was Defence Minister himself and then Ambassador in New York and Moscow – anyway, he was the big man, and he was sitting next to me on the aeroplane. I didn't have a visa to get in. Being on the move all the time I had not had time to send in my passport to the consulate to get a visa. But I thought I'd be all right – I thought I'd get in because I'd been invited to go there. I'd gone before to Czechoslovakia without a visa – that was very strict, but they knew who you were. In Russia and all those states they always came aboard the aeroplane and checked all the passports. On this occasion they looked at mine and said – in Russian – you have no visa. And this man I was with, who knew languages, explained the situation. He said, "Don't worry, as soon as I get off the plane I'll clear it up. You'll soon be off." Everybody left the plane except me, and a soldier sat down next to me with a Kalashnikov rifle to guard me. I wasn't allowed off the plane. Time went by and the aeroplane started to fill up with people again because it was flying back to Stockholm. What could I do? I just sat there and went with the plane back to Stockholm. But before we arrived, the captain of the aeroplane came to me with the message that I had to see the border patrol in Stockholm straight away because they knew all about it.

'When we got back to Stockholm they were waiting there with apologies from the people back in Russia that there had been a mis-understanding. But by that time, with my short temper and all that, I was so worked up that I said, "Never again, those f——ing Russians, I never want to see them ever again!" They said all I had to do was hop on the next plane, that the tickets were arranged and they were waiting there for me. But I went and bought myself a ticket and flew back to Malmo. Afterwards I received a very nice letter from the chairman of the Communist Party of Sweden – who was the most devoted Red they ever had there – a letter from him saying I shouldn't worry, that I should understand them and also understand that it was partly my fault, and he apologised for his comrades in Russia. But even though it cost me my chance of another World Championship, I decided I would not go there.'

In a feature entitled 'It is Tough at the Top' in *Speedway Star & News*, writer Jim White analysed Fundin like this: 'My own theory is that Ove is too volatile a personality for many speedway followers to get used to at once. He would pass unnoticed on the football field, but the speedway crowd is used to nothing more than a touch of gloves at the end of a race, or a slight wave to acknowledge the cheers. Not so with Ove. If the champ gets crossed, whether by an opponent or a referee – and let's face it he is rather sensitive on many things – he shows it and doesn't care who knows. Ove is the biggest draw in the sport. He wants to win so much it hurts. To alter an old phrase one ought truthfully to say, "Hell hath no fury like Fundin in second place." Yet off the track Ove is a gentle person, happy and willing to chat with anyone who might wish a few words with him or perhaps an autograph.'

Dave Lanning says: 'Men like Ove Fundin happen only once in a lifetime. We should be grateful we have had the chance to see him, because our grandchildren will certainly be talking about him as they wheel us into speedway meetings in 2021.'

# EPILOGUE

*'When I ride now I still like to win, but you are always a little bit nervous. Can I slide it round the first corner? But it comes back like riding a pushbike. Of course it's not fast, but it's there.'* – Ove Fundin

Ove Fundin was still going strong well into the 1970s. In 1974 he joined the star-studded Briggs-Mauger World Champions Troupe to race on the West Coast of America and in Texas at the Houston Astrodome, as well as Australia and New Zealand. In 1976 he toured Israel with a Rest of the World side against the Americans, when he and Barry Briggs were the series' joint-top scorers.

He says: 'In Tel Aviv, so as not to ruin the tracks there, because they were made for running, we cut all the tread off brand new tyres so they were smooth – and that was a fantastic idea. I heard somewhere that there was some talk about using those kind of tyres in speedway, which would slow everybody down a bit and make it more even. We had some very good racing on them and we didn't tear up the tracks. We got lots of spin, but it suited me because I had always been good getting traction. That way it would be a disadvantage to have too strong an engine, and they should do away with those four valves. That has also ruined speedway a bit. They are too costly. They could go back to the old ones. On slick tyres a JAP would be perfect. Maybe they would have to start making something like the JAP again.'

He has always maintained an interest in the sport he graced with such brilliance, and over the years has been a regular at the annual dinner of the Veteran Speedway Riders' Association in Britain, being elected president in 1993. He says: 'Like many others, I have got back my interest in the sport thanks to the television coverage. I think we are all grateful for that, and the Grand Prix.' Now, half a century on, his views on how the sport has developed are equally as forthright and vociferous as ever they were during his controversial prime. He says: 'I think it's disgraceful the way riders in Britain have different teams each year because of the points limit. It destroys club loyalty by virtually forcing riders to switch teams every season. I would never have dreamed of doing that. I was with Norwich until they closed. Of course, we keep coming back to "our days" – the time of Ronnie, Barry, Peter Craven and me. Peter was with Belle Vue all the time, except when he started out at Liverpool. He was not with Belle Vue one season, next season Wimbledon and next season somewhere else. Ronnie was a Wimbledon rider, I was a Norwich rider. Barry moved around a bit but not as bad as today. Not with that silly guest system as well. That's a farce. One week they ride with you, next week they ride against you. What kind of team spirit would that give? The likes of me were not very good team men – the way I rode was very selfish – but at least I stayed with the team.

'A team should not be built around just one or two star riders, so that it virtually ceases to exist because of the demands of the Grand Prix, or because they are foreigners and are sometimes ordered to return to their own country to ride. I guess I was a star man at Norwich, but I had to do what my national controlling organisation told me to. When SVEMO said jump, I jumped. Even if they ordered me to return to race in a crap meeting, I had to go. If the star men have to be away, for whatever reason, then that gives the up-and-coming ambitious youngsters their chance.

'Some of the top riders are holding the sport to ransom these days – and it's not really the riders who are to blame, but the managers they employ to negotiate for them. Too many are greedy and are asking for too much money. In my day managers were unheard of. In all my years of riding I never received one penny more than the permitted start and points money. Riders should realise that speedway is not Formula 1. The sport doesn't justify someone having lots of bikes and a big transporter, and the money is not as compensation for the risks involved either. I'm quite sure that none of them consider the risks – except the risk of investing in another speedway bike. When I was offered the use of an EsO machine – now JAWA – I was never given any money, the factory just supplied me with bikes.'

Fundin can often be seen at modern Grands Prix and, after due consideration, admits that he would have enjoyed riding in the series. But he questions the qualification system. 'It's crazy,' he says. 'There should be qualifying rounds for everyone, which would open the competition up to many more faces. At the moment there is a danger of the public seeing the same riders all the time – just like Formula 1, where you can practically calculate who is going to win that before the season even starts. We don't want to see the same names every year. By doing this they make it a closed circuit like F1. For someone else to get in there it will be difficult. I think eventually it will be a completely closed circuit. There has to be a better system. Now there is automatic qualification for some riders, but when I was in the World Championship even the winner had to go through all the qualifying rounds just like everyone else.

'Don't think that I'm against the Grand Prix system and all that, but it makes me sad when they say that it was so much easier in our day, and also of course it is good for speedway because we have not seen those sort of meetings for a long, long time. The sport has been brought back to the big stadiums, which is good, so we should be grateful for that. Why am I saying all this? Because, like many others, I have got back my interest in the sport thanks to the television coverage. I think we are all grateful for that.'

Benfield Sports International, having taken the old World Championship by the scruff of its neck and transformed it into the speedway Grand Prix, revitalised the moribund World Team Cup at the start of the new millennium. As befitted the razzmatazz that they had injected into the world individual competition, they needed something classy and eye-catching to make not only the speedway world but the media sit up and take notice. They settled on a handsome new £10,000 trophy, and they named it after Ove Fundin.

'I am quite friendly with John Postlethwaite, the chief executive at Benfield,' says Ove. 'I know him quite well, and they first invited me to the press conference after one of the Grands Prix to announce the new World Team Cup and show the trophy. They took care of me very well. I have never seen anything like it in speedway. They sent me air tickets, there and back, first class. They sent a taxi to pick me up at the airport, and they put me up in the nicest hotel there was, the hotel where they stayed themselves, John, and all his gang. When I came into the hotel there was a big bouquet of flowers and two bottles of wine. There was a card saying welcome. They wrote to me a few times and asked me if I minded them naming the World Cup after me. Of course I said I would be more than honoured.' The sterling silver trophy, designed by Asprey and Gerrard, the Crown jewellers, who also created trophies for the US Masters golf tournament, the PGA golf championship and the rugby World Cup, is two feet high and is in the shape of a gilt globe of the world surrounded by an authentic speedway rear gear sprocket.

Nowadays, when the fancy takes him, Ove gets back on a bike, his BMW R1300 RT, and takes a trip from France to Sweden to see a Grand Prix. You may find him roaring round the Pyrenees for the weekend on a jaunt with half-a-dozen other motorcycle enthusiasts who just happen to be airline captains – fellow pilots. Ove has recently passed all his medical tests and has been cleared to fly for another year. He rode the bike 600 miles from his home to visit me in southern Spain to be at the launch of our Speedway Amigos Europe group, made up of expats who have decided to keep the speedway flag flying on the Costas. Then there is the occasional Golden Greats meeting.

'Of course, when I ride now I still like to win,' he says. 'But I wouldn't take it too far because I would hate to fall off and break a leg or something like that. I wouldn't want to walk around in plaster for six months. The Golden Greats are fun. It's amazing. I only do it once a year and in between times I never go near a speedway bike. I don't have one and I don't go near the places. And there is no practice or anything. You are always a little bit nervous. Can I slide it round the first corner? But it comes back like riding a pushbike. Of course it's not fast, but it's there.'

Have there been any regrets?

'I would have had regrets if I had not been successful,' says Ove. 'I don't look back on my racing career – only when I'm reminded of it. Then of course I do. Sometimes I even wonder if I did it. One thing

I do, or I can say off-hand, is that I was never friendly enough with everyone else, especially Les. You must remember I had red hair and they always say that red-haired people are aggressive and hot-tempered, which I certainly was. And poor Les. If we had gone to a meeting and it had not gone well for me, no doubt I would be swearing till I fell asleep. So that is one thing I do regret. But not with riding.

'The only thing that mattered to me was winning. If I didn't win I felt sorry for myself – no, sorry is the wrong word. I felt angry with myself because I knew that if I had gone harder into that corner, came better out of that corner, had missed that bump, whatever, I could have won. So I was always angry with myself if I didn't.

'Maybe sometimes I regret that I didn't take it seriously enough. Today I would have taken it even more seriously. Knowing what I know now, I could have spent a bit of money and bought my own equipment, for instance, and I could have made sure that I had the back-up like they have today. And maybe I would have tried harder. I gave up too easily once or twice.'

# INNERVIEWS

*'Well, after a couple of World Finals I thought, "I can win this." And of course that was my aim. I wanted to win everything. I was very good at forgetting the last meeting and concentrating on the next.'* – Ove Fundin

While compiling this book a great deal of material was gathered. Some of it, for one reason or another, I felt did not comfortably fit into the running story, but I didn't want to discard all of it and see it end up on the cutting room floor – or 'the spike', as we say in the journalistic trade. So I have called the collection 'Innerviews', inspired by the editor of an American speedway magazine who was very happy to print all the stuff I wrote for him, but was never equally as happy to pay me, and to this day still owes me money.

'Speedway has always had its men to hate. Nine out of ten are the perfectionists whose only fault was that they could beat everybody practically all the time... and make it look simple. For the nearest piece of humanity to speedway perfection, then Fundin must be your man. Mind you, he was not the greatest sportsman I have ever seen. He would accept defeat but he would not like it. And that occasionally showed. The crowd saw it and didn't like it. Being a winner was almost a religion with him. The trouble was he let his feelings show, and that made him appear a bad loser.'
– Angus Kix, writer.

'I was always pessimistic. And not just for World Championships, but for any ordinary meeting. Quite often, if it was anything important

and the sky started to get dark, I would more or less say, "Please God let it rain so I can get away and I don't have to ride."'
– Ove Fundin.

'I liked and respected Ove as a rider. I've always respected him as a rider, because I think he was one of the top riders that ever was – but you couldn't say that you liked Ove when he was riding because he didn't have time for anyone. There was only one thing in his life. When it is said he was not likeable to people, I don't think it was an aggressive attitude towards people. I think it was just that his mind was on one thing. He was absolutely focused.

'He would have been good at anything he took on. His transport business was out of this world. Absolutely. I went to stay with him in Sweden and went to his office. It was in the early days of computers and everything was there. Wonderful. But that was him. Anything he took up he would have been the top man. Like this walk he's done, like the cycle ride he did, and of course the number of parachute jumps he's made. The thing about him, he had 'the killer instinct' to win.

'I was an announcer and I've refereed. But I never got close to Ove while he was riding. I must say, quite out of the blue, he invited my wife and I to Sweden for a holiday, and he did everything for us. He was most hospitable. He was fantastic. And he said to me one day, "I didn't like you. You were chairman of the supporters' club and you gave every other rider a bloody engine and you didn't give me one." He has never forgotten that. He knew he was the figurehead who brought in the crowds, so he thought he should have been given an engine as well. I had to explain to him that the other riders didn't get the wherewithall [money] that he got – but he has never forgotten it. And he still doesn't understand why he didn't get the engine.

'I don't ever remember him doing a dangerous thing to another rider. There have been dust-ups afterwards because he'd gone past somebody, a sort of, "Get out of my way," as he went through on the inside. He expected everybody else to do the same. Peter Craven and Ove had a lot of respect for each other. I once stood with Fundin at the Belle Vue pit gate and Craven came down the straight, and you know how he used to bring his foot up. Fundin said, "He will have only one crash – because it is all done on balance." Craven once said to me, "You get behind Fundin, you wait for him to make a mistake. Fundin gets behind me and he waits for me to make a mistake."

'It was hard work getting the crowd going at King's Lynn. I finally cracked it by asking people to write to me with the war cries they wanted read out. This particular one... how did it go now? "Two, four, six and a bit, who's got King's Lynn in the shit!?" I said, "Oh, we can't have that. Would you like to hear it again?" And they shouted, "Yes!" And after that we got them going.

'Ove used to miss the second halves sometimes. But I think he was so good that the crowd would forgive him anything. They just accepted he had to get to London and a meeting somewhere on the Continent. Gordon Parkins was very good, he used to give me stuff to tell the crowd: Fundin was riding in Sweden – and I remember him riding in five different countries in nine days and dropping only three points. Incredible when you think about it.

'I was staying with him once in Belgium. We dropped our wives off at Ostend where he kept his aircaft and he said, "Today we fly to Le Touquet." When we got there I said, "Shall we get a taxi?" And he said, "No, we walk into town." It was about three miles. He said, "We don't want too much to eat, we'll eat tonight." I was about sixty-five then and said, "Shall we get a taxi back?" And he said, "No, no, no. We'll walk another way and look at the beautiful houses." He was so fit.

'The thing about Norwich was that every rider you spoke to loved the track and they loved the atmosphere of the social scene after the racing in the club room. I don't know how some of them got back to where they were supposed to. When I think back about that stadium it was like a potential fireball. I had a wooden plank to cross and a rope to hang on to to get to my announcer's box. You could sit and smoke. If that lot had gone up I couldn't have got out.

'The Norwich directors had a very 'old-fashioned' approach – a good manner and bearing – and Gordon Parkins could sort out squabbles very quickly. He'd listen to both sides and he'd have them shaking hands in no time. He was a diplomat, but of course he was ruled by a

very, very hard bunch of directors. They had a very rich farmer, Harry
Wharton, as chairman who didn't understand much of what was going
on. They had another director who was the managing director of a big
clothing company who was the brains behind it, George Mann. But
they were in it for the money. When I was chairman of the supporters'
club, they had a massive club room with a marvellous Canadian beech
floor. I wanted them to make it bigger and put a top on and open a
proper restaurant that would operate seven days a week, and then put
in an indoor bowling rink. A leisure centre. It was unheard of in those
days. And they laughed at me.'
– Bill Smith, former announcer at The Firs, speedway referee and
Norwich supporter's club chairman.

'We were racing in Czechoslovakia, in Pardubice, where they do that
Golden Helmet every year. In those days alcohol was so very expensive in Sweden, so everybody used to try and smuggle. I didn't drink
any of it so it didn't matter to me. I won a barrel of beer – a whole
barrel. I knew I couldn't take it home. So the Russians said, "We'll
take it for you." Because they had a bus with all the things in. On the
ferryboat I bought quite a few bottles of vodka, whisky, whatever. I
put everything in the Russians' bus. They didn't check on them. They
checked on me.

   'Igor Plechanov helps out at a go-kart track these days. He instructs.
And Boris Samorodov, he is a riding instructor at a motocross school.
They didn't want to talk to me too much about what they did when
they gave up speedway. But from what I gathered, Plechanov has been
married twice and both his wives died – the last one hanged herself.
He has one son who lives in Moscow. Boris still is married. When they
first quit racing they were taken care of by the state. They would have
been well off had it not been for the collapse of the Soviet Union. But
Boris says now they have nothing. Not a decent home, not a motor
car. The bikes they rode were never theirs. The clubs of course owned
their speedway bikes. The clubs were owned by the police, the military,
the trade unions. One season I took up ice racing so that I could go
to Russia. I wanted to see Russia and as a tourist I couldn't go. I am

interested in any country. Jack Fearnley, who ran Belle Vue, he had contacts in Russia because he used to go there to arrange circus acts and animals. He took the Belle Vue team to Leningrad when I did that short season with Belle Vue.'

– Ove Fundin.

'I took Ove and a Scandinavian team to South Africa in 1955. If we had a party, and maybe there were girls there, like, he would sit in the corner. Shy, he was. Later on he changed completely. He was the same as me. When we were in England we had to go to the next meeting. So you couldn't piss about really. Make sure you get to bed and get up in time. You had to establish yourself before you started messing about. Oh, yes there were opportunities. The girls would come looking for you, but then you would think: Oh, I can't go there. I think Ove was always looking towards the next meeting, and on race day it was no good even talking to him. He was concentrating. As soon as he got up he was focused. The programme in Norwich was: a bit of breakfast, then he would go to the pictures. That finished about five o'clock. Then it was down to the stadium, get ready.

'In South Africa we went to the Kruger Park. I had a car and my wife was with me there. A big baboon turned up and she jumped in the car and shut the door and then the baboon – they look horrible, don't they? – went for Fundin. The baboon was behind him and it chased him round the car. He was shouting, "Open the door! Open the door!" He didn't like that bit. He was really frightened. We opened the door for him in the end. We did it to scare him a little bit. He wasn't very pleased.

'We also travelled to Austria. He was very popular in Austria. There was this huge stadium in Vienna. We had brilliant hotels. There was Barry Briggs, Jack Young, Ronnie Moore, Trevor Redmond, Howdy Byford, me and Fundin. Really good teams. I think with Fundin he built up the speedway there. And they took us out to these nice places, nightclubs and things.

'I played a trick on Fundin. We came walking back in the evening, and I said, "What's that hanging up there out of the window?" He looked up and said, "Oh, my f——ing bike." I had got a rope and hung the bike out of the window, third floor up. I did a lot of stupid things. But Fundin was never like that. He was 100 per cent sportsman. Always clean. Always doing his best. The riders today have all these wonderful bloody kevlars and equipment to ride in. He never had any really nice leathers. He had gloves with holes in, his boots – the soles were always coming off them. He had to tape them together, and things like that. I don't know if that was a good luck charm. He wouldn't go looking pretty or anything like that. He was arrogant and obviously he could have been more popular. If you want to be popular you have to sign more autographs. Speak to people. He did that later on. Michanek was worse than Fundin. He was an awful bastard.

'What was it that made Fundin so special? Well, I think he must have just picked up how to ride a speedway bike so well, but not with other forms of motorcycling. I suppose once you get up with the top boys, you don't think of them as the top boys. It's like if you see them in the pub every evening. You get used to them, and then you probably know a little bit more about them so you know how to beat them. You are not overawed by them any more. I tried to suss him out and try and beat the bugger, but I couldn't. And once he got on that line – I mean they rode the line in those days. He'd got what it takes to win at speedway. Win the gate. Being tough. He wasn't very polite. You can't be, can you? Like Tommy Price said, "I've got no friends in speedway. If you want to get on in this game don't have any friends." Which means: if you need a point, just run into them.

'I remember when Tommy Price came to Sweden one time. It was a big meeting. I think Fundin was there, and Rune Sormander. And a big crowd. And Basse Hveem was there. He wasn't a very good speedway rider, he was a long-track rider. At the end of the meeting Tommy Price was going out with Basse Hveem. I said to Tommy, "What about having him sorted so that I can win the meeting?" And he said, "I'll see what we can do." Stone-last came Basse Hveem. Tommy took him out. I just wanted to get Basse Hveem less points. Tommy was the man to do it, the way he told me in England.

'Fundin was a brilliant man. I think he is one of the most edu-
cated riders. He read a lot. When he came to big cities he went round
and looked at things. You wouldn't think he was a speedway rider. We
never fell out. We were always friends. He was just a guy who was a
good speedway rider who was doing his best. In the beginning he
did run people down. Barry Briggs was the same. But you want to
show people you can do it. It takes time. It is not an easy sport, going
round a circuit with a fence. It is easy when you know it, but it's difficult
to learn – but it's bloody difficult when you have all that power and you
have to go facing that way and then all of a sudden facing that way. And
then you have to race four of you. That is why lots of people are good
on their own, but they are not so good when they get in traffic.

'When Fundin finished riding I was disappointed with Sweden, and
I did tell them. A guy like that who got all those World titles, and all
those World Finals for Sweden, when they finish one day they don't
even get a thank you letter. Not like England – where Henry Cooper,
the boxer, goes round thirty years after he is finished. I wanted Fundin
to be like that in Sweden.

'I tell you how powerful Fundin's influence was. We were about to
ride in a meeting in Czechoslovakia and the promoter had said they
were going to pay us in dollars. We didn't want any of their money,
because you couldn't take it out. You had to buy things with it. So
I said, "Show us the money now." And they said they hadn't got the
money then, they would get it later. So we said, "If you can't produce
the money in dollars now, we won't ride." So we went and got changed
out of leathers. There were 30,000 people there. So they came back
and said they had the money, so we went and got changed and came
out again. Then they said they had half of it. So we went back in and
changed again. That's how it went for an hour. In the end we got
the money – in dollars. And the meeting was hard for me – it was so
bumpy. But Fundin, he went round there and won it. That was the
only time we were striking to get our money. But it was only because
of Fundin. It wouldn't have worked with anybody else but Fundin.'
– Olle Nygren, friend, Swedish international teammate and Norwich
teammate 1962-1964.

'The World Final promoters were cheapskates, weren't they, when you think how many people were in Wembley Stadium on a World Final night? What a riot there was when we wanted more than just the £500 for winning the title laid down by the FIM. It was ridiculous, the money we were paid, it was just bloody daylight robbery. How many people do they need now to substantiate riders being paid a couple of grand a meeting? It's sad that people don't understand what speedway was about. You go in front of 50,000 people all the time. And those Wembley boys were riding in front of 70,000 people every week. The promoters couldn't dig shit, could they? I don't think they even thought about the sport. You look back and see how they ran World Finals. They just happened and they happened in front of 75,000 people. They didn't go out and bang any drums or do a master promotion. And that's what happened to speedway. When it wasn't controlled it was in freefall. Like Eccleston in Formula 1. It's a crap sport, I think, but as soon as Bernie sees something going wrong, he changes the formula or does something to even it up. The Speedway Control Board, they were all nice blokes, but they never lost money out of their own pockets. The surest way to learn what to do and what not to do as a promoter is to lose a packet of money.'
– Barry Briggs, rival, friend and four times World Speedway Champion.

'As a person Ove is fantastic, but that is because he is now away from speedway. We have an understanding: if he comes to New Zealand he has a bed at my place, the same for me when I go to France. Speedway rider and an opponent: tough as hell, not dirty, but tough.'
– Ronnie Moore.

'Not all of us have clear memories of my father competing, even if I have some pale memories from the racetracks when he came home with one or two bikes heavily stuffed in the back of our Mercedes Benz! One memory I would like to share is when we played a game together, and this one tells us a lot about his urgency to win in everything he does. He is extreme in this sense; not always in a healthy way, for him or others.

'I was around eight or nine years old, I guess, in the beginning of the
1970s. My parents were divorced and I was visiting, and that was also
always my feeling – it was a visit, with one of my brothers or sisters,
can't remember who it was now. We were only allowed to visit one
or two at a time. We were playing a game at home, in Swedish called
Fia Med Knuff, or I believe in English, Ludo. It's a game where you
throw a dice and you push or bump the others off the table, meaning
that they have to start all over again. Ove's wife at that time, Catharina,
was also playing. After a while when it seemed like my father was
winning I came up from behind and pushed his piece off the board
– after he had done it several times with us, every time laughing, and
criticising me for being a sourpuss. When he realised that he would
have to start all over with his piece and probably couldn't win, he
went completely mad, raised and grabbed the game table with all the
pieces and dice, and chucked it into the wall. Smash! Boom! Crash!
He yelled at us and ran into his bedroom and came out of there not
until next day. There I sat in the sofa, startled and scared. He couldn't
take a loss even if it just was a party game between him, his wife and
his own children.

'This is an example of how it always has been, and always will
be. Recently when I and my own children, two boys, Karl and
Gustaf, went down to France to visit my father we went out to play
boules. My youngest boy Gustaf is also very, very anxious to win.
He is eight now but was six at that time. The game ended up with
my father leaving the field/playground angry, not fulfilling the
game, and Gustaf crying and yelling and very angry with all of us
and especially with his grandfather. They exasperated each other
into fury!

'Of course the actions of my father also has affected us children a lot.'
– Niclas Fundin, Ove's youngest son, born in 1966.

'Ove was complex. He didn't mix and laugh like other riders. He was
there to win. Occasionally I would beat him, mostly at Wimbledon,
and he would park his bike on the track after the race to make out
it had developed a fault. When it was pushed into the pits it was just

filled for his next race, so there was nothing wrong with the bike. But I could never convince anyone that I had beaten him fair and square. Many a time I saw him in tears after he had been beaten. My strategy at Wimbledon was if I beat him to the first bend, which I did at times, I would ride an inch from the white line, then go down the straights about six or seven feet from the inside line. Because Ove would not go around you, so you knew at every bend he would be trying to pass on your left. This only worked at Wimbledon and New Cross.

'Fundin was the ultimate in gating – his reactions were so good. In Sweden there was a gaming machine on a wall in a certain café. There you put in a krone, which sat at the top of the machine. Then, after about three to eight seconds it dropped and if you could press a button and stop it getting to the bottom you got it back (not good odds). Now Briggo, always wanting to be one up on Ove, would try it too. Ove's coin would travel down about two inches, and he would stop it and get his coin back. Briggo always lost his coin. It went the whole twelve inches. He lost all his pocket money that way. Poor old Briggo would even try and listen to the mechanism to see if there was any trickery.

'In 1958 in South Africa Ove and I were asked to go to Johannesburg from Pretoria to pick up some cars for a local dealer. We went for a walk together around the city and Ove bought a big bunch of grapes from a street vendor. I thought, well he will share them with me, so I bought a bunch of bananas to share with him. He ate about half a pound of the grapes and still had heaps left. Then he just found a rubbish bin and tossed the rest away. So I said to him, "Do you want a banana?" And he said, "If I wanted a banana I would have bought some." So that was Ove, he didn't need friends. But now he is such a delightful person.'
– Bob Andrews, World Pairs Champion with Ivan Mauger 1969, World number five 1961, England international, Wimbledon, Wolverhampton, Cradley Heath and Hackney, now retired and living in New Zealand.

'I asked around once. They told me that being on drugs was good for you. What bloody advantage can there be in that? It's not like running,

or skiing or something where you have to get the most out of yourself. A doctor friend of mine explained to me that the advantage that they get out of it is that they have no fear. They think, "I can live for ever, I can do anything." They can go into a corner at twice the speed that any other human being can. And that was the advantage – they lost the fear. Because all of us have something built into us, if we are clever enough, we have something tell us we have to brake here. Like when you drive your car. But when you are on drugs you think, "It doesn't apply to me." And because a speedway race lasts less than sixty seconds, you don't have to build yourself up to be exceptionally physically strong. Josef Angermuller, of Germany, he was very ordinary, but he could have been so much better. In Israel in 1976 we stayed in a big hotel, all of us. Back at the hotel he was behaving as a drunk. Myself and Barry, we shared a room – that's another argument to use that we are friends – and this one night Josef seemed to us to be very drunk. One of the Americans, Sonny Nutter, said to myself and Barry the following morning, "We gave Josef a little bit of our 'medicine'."
– Ove Fundin

'Of course he never hardly broke traction. He seemed to ride the bike in a straight line. And he rode a Rotrax frame with a very short back end, which is very hard to ride. But he was the sort of rider who could master it. It pulled so hard, being a short frame. It was tough to hold it and he was absolutely 100 per cent fit. When we used to go away he used to have a bag of apples by the side of him and he'd eat them all the while. Reg Trott had an almost identical bike, with a slightly longer frame. Ove used to get on that and win races. I've seen him beat Craven round Belle Vue on it in a Match Race.

'When I first started at Norwich I was at work in Norwich as a mechanic and I was getting about £2 10s a week. I went up to The Firs and had a few practices and Gordon Parkins said, "We'll put you on a contract." I got £8 10s a week – maintenance money. I don't know if they all used to do it, but that's what Norwich used to do – a sort of retainer, I suppose. Pay rates were at the time £2 a point and 10s a start and a weekly retainer. It wasn't that bad then. We used to pay about £75 for an engine and towards the end they were about £100. Now a GM engine off me is about £1,600 plus VAT. I reckon today's top riders are on two grand a meeting.

'There were two riders who used to come to Norwich who could get the better of Fundin – and they were Ron How and Ronnie Genz. They were white liners and Ove wouldn't go past them on the outside.'
– Trevor Hedge, World Finalist, England international, Norwich team-mate 1961-1964 and now a major engine tuner.

'I've got the mission to tell about Ove's eating habits. Of course I can only talk about the time since we have met, some sixteen years ago. He avoids as much as possible eating meat. He likes vegetables, the Mediterranean style of cuisine with olive oil, garlic, lots of fish, shrimps, salads, rice – especially wild rice – and pasta. He likes even the Romanian-Italian polenta accompanying a French-Romanian ratatouille. Ove eats with pleasure vegetable gratins, cauliflower, broccoli, zucchini. He loves Romanian eggplant salad, called caviar d'aubergines here in Provence, and he enjoys some Thai or Chinese dishes that I cook now and then. But he could live on cheese, crispbread and tea, cornflakes, muesli and fruit yoghurt. He likes, of course, fruit: apples, oranges, pineapples. And ICE CREAM and CHOCOLATE! Ove only has a 'tea and cheese on brown or wholegrain bread' lunch. Our principal meal is dinner around seven in the evening, most of the time accompanied by wine, prefering the whites from Alsace or Bourgogne, now and then even reds from Bordeaux or Cotes de Provence. The source of Ove's well-being is in the saying 'one is what one eats' and, I am pretty sure, the fact that he is almost addicted to motion. Golf, his pushbike and those long, long walks.'
– Ioanna Fundin

'I reckon a lot of my early success was due to the good advice given to me by Ove. Many times in my early days at Norwich he told me, "You are trying too hard, Hendriks. Keep more to the inside and you will win races. Out there on the boards you merely collect dirt and get nowhere." Sometimes I ride with Ove and then I could understand the reason for his greatness. Ove was the best line rider in the sport

and could slip through openings that I personally just could not see. I found trying to team ride with Ove hard. His pace was too much for me. One occasion, when Ove did wait for me to follow him over the finishing line, riding full throttle and not slowing for a second I nearly went across first. Back in the pits, a grin playing around the corners of his mouth, Ove wagged a reproving finger at me and said, "Don't you spoil my maximum, Hendriks."'
– Arne Hendricksen, teammate at Norwich 1958

'After I'd stopped speedway I met a couple of guys on an exhibition demonstrating parachutes. I asked them what it was all about and they invited me to have a try. So I went and signed up for a course, which lasted over two weekends. Then I wanted to jump. I wanted to see if I could dare to do it. I had done the same with ski jumping, just to see if I could dare to do it – like Eddie the Eagle. That was when I had my speedway career. And I regretted it. When I stood up there and looked down I was scared! But I managed to do it. With a parachute it was just the same. And there again I regretted it so much. I was afraid of dying, I think. You sit there and the ground is about 1,000ft – that's the lowest you jump from. And the wind comes at you. The plane can't go slower than 100 miles an hour. And suddenly they say to you, "OK. Jump!" You have to go. And if you hesitate the aeroplane has travelled so far you will be landing somewhere that is not suitable. I was so scared. But I did one and said to myself: it wasn't so bad, and I wanted to do another one. Then I found out in the aeroplane you are on a static line, so I could have fallen out of the aircraft and that thing would have opened up. It was no test. Nothing to it.'
– Ove Fundin

'I was challenging Ove for the Golden Helmet in 1961 and my bike let me down a couple of times. I was very upset. Well, you don't go home laughing. Maybe I was disappointed more than upset. I had beaten Ove 2-1 in the first leg at Wimbledon and was leading him in the first heat in the second leg at Norwich when on the last lap I had a partial sei-zure, which frees itself if you put in a new plug and a bigger jet. I won the second race and then the same thing happened in the third race – another partial seizure. So Ove kept his Match Race Championship.

'Belle Vue were there and Peter Craven came to me after the first race and said, "Bad luck, Ron. Borrow my bike. You're welcome any time." Peter always carried two bikes, and it was very nice of him to offer – I always liked Peter Craven because he was one of our greatest riders ever as far as I am concerned. It was a tricky situation, that, and I said thanks a lot Pete but I don't like to because things might happen to it.

'I was a great admirer of him. I even went to his funeral. It was up at Liverpool and I got fined by the Control Board because I should have been at a meeting at Wimbledon. But I thought I ought to pay my respects to my England captain. I thought I ought to be there, so I just went off and I got fined for not turning up at the meeting at Wimbledon. I was the loser because it cost me money. But if you have respect for somebody, as far as I'm concerned I go with what I think is the right thing to do at the time.'
– Ron How, Harringay, Wimbledon and Oxford. One of the few riders who consistently beat Ove.


'At Houston the racing was good and the track was good. I only wish I'd had a decent bike because I enjoyed that night, beating all those young Americans. We stayed in Hawaii one time and we had Zenon Plech with us. In Hawaii it always rains every day – you know, a shower. If we got really wet we could change, but poor Zenon Plech had only one pair of pants and Barry went out and bought him a pair of trousers.'
– Ove Fundin.


'I was there in the great days before the Second World War. I helped Max Grosskreutz for quite a while. But then he went to Norwich and he pleaded with me to go with him. I didn't fancy over-reaching myself and going to Norwich. He rode and then he managed them for quite a while. He made quite a success of it there. He was a gentleman, a nice bloke. I had a very good grounding at Belle Vue, because I was

very, very friendly with the Langtons – Eric and Oliver – and of course, Bob Harrison. He was an excellent mechanic, knew what was what and knew all the ways round it. I spent a lot of time with them and picked up a lot of good knowledge from them. The Belle Vue boss, E.O. Spence, he was a gentleman and he came to my house to employ me. They were going through a bad time on the mechanical side just after the Second World War. I was working in a garage for John (J.D.) White, the old Sheffield rider, I was managing a garage for him. I had an engineering degree and I'd been in the motor trade all my life. After a year or two I got a bit tired and one day E.O. Spence came round and pleaded with me to go back. I stayed there for about seven years. I think that was about 1949 and I stayed there for quite a bit. Speedway now? Well, they don't race like they used to. I think we saw the golden era.'
– Harold Gardner, Belle Vue mechanic.

'Ove was a more relaxed rider by that time, and got on well with the team. I drew the short straw and became his partner and, of course, ended up with the gate positions that Ove did not want. However, I do recall winning one race while paired with Ove and he finished at the back, probably the only time that I beat him. I also got an extra £1 per race for being partnered with him. Now you know why I am so rich! He didn't last the season with us but there were no problems.'
– Vic White, Ove's race partner, Long Eaton 1966.

'Trevor Redmond took me out to South Africa and we stayed in a hotel owned by one of his business partners. One night Olle Nygren went on the phone in the pits to the referee to make a complaint about an incident on the track. Well, Trevor was racing with us, but it turned out that Trevor was also the referee and he was the timekeeper, and everything had been worked out beforehand. So when he won a race it was a new track record, for sure, and all the timing and the programme had been filled in by hand before the meeting even started. There wasn't a proper referee, and we probably had a bit of elastic for the starting tapes as well. Trevor said, "It's no use you trying to phone the referee, because the referee, that's me." And Olle went and got a big hammer and smashed the telephone to bits, and said, "In that case there's no need to have a bloody telephone either."

'The financial deal with Trevor was something I can't really remember, but he paid for my hotel and I was probably on about £25 a week or something like that. A straight deal. Normally we never did less than three meetings a week, sometimes more. They were so primitive. I remember one track that Trevor hadn't apparently been to look at. It was an agricultural showground and we were supposed to race at night in the dark, But there were no lights. So cars were parked all the way round the track and their lights were aimed so that they didn't blind you. They did blind you, of course. There was no fence either. The track was marked out with a few straw bales.'
– Ove Fundin.

'On our one and only speedway trip to America and Israel for the Briggo/Mauger World Champions Series, USA *v.* Rest of the World, the Yanks, including Bruce Penhall, Rick Woods etc, were all out chasing the Israeli girls. But Ove would spend his free time going round museums and visiting places from the Bible. While everyone else was painting the town red, Ove was adding to his cultural knowledge. It didn't do him any harm, either, as he was still super-fast out on the track. Ove kept himself pretty much to himself on these trips, but he certainly took no prisoners on the track. I always got on very well with him, but I remember that crazy American, Danny 'Berserko' Becker trying to run Ove into the fence only to finish up going through it himself after the old fox got his own back.'
– Bert Harkins, one of Scotland's finest and Ove's Wembley teammate in 1970.

'It would be fair in saying that winning a World Championship was not high on my list of ambitions. Every time I sat on my bike I gave 110 per cent, but on the big nights nerves did appear to get the better of me. When competing in qualifying rounds I would sail through virtually unbeaten but come World Final night it never seemed to happen. My main priority was to give my best for club and country, which is not the same as being World Champion but it gave me just as much satisfaction, as the averages of the time prove.

'Ove did pass on some valuable advice to me in that "when you are broadsiding you are going sideways, but when your wheels are in line you are going forward." We had many good tussles throughout our time together, and his riding was permanently faultless. When riding against other star riders they would pull back at the start and go down the back straight and do a practice start to put stress on the opposition and distract them at the gate. But not Ove. It wasn't his way of doing things. In that era the Swedes were a force to be reckoned with. Test matches between them and Great Britain were great draw cards.'
– Nigel Boocock, World number four, 1969, England international and Coventry star.

'I first encountered Fundin at the start of my journalistic career, working as a teenage hopeful for Reg Hayter's Sports Reporting Agency in 1960-61, and immediately was impressed with his seemingly metro-nome-like consistency and ability to beat even the other members of the Big Five of the day – Briggo, Moore, Craven and Knutsson. When I saw him win the 1961 Internationale at Harringay, nothing seemed more pre-ordained than that he should win the first World Final away from Wembley… and of course he did win in Malmo, which I reported upon for the *Daily Express*. Fundin drew roars of approval from the Malmo crowd when, his title won, he throttled back to allow Gote Nordin to beat him to the flag in his final ride, thus giving Nordin a shot at third spot that eventually gave the Swedes a 1-2-3 on the night. The fact is, though, that Bjorn Knutsson was the fastest and best rider on the night and, just as Ole Olsen did at Wembley in 1972, he won four rides in quite brilliant fashion but in an uncannily similar moment of madness forfeited the crown because of a crash. Knutsson's faux pas, as was Ole's eleven years later, was the result of trying too hard too soon to pass when another lap would probably have done it. The moral of both stories is that there's a lot to be said for being a fox. Ove and I came back to the UK on the same plane because he was racing at Norwich the next night, and I rushed to the airport kiosk to buy an *Express* to see how my report had turned out, the contents of which were then examined closely by Fundin himself!

'Even now Ove is a god in Norwich and around Norfolk. Stories about him abound, and some may even have been true, but true believers up there will not have it any way other than that this was the most fantastic rider who ever lived. Like all who march to a different tune, Ove occasionally would simply go missing when expected for a UK domestic meeting, yet the capacity of his adoring followers to forget and forgive was almost inexhaustible. That said, when he didn't front at King's Lynn with Wembley in 1970 – the Lions had just come back into the British League and Fundin's expected appearance pulled in a huge number of extra fans for the occasion – a lot of the natives were restless. Ove was reported delayed, but some (including the announcer) were sceptical and I told Trevor Redmond, the Lions' promoter, that he could get on the mike and tell the crowd because no way was I going to face their wrath!

'Funnily enough I was in Sweden in September 1969 on a whistle-stop tour that took in the World Pairs Final and a Great Britain v. Sweden international and was surprised to see Trevor Redmond at the Test match. He had been out of speedway for a while and was close to being the last person you might have expected to see on such an occasion. What later emerged was that he had flown in to take Ove into his confidence about his and Bernard Cottrell's plan to re-open Wembley and to sweet-talk Fundin into leading the campaign, which, of course, he did.

'Seeing the man thirty-odd years on, when he and his latest wife visited the Maugers on the Gold Coast while on a round-the-world trip a year or two ago, it was impossible not to marvel at his leannes and age-defying fitness. The two old warriors cut an impressive dash as they talked over some old times and happily pandered to the needs of the local scribe and photographer whistled up for the occasion. Not only do old speedway World Champions never die, it seemed that these two don't even have the good grace to fade away.'

– Martin Rogers, speedway journalist, track announcer and promoter at Leicester, Peterborough and King's Lynn.

'Fundin rode for Belle Vue for part of the season – and he won the
World Final. Harold Gardner, who was the head mechanic at Belle
Vue, built Ove's Fundin's bike, frame and everything. Ove will tell you
that he owed a lot to Harold and Isobel Gardner when he came into
Belle Vue. Harold – he's now in his eighties – had been in speedway
all his life. He and Ove were a good match and Ove fitted in well at
The Zoo. I mean, the Belle Vue and Norwich tracks were virtually
identical. It was like coming home to him. There was the odd flash of
temperament – he had a very short fuse at times. He is also a beautiful
ballroom dancer. You wouldn't think he was an ex-World Speedway
Champion. It's a pity he wasn't at Belle Vue a bit longer. He could
beat Craven nine times out of ten. If Craven was in front, he would
always run his front wheel as near as possible to Peter's leg. He could
always put the wind up Peter. If there was one rider I would back to
beat Peter in British speedway it was Fundin. Everybody has that one
little weakness and it was Fundin with Craven.'
– Allan Morrey, clerk of the course at Hyde Road Stadium, Belle Vue,
since 1958, now retired.

'Ove hasn't changed over the years. I only became involved with him
when he came to Belle Vue. He didn't stop very long. He had been
there no more than a week or two before he rode in the World Final.
I was doing a few motors for Belle Vue at the time. Harold Gardner
used to do the frames. You see, in those days they had good people at
speedway who could do things. Ove didn't ask for anything special.
He was the dead opposite.

   'I looked after quite a lot at Belle Vue. They had a team of Harold
Jackson and Harold Gardner. I worked for myself. They said, "Would
you do an engine for Fundin?" I went up to him and said, "How do
you want it?" I think the words he said to me were: "Give me an
engine that will get me round the first turn five times out of six and
I will look after the rest." There's more bloody rubbish talked about
engines nowadays. I mean the best guys in England are now doing
engines – you get Peter Johns, he's quite good. He's an old rider, he
knows what it's about. You get Eddie Bull and you get Trevor Hedge

– they know what they're doing. Norwich was a lovely place. There isn't a place as good now anywhere. People think it was rubbish in the old days, but it wasn't, it was better.'

– Guy Allott, world-renowned engine tuner and former rider.

'There was a Test match. Some Swedes had come over and they were all staying at Fundin's flat in Norwich. We were on our way to Wimbledon and there were about five of them in the car. I was driving with all the bikes on the back on a trailer. We came up the A11 into the main driveway in Newmarket. I saw the 30mph up front but the lights were with me so I let it go. I'd just gone through the lights and I twigged this radar. There was a police sergeant standing there with three constables. I stopped, wound the window down, and he said: "Good afternoon, sir. You realise you are in a 30mph limit?" For some unknown reason I just sat there and looked. He said, "Did you hear me?" Ove was sitting in the back. I looked at him and he looked at me. He leant across and said, "What's the trouble, sergeant?" The sergeant said, "Who are you?" Ove said, "My name's Fundin and this is my car. It's no good you saying anything to him, he doesn't understand a word you're saying, he's Swedish." The sergeant said, "Mr Fundin, would you convert 30mph to kilometres, and just tell him to keep his speed down?" Presumably he then thought of all the paperwork he would have to do and sent us on our way. After a while Ove looked at me and said, "You're a clever bastard. How did you think of that?" I said, "Well, I just thought the best thing to do was to keep my mouth shut and see what happened. Obviously we were on the same wavelength because you twigged it as quick as that." He had filled in for me and we got away with it.'

– Les Mullins, former chief mechanic, Norwich Speedway.

'Speedway is quite a dirty sport. By dirty I mean you get filthy. And later on when I started meeting other sportsmen, I used to run into the Swedish tennis players who travelled around living in first-class hotels, smartly dressed, nice and clean always. I played a game now and then. And there I was, riding nearly every night, and I was dirty

and filthy. I never thought of the risks. You don't when you are young. Not even later on, like even today, when I do demonstration races. Knutsson used to do them but he won't do them any more because it is too risky. Quite a few won't do it. You see only myself and Barry of the 1950s riders, don't you? The others are too scared. Fred Williams won't do it. Reg Fearman would never do it. He's said he'll never get on a bike. I am not going to take any risks voluntarily. But you always take a little bit of risk here and there, going out anywhere, crossing the road or riding your bike down to St Tropez.'
– Ove Fundin.

'I shared a room with Ove in South Africa on the 1957/58 tour. I was booked in with Trevor Redmond. My most vivid recollection of Ove Fundin was that I was going to kill him during a meeting. He jumped the tapes. He wouldn't adjust the races to make it look good. Speedway wasn't doing too well at the time, and what we wanted to do was get people keen on it. Trevor used to say, "Make it look good boys." Olle Nygren would, and we'd all join in. But Ove wouldn't – he wouldn't hang back and make it look good. "No," he said. "If you want to beat me, beat me, but I am the World Champion."

'Anyway, we were at a meeting out in the bush somwhere, and Ove jumped the gate, really going for it. Catches the tapes. They were strong ones and they broke, but the long bit went across my neck. We didn't have anything on under our leathers because it was so damned hot – and we all went off. The tape went across my neck, it burned me and it was red raw. By the time the race finished I was in a blinding red rage and I was going to kill Fundin. I went for him and Olle Nygren acted as a peacemaker and he hauled me back to earth. "Hold on, boy," he said. "This is Ove's temperament." "But," I said, "I've been in the same room with the guy for months – what is his problem?" And Olle just said, "Oh, he's just like that – forget it." And that was it.

'But, honestly, he would go a couple of weeks without saying a word to me. Really. I wrote one letter to my wife and told her that Ove was "objectionable". He was always writing to his wife – his then wife – Mona, at the time. He wrote dozens of letters to Mona

– I took it. But he never came with us anywhere socially. What he did with himself was a bit of a mystery, to tell you the truth. The few get-togethers there were, Ove was very low key. Very quiet. Rather subdued, you might say. It was only when he got on that bloody bike that he came to life. And went crackers, too.

'I don't know how I came to be in the same room with him on that tour. That was a mystery. I suppose they had told him, "Roy's a pretty quiet and capable sort of chap, you'll be safe with him. He won't chuck you over the balcony." If we went out he'd either be in bed or he'd come in late. He never went out for a drink or anything. It was a good lark. And that's what Ove missed, I think. He missed all the fun. He came down to Durban once with us, Trevor Redmond and Olle Nygren, in Olle's car. We put on a few races in which we should have been putting on a show for the customers – but he wouldn't. "No, I'm champion," he said. Coming back from Durban with Olle and Trevor, I was driving and and we had a little contretemps – no, not any women, women weren't involved, they were banned, I wouldn't have any of that. Olle was a different character – more ebullient.

'During the meeting some guys had talked to Olle, and it turned out they were off a Swedish boat. And Olle said, "We're going back to this Swedish boat." So we go back and had a fair drop of whatever they drank. It was beautiful stuff, you didn't get a real hangover on it. We had a fairly late session and we left late and had to drive back to near Pretoria – about 500 miles as I remember, a fair distance anyway. We were sharing the driving and suddenly something jumped out in front of us. And we hit it. Whatever it was disappeared over the top of the car. We came to a halt a bit further on to assess the damage – which was minimal. But Ove wanted nothing to do with it at all. He was asleep, he knew nothing. That is just for instance.

'He was obsessive about washing his shirt. He travelled lightwieght. My first recollection of Ove was in the foyer of a hotel – a very nice place run by a lovely old boy, a Dutch-South African. I noticed that Ove's dress was economical: shirt, jacket, trousers, and his shoes with the sole coming off. Sand boot things. I said, "Have you been scuffing them a bit, Ove?" That didn't go down at all well. And I thought, "Oh, he'll get some new ones tomorrow." But I don't think he ever did. But his shirt... he would type a letter to someone every day, religiously. And he always washed his shirt. It was called seersucker then and it always dried quick. That was the advantage, I suppose. He had everything worked out to the minimium. He'd wash his shirt, hang it up and put it on the next day.

'We used to play badminton up at the old fire station. We used to use their gym. We'd have a good old bash about there. But old Ove was very awkward with a bat. He just wouldn't talk. And that didn't change – not for years. After that he was still the distant Mr Cool. They used to say Bjorn Borg was the "Iceman of Tennis", didn't they? Well Ove was the "Iceman of Speedway".

'He's a totally different person now. Beautiful. A different guy. A gentleman.'

– Roy Bowers, Yarmouth, Weymouth and Oxford.


'If I was on the track with Ove now, given half a chance, he'd still run over my foot.'

– Barry Briggs.

# OVE'S CAREER RECORD

**BRITAIN**

World Champion: 1956, 1960, 1961, 1963, 1967.
Runner-up: 1957, 1958, 1959.
Third: 1962, 1964, 1965.

World Final appearances: 15. Points: 173. Average: 11.53.

World Team Cup Champion: 1960, 1962, 1963, 1964, 1967, 1970.

World Best Pairs Champion: 1968 with Torbjorn Harrysson.

European Champion: 1956, 1958, 1959, 1965.

British Match Race Champion: 1957-1964. Won: 19. Lost: 6.

Internationale winner: 1961, 1962, 1963.

**League**
Norwich 1955-1964
Matches: 147. Points: 1,830. Bonus points: 21. Total: 1,851.
Maximums: 57. CMA: 10.76.

Long Eaton 1966
Matches: 5. Points: 53. Maximums: 2. CMA: 9.636.

Wembley 1970
Matches: 14. Points: 115. Bonus points: 2. Total: 117. CMA: 7.932.

**SWEDEN**

Swedish Champion: 1956, 1957, 1960, 1962, 1964, 1966, 1967, 1969, 1970.

International appearances: 83. Total points: 1,011.

Swedish Pairs Champion: 1960 (with Bengt Brannefors).

**Swedish League**
Filbyterna 1951-1957
Points: 1,045. CMA: 12.358.

**Kaparna** 1958-1970
Points: 967. CMA: 10.66.

Ove won two Swedish League championship medals with Kaparna in 1968 and 1970.

# Other titles published by Tempus

## Norwich Speedway
NORMAN JACOBS & MIKE KEMP

Norwich has been one of the most famous and best-loved teams in the history of speedway. From the early days in the 1930s, through the remarkably successful '50s and up to the closure of the promotion in the '60s, this pictorial history brings the city's rich speedway heritage to life. Containing over 200 images, including action shots, rider portraits and programme covers, many of Norwich's galaxy of star names are featured, such as Max Grosskreutz, Billy Bales, Aub Lawson and Ove Fundin.

0 7524 3152 8

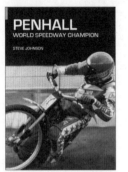

## Penhall: World Speedway Champion
STEVE JOHNSON

In less than five years, Bruce Penhall, the blond-haired, blue-eyed golden boy of America, had gone from British League novice to World Speedway Champion and was hailed as arguably the most popular champion there has ever been. Overcoming personal tragedy at eighteen to become World Champion again in high-speed powerboat racing and subsequently a Hollywood movie star, the story of the charismatic Bruce Lee Penhall is an exhilarating read for every speedway fan.

0 7524 3400 4

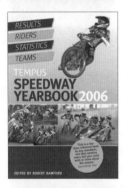

## Tempus Speedway Yearbook 2006
EDITED BY ROBERT BAMFORD

For speedway fans across Great Britain, Tempus present the latest edition of the sport's definitive annual. Once again featuring comprehensive statistics, team and rider information and superb colour photography, this is the guide to the 2005 season that supporters have been waiting for.

0 7524 3692 9

## Chris Morton: Until the Can Ran Out
CHRIS MORTON & BRIAN BURFORD

Chris Morton is regarded as one of Britain's greatest ever speedway riders as he won almost every honour that was open to him. A talented racer, he was respected by his rivals and was one of the most exciting riders of his generation. *Until the Can Ran Out* takes the reader on an enthralling journey to the highest level of the sport – a ruthless place where all that matters is to be a winner.

0 7524 3473 X

If you are interested in purchasing other books published by Tempus, or in case you have difficulty finding any Tempus books in your local bookshop, you can also place orders directly through our website

www.tempus-publishing.com